New Perspectives on Transfer in Second Language Learning

MIX
Paper from
responsible sources
FSC® C014540
www.fsc.org
FSC®

SECOND LANGUAGE ACQUISITION

Series Editors: **Professor David Singleton**, *University of Pannonia, Hungary* and Fellow Emeritus, *Trinity College, Dublin, Ireland* and **Dr Simone E. Pfenninger**, *University of Zurich, Switzerland*

This series brings together titles dealing with a variety of aspects of language acquisition and processing in situations where a language or languages other than the native language is involved. Second language is thus interpreted in its broadest possible sense. The volumes included in the series all offer in their different ways, on the one hand, exposition and discussion of empirical findings and, on the other, some degree of theoretical reflection. In this latter connection, no particular theoretical stance is privileged in the series; nor is any relevant perspective – sociolinguistic, psycholinguistic, neurolinguistic, etc. – deemed out of place. The intended readership of the series includes final-year undergraduates working on second language acquisition projects, postgraduate students involved in second language acquisition research, and researchers and teachers in general whose interests include a second language acquisition component.

Full details of all the books in this series and of all our other publications can be found on http://www.multilingual-matters.com, or by writing to Multilingual Matters, St Nicholas House, 31-34 High Street, Bristol BS1 2AW, UK.

SECOND LANGUAGE ACQUISITION: 92

New Perspectives on Transfer in Second Language Learning

Edited by
Liming Yu and Terence Odlin

MULTILINGUAL MATTERS
Bristol • Buffalo • Toronto

Library of Congress Cataloging in Publication Data
A catalog record for this book is available from the Library of Congress.
New Perspectives on Transfer in Second Language Learning/Edited by Liming Yu and Terence Odlin.
Second Language Acquisition: 92
Includes bibliographical references and index.
1. Language transfer (Language learning) 2. Second language acquisition. I. Yu, Liming, 1952- editor.
II. Odlin, Terence, editor.
P118.25.N49 2015
418.0071–dc23 2015019562

British Library Cataloguing in Publication Data
A catalogue entry for this book is available from the British Library.

ISBN-13: 978-1-78309-433-2 (hbk)
ISBN-13: 978-1-78309-432-5 (pbk)

Multilingual Matters
UK: St Nicholas House, 31-34 High Street, Bristol BS1 2AW, UK.
USA: UTP, 2250 Military Road, Tonawanda, NY 14150, USA.
Canada: UTP, 5201 Dufferin Street, North York, Ontario M3H 5T8, Canada.

Website: www.multilingual-matters.com
Twitter: Multi_Ling_Mat
Facebook: https://www.facebook.com/multilingualmatters
Blog: www.channelviewpublications.wordpress.com

The policy of Multilingual Matters/Channel View Publications is to use papers that are natural, renewable and recyclable products, made from wood grown in sustainable forests. In the manufacturing process of our books, and to further support our policy, preference is given to printers that have FSC and PEFC Chain of Custody certification. The FSC and/or PEFC logos will appear on those books where full certification has been granted to the printer concerned.

Typeset by Deanta Global Publishing Services Limited.
Printed and bound in Great Britain by Short Run Press Ltd.

Contents

Contributors

Jinting Cai is vice president of the China Second Language Research Association. He has published extensively in China, including more than 30 research articles in *Foreign Language Teaching and Research*, *Modern Foreign Languages* and *Foreign Language Research*, as well as four monographs, including *The Effects of Multiple Linguistic Factors on the Simple Past Use in English Interlanguage*, *Research on Chinese-Speaking Learners' English Interlanguage* and *Empirical Studies of EFL Learners' Acquisition of English Tense and Aspect in China*, and a co-authored work, *The Dynamic Influence of Learner Factors on University Students' English Proficiency Development*.

Hui Chang received his PhD in second language acquisition from Shanghai Jiao Tong University, where he now teaches. His research interests include the acquisition of syntax in L1 and L2, the syntax–discourse interface and the syntax–semantics interface. His recent publications include *Asymmetries of Null Subjects and Null Objects in Japanese Speakers' Chinese* and *The Acquisition of Chinese Double Object Constructions and Dative Alternation Constructions by English and French Native Speakers*. He has recently received a national grant for a project entitled Acquisition of L2 Chinese Syntax by Speakers with Different L1 Backgrounds.

Yusong Gao is professor of applied linguistics at Northwest Normal University in Lanzhou, China. He received his PhD in linguistics and applied linguistics from Guangdong University of Foreign Studies and his MA in English language and literature from East China Normal University. He is the author of *L2 Acquisition of the English MC and Its Related Structure by Chinese and Korean Learners: Towards an Event Structure-Based Account* (Science Press, 2010). He has published articles in several journals including *Foreign Language Teaching and Research*, *Contemporary Linguistics* and *Modern Foreign Languages*.

Scott Jarvis is professor of linguistics at Ohio University in the United States, where he teaches courses in second language acquisition and language assessment. His current research interests deal primarily with cross-linguistic influence and lexical diversity, and within these areas he has focused on modeling and measuring the relevant constructs. He completed his PhD in linguistics at Indiana University in 1997 with a concentration in second language acquisition and a minor in semiotics. From 2007 to 2011, he served as an associate editor for *Language Learning*, and since 2011 has served on the board of directors for this journal.

Hong Li is professor of applied linguistics at Chongqing University, China. She has authored *SEMANTIC Processing: The L2 Lexical Competence Perspective* (Higher Education Press, 2007) and *Empirical Investigations on the Bilingual Mental Lexicon* (Chongqing University Press, 2007). She is a member of the editorial board of the *Journal of Chongqing University (Social Sciences Edition)* and *Chinese Journal of ESP*. She has published articles in professional journals such as *Bilingualism: Language and Cognition*, *Modern Foreign Languages*, *Psychological Science* and *Foreign Languages in China*.

Jia Li has published articles in several journals in China including the *Journal of Sichuan International Studies University, Foreign Language Education* and *Modern Foreign Languages*.

Shaopeng Li holds a PhD in second language acquisition from Shanghai International Studies University and is a lecturer in EFL at Shanghai International Studies University in China. His research interests are in second language acquisition and EFL teaching and more specifically in dynamic perspective on second language development and inter-individual and intra-individual factors influencing second language acquisition. His publications appear in such journals as *Studies in Second Language Learning and Teaching, Cambridge Journal of China Studies, Journal of Foreign Languages, Contemporary Foreign Languages Studies and Foreign Language Research*. *Contact details*: School of Economics and Finance, Shanghai International Studies University, Shanghai, 200083.

David Mitchell is a doctoral student in the Linguistics Department at Ohio State University, Columbus, Ohio. His primary focus of study is morphological change in the African American Vernacular English (AAVE) verb system, including folk perceptions of AAVE from the perspective of AAVE speakers in Columbus. Another project involves the compiling of the slave narratives from the Federal Writers Project into a searchable linguistic corpus. Having recently relocated to Denver, Colorado, he is an instructor at Metropolitan State University.

Terence Odlin is the author of *Language Transfer: Cross-Linguistic Influence in Language Learning* (Cambridge University Press, 1989) and is the editor or co-editor of four other volumes. He has published articles in several journals including *International Journal of Multilingualism, Language Awareness, Language Learning, Modern Language Journal, Studies in Second Language Acquisition* and *TESOL Quarterly*. He has also published chapters in several edited volumes including *The Handbook of Second Language Acquisition, Handbook of Cognitive Linguistics and Second Language Acquisition* and *The Oxford Handbook of Applied Linguistics*. Recently retired from Ohio State University, he lives in Columbus, Ohio.

T. Sima Paribakht is the director of graduate studies at the Official Languages and Bilingualism Institute, University of Ottawa, Canada, and is also a professor at the same institution. Her research focuses on second language vocabulary acquisition including the effects of the first language on second language lexical processing and development, second language vocabulary instruction and assessment of lexical competence. Her recent book (with Marjorie Wesche), *Lexical Inferencing in L1 and L2: Cross Linguistic Dimensions*, was published by Multilingual Matters (2010).

David Singleton took his BA at Trinity College, University of Dublin, and his PhD at the University of Cambridge. He is an Emeritus Fellow of Trinity College Dublin, where he was, until his recent retirement from that institution, professor of applied linguistics, He now holds the title of professor at the University of Pannonia, Veszprém (Hungary) and at the School of Higher Education, Konin (Poland). He has served as president of the Irish Association for Applied Linguistics, as secretary general of the International Association of Applied Linguistics and as president of the European Second Language Association. His publications number close to 200, his books and articles ranging across a wide spectrum of topics but focusing mainly on cross-linguistic influence, the second language lexicon, the age factor in language acquisition and multilingualism. He is the founding editor of the Multilingual Matters SLA book series.

Chuming Wang, professor of English at the Center for Linguistics and Applied Linguistics, Guangdong University of Foreign Studies, China, is president of the China Second Language Research Association. He has published articles in journals such as *Language Learning, Applied Linguistics, Foreign Language Teaching and Research, Foreign Languages* and *Modern Foreign Languages*. He is the author of several books including *Applied Psycholinguistics: Studies of L2 Learning* (1990), *Chinese Students' Self-Concept of EFL Learning* (co-authored, 2008) and *How Foreign Languages are Learned* (2010).

Marjorie Bingham Wesche formerly taught at the Official Languages and Bilingualism Institute of the University of Ottawa. Her research specialties are in L2 vocabulary acquisition, performance-based testing and content-based instruction including immersion.

Lianrui Yang is currently professor and dean of the School of Foreign Languages, Ocean University of China. His research interests focus on interlanguage linguistics and various topics in second language acquisition and attrition. He is currently an editorial board member of *System, Language Learning Journal* and *International Journal of Language* and *Society and Culture*. His recent books include *China SLA Studies, Multi-Disciplinary Studies in SLA* and *Second Language Acquisition and Foreign Language Teaching in China*. He has published more than 100 research articles in academic journals. He has assumed a number of posts of academic organizations in China, including vice president of the China Educational Linguistics Association and secretary general of the China Second Language Research Association.

Liming Yu joined the faculty of the School of Foreign Languages of Shanghai Jiao Tong University on receiving his doctorate from the University of Toronto in 1996. Recently retired from Shanghai Jiao Tong University, he is now a guest professor at Shanghai International Studies University and president of the China Educational Linguistics Association. His research interests have focused on language transfer in second language acquisition, the disciplinary nature of second language acquisition and theory and practice in bilingual education. He has published extensively, including *Language Transfer in Language Learning: Review, Reflection and Research* (Shanghai Foreign Language Education Press).

Lei Zhang has published several articles in *Journal of Xi'an International Studies University, Journal of Chongqing University (Social Sciences Edition), Journal of University of Electronic Science and Technology of China (Social Sciences Edition)* and *Journal of Hefei University of Technology (Social Science)*. He is now a PhD student at Beihang University in China.

Lina Zheng is a lecturer at Shanghai University of International Business and Economics, China. She received her PhD in second language acquisition from Shanghai Jiao Tong University. Her research interests include L2 acquisition of syntax and lexicon. Her recent publications include *Word Order Parameter Resetting in English Speakers' Chinese* and *A Case Study of the Acquisition of Chinese Negative Constructions by Two L1-English Speakers*.

Ling Zhou recently completed her MA thesis on the acquisition of word stress patterns in English by Chinese learners. She works at Chongqing University and lives in Chongqing, China.

Acknowledgments

We would like to thank the anonymous reviewer of the volume for several valuable suggestions and also Laura Longworth and the staff at Multilingual Matters for their help and patience with the project.

1 Introduction

Terence Odlin and Liming Yu

What is Language Transfer?

The word *transfer* has had many specialized uses and not just in linguistics: for instance, *transfer* and *transference* have long appeared in psychology, with different movements (e.g. psychoanalysis and behaviorism) using the words as terms with quite different meanings. Likewise, in linguistics the technical meanings of *transfer* are far from uniform. Some of the varying uses will be mentioned a little further on, but for now, the working definition that will inform this chapter is as follows: 'Transfer is the influence resulting from the similarities and differences between the target language and any other language that has been previously (and perhaps imperfectly) acquired' (Odlin, 1989: 27).

The definition deliberately includes 'any other language' because there are many cases of people learning not only a second language (L2) but also a third (L3). For example, in China many native speakers of Uighur (a Turkic language) have Mandarin Chinese (a Sino-Tibetan language) as their L2 when they begin to study English as their L3, and so similarities and differences between Chinese and English as well as similarities and differences between Uighur and English might affect such learners' acquisition of the L3. Although relatively little study has yet been done on this particular trilingual situation, the steadily growing research field dealing with multilingual settings has documented many cases of both first language (L1) and L2 influence on an L3 as well as the influence of an L3 on an L4, etc. (De Angelis, 2007; De Angelis & Dewaele, 2011; Gabryś-Barker, 2012; Hammarberg, 2009). In our volume, Chapters 3, 11 and 13 consider trilingual or multilingual cases, but the other chapters focus on L1 → L2 transfer.

Even when only two languages are involved, cross-linguistic influence (which is a synonym for transfer) can be manifested in different ways, as will be seen. Moreover, while an L1 can influence an L2, the reverse is also common (thus constituting L2 → L1 transfer). For instance, Porte (2003: 112) investigated the English of several native speakers of English who were teaching English as a foreign language (EFL) in Spain and found many examples of L2 → L1 influence: e.g. *I was really shocked when I first saw how molested some teachers got at my criticising the system*, where *molested* has the less pejorative meaning of Spanish *molestar* ('annoy') as opposed to the English *molest*, which is often used to denote criminality (e.g. *child molester*). The teachers in Porte's study seem to have been influenced both by some direct knowledge of Spanish and by their relatively long residence in Spain, especially since the *molested* example could just as easily come from a native speaker of Spanish using English (Nash, 1979). It is also clear that L2 → L1 influences in grammar are rather common. For example, Pavlenko (2003) found that Russian speakers residing in the USA sometimes used the perfective/imperfective system of verbs in Russian in ways quite different from monolingual speakers in Russia and in ways quite like those found in the L2 Russian of L1 English speakers. Sometimes, the difference between the L2 → L1 influence and what is called code-switching is subtle or even non-existent, and there likewise exists a large body of research on code-switching (e.g. Isurin *et al.*, 2009), though none of the chapters in our volume focuses on that phenomenon.

In many immigrant situations, both L2 → L1 and L1 → L2 transfer are likely in the same community, but an opportunity to study a different kind of bidirectional transfer comes from international schools, where, for example, Italian children who might or might not become permanent residents of England study English, and where English-speaking children study Italian in international schools in Italy. Rocca (2007) investigated just this kind of parallel transfer (L1 Italian influence on L2 English, L1 English influence on L2 Italian) with regard to tense and aspect structures in the target language.

The most typical cases of transfer – and usually the ones that preoccupy language teachers – involve divergences between the source language (whether the L1 or perhaps the L2 in cases of L3 acquisition) and the target language (i.e. the language that learners are seeking to acquire). Such divergences can result in negative transfer, which is often evident in vocabulary problems as when a native speaker of Spanish uses *molest* in English as a synonym for *annoy*. Along with such vocabulary problems, negative transfer is often evident in syntactic structures, as in the following sentence from a native speaker of Vietnamese: *She has managed to rise the kite fly over the tallest building* (=*She has managed to fly a kite over the tallest building*), where the use of *rise...fly* indicates the influence of Vietnamese grammar (Helms-Park, 2003). The pronunciation and spelling patterns of L2 learners likewise show many instances of negative transfer related to pronunciation problems, as seen in a spelling error of a Finnish student who writes *crass* instead of *grass*. The Finn's misspelling of *grass* with either the letter <c> or the letter <k> reflects a phonological fact about the native language: Finnish does not have a phonemic contrast between /k/ and /g/, and learners of English in Finland thus have to learn a new consonant contrast.[1]

While divergences involving pronunciation, vocabulary and grammar naturally compel teachers' attention, a topic just as important for anyone wishing to understand transfer is the complementary phenomenon of positive transfer, which does *not* involve errors. For example, it now seems clear that some errors such as omitting articles are less likely to come from speakers of some L1s in comparison with others (e.g. Luk & Shirai, 2009; Master, 1987; Oller & Redding, 1971). Such research indicates that although speakers of languages with articles may still have problems with articles in a new language, they have fewer than do speakers of languages that do not have any articles. In other words, omissions and other article problems are less characteristic of some groups, as in a sentence taken from a corpus of EFL writing[2] that focused on events seen in a film: *Old woman say to baker: Girl take it, not man* (with four articles being omitted along with the problems of punctuation and the erroneous verb forms). In principle, omissions might be found among any L1 group, but in reality they are much less common among native speakers of Swedish, a language that has articles, than among native speakers of Finnish, a language that does not. The example just given comes from a speaker of Finnish, whereas the facilitating influence (i.e. positive transfer) of L1 Swedish is reflected in many passages in the same corpus, cases that would not, as far as article use is concerned, cause any concern for language teachers: e.g. *But the old woman came and she said to the man that it was the woman ho tok [took] the bread.* The advantage of L1 Swedish speakers over Finnish speakers in regard to the positive transfer of articles is now amply documented (e.g. Jarvis, 2002; Odlin, 2012a; Ringbom, 1987).

A number of researchers including Corder (1983: 92) have criticized the term *transfer* for its metaphoric suggestion when in fact 'nothing is being transferred from anywhere to anywhere'. The notion of movement inherent in *transfer* has sometimes been seen as one manifestation of a larger group of metaphors which Reddy (1979) dubbed 'the conduit metaphor'. Corder's criticism might be best viewed as a warning against an unreflective use of metaphors, which can indeed cause misconceptions, as discussed by various specialists (e.g. Lakoff & Johnson, 1980, 1999; Vervaeke & Kennedy, 2004). Even so, *transfer* has long served as a useful cover term for a variety of phenomena that require detailed non-metaphoric analyses. The conduit metaphor is also evident in two other terms: *translation* and (somewhat ironically) *metaphor*. The latter seems less closely related to *transfer*, but Dechert (2006) observes that the etymologies of both *transfer* and *metaphor* suggest that something is carried from one place to another, *transfer* coming from the Latin *trans* (across) and *ferre* (carry) and *metaphor* from the Greek *meta* (across) and *phor* (carry). The verb *translate* has essentially the same etymology as *transfer*, since the word *latus* is a participial form of the irregular Latin verb *ferre*. Of course, there are undeniable differences between the phenomena of transfer, translation and metaphor; nevertheless, the semantic kinship of the terms seems significant. Specialists such as Lakoff and Johnson have emphasized that metaphors permeate the everyday use of language, as people often seek to comprehend the world and their own lives, and it is thus not surprising that the image of carrying over has seemed useful to both specialists and non-specialists in discussing language, whether the topic is translation or transfer (Odlin, 2008).

The phenomena of translation and transfer do in fact show more than simply an etymological overlap. The *molest* example given above illustrates a pitfall for both translators and language learners, who are often warned about 'false friends'. Sometimes, the overlap is more subtle, as in the prepositional error seen in *They sit to the grass* (=*They sit on the grass*), which was written by a native speaker of Finnish in describing a scene in a film and which reflects the semantic influence of a Finnish inflection –*lle* (meaning 'to' or 'onto') as in the word *nurmikolle*, translatable literally as 'grass-to' (Jarvis & Odlin, 2000). Yet, even though many cases of lexical and grammatical transfer involve some kind of translation or, as Weinreich (1953) preferred to phrase it, some 'interlingual identification', it would be a mistake to conclude that the two phenomena are really one and the same thing. Not all transfer behaviors involve translation. For example, hypercorrections such as a Finnish writer's use of *gomes* (=*comes*) differ in a remarkable way from the error *crass* discussed earlier. As already noted, Finnish has a voiceless velar /k/ but no voiced counterpart /g/. The *crass* example involves a simple carrying over, so to speak, of the voiceless /k/ to an inappropriate target language context, but the use of the letter <g> in *gomes* represents a rejection of both the Finnish letter <k> and the Finnish phoneme /k/, even though *comes* or even the misspelling *komes* would constitute a valid interlingual identification between an English and a Finnish phoneme. Unlike translation errors such as *molest* and *to the grass*, where learners overestimate the similarity between the L1 and L2, hypercorrections arise when learners underestimate the actual similarity.

Although errors involving mistranslation or hypercorrection naturally loom large in the concerns of language teachers, some manifestations of negative transfer lie on the borders of language itself. One such area involves what is sometimes called *contrastive rhetoric* and sometimes *contrastive pragmatics*. For example, Blum-Kulka (1982) found that requests in L2 Hebrew by L1 speakers of English were often too indirect by the norms of the target language. Such research entails comparing cultural norms, which, of course, vary a great deal from one society to the next. Not surprisingly, the norms sometimes prove challenging to study, due in part to the fact that they can vary over time, as seen in a study of Chinese rhetoric through the centuries (Bloch & Chi, 1995). Along with the cross-linguistic variation in rhetoric and pragmatics (aka discourse), the complexities of cultural norms are also manifest in paralinguistic behaviors, with the variation sometimes conducive to transfer as evident in recent work on L2 gestures. A wide repertory of gestures is typically available to native speakers as when, for instance, French speakers often provide information about the path of a moving object, a pattern in contrast to that of Dutch speakers, who tend to provide information about the object as such (Gullberg, 2011). Transfer of L1 gestural patterns has been evident in a wide range of studies discussed by Gullberg (2008), and as might be expected, L2 → L1 influences are also evident (Brown, 2007).

When did Interest in Transfer Begin?

SLA research frequently shows references to a book by Robert Lado (1957), who does indeed use the word *transfer*; however, use of this word as a term for cross-linguistic influence occurs well before Lado's book, as seen, for instance, in a book by Uriel Weinreich (1953), whose work Lado cites. In fact, the term *transfer* goes back at least to the 1880s and two German words that correspond to it are likewise evident in the 19th century. The earliest discussion of transfer as a psycholinguistic phenomenon may be in a work published in 1836 that ponders the relation between language and mind. Its author, Wilhelm von Humboldt (1767–1835), briefly considered second language acquisition (SLA) with regard to the cognitive effects involved in learning a new language, and he used the term *hinübertragen*, the literal translation of which (over-carry) clearly resembles the Latin *transferre*, which was discussed in the preceding section. A related term, *übertragen*, appears occasionally in an 1884 study by Hugo Schuchardt (1842–1927), looking closely at the German and Italian used by speakers of certain Slavic languages including Czech, Polish and Slovenian. Clearly a pioneer in SLA research, Schuchardt ([1884] 1971: 150) may have also been the first linguist to note the possibility of multilingual transfer (e.g. an L2 influencing an L3) as part of the phenomenon of cross-linguistic influence.

The earliest use of the English form *transfer* to designate cross-linguistic influence may be in an 1881 article by William Dwight Whitney (1827–1894), but a variant of the term, *transference*, also appeared shortly thereafter in a review of Schuchardt's book published in 1885 in the *American Journal of Philology* (and the review is reprinted in the 1971 edition of Schuchardt's work cited above). The author of the review, Aaron Marshall Elliott (1844–1910), also used *transfer* in an 1886 discussion of language contact in Canada. It seems quite possible that the two American linguists' use of *transfer* came about as translations of *ubertragen* or *hinübertragen*. Both men had studied in Germany (Marshall in Munich and Whitney in Berlin and Tübingen), where the topic of language contact had become increasingly prominent in historical linguistics. The 19th-century uses of *transfer* show that, contrary to the beliefs of some SLA researchers, the term did not originate in the 1950s. Moreover, the word *transfer* in the sense of cross-linguistic influence also appears in introductions to linguistics by Edward Sapir (1921) and Otto Jespersen (1922), and so there is clear continuity in its use from the 19th to the mid-20th century.

Even a casual look at the writings of Humboldt, Schuchardt, Whitney, Elliott, Sapir and Jespersen will show that linguists were using *transfer* (and translation equivalents) without reference to any particular theory of psychology. This point matters because the behaviorist use of the word *transfer* (e.g. Osgood, 1949) is sometimes equated with its use in linguistics, thus leading to a mistaken conclusion that the theoretical foundation for ideas about transfer is to be found in behaviorist psychology. It is true, however, that Lado took a behaviorist stance, as Selinker (2006) observes, but Selinker also studied with Lado's mentor Charles Fries, and he states that Fries did not subscribe to behaviorism. In his preface to Lado's book, Fries did refer to the 'habits' arising from a learner's L1 in relation to transfer, and so it is not surprising that in the challenge to behaviorism that arose in the 1960s, Fries and Lado would both be considered behaviorists. Nevertheless, other structural linguists who were not behaviorists also found the words *habit* and *habitual* convenient for alluding to the psychology of language (e.g. Edward Sapir and Benjamin Lee Whorf). Like *transfer*, then, the word *habits* had a life in linguistics quite independent of its uses in psychology.

Well before Humboldt, there was some interest in cross-linguistic influence, although the interest seems to have focused less on psychological and more on historical questions such as why Romance languages such as French and Italian differed so much from Latin: perhaps there were linguistic influences from groups subjugated by the Romans on the language of the conquerors (Odlin, 1989). In any case, the field of language contact has maintained a strong interest in transfer from the earlier studies reviewed by Weinreich to recent studies of both creoles, which are usually viewed as new languages that have arisen in bilingual or multilingual environments (e.g. Migge, 2003), and certain dialects viewed as varieties of an already existing language (e.g. Filppula *et al.*, 2008; Klee & Ocampo, 1995). Such work focuses on social as well as historical contexts that foster cross-linguistic influence. While arguably different in their main orientations, SLA and contact linguistics remain connected. Contact research (e.g. Mufwene, 2010; Siegel, 2012) naturally draws on psychologically-oriented studies of transfer, and some SLA research (e.g. Helms-Park, 2003) has likewise put contact studies to good use.

How Can Any Effects of Transfer be Demonstrated?

The skepticism about transfer that developed in the 1960s and 1970s has been closely examined elsewhere (e.g. Larsen-Freeman & Long, 1991; Odlin, 1989), and so there will not be a lengthy consideration here. Nevertheless, one especially relevant detail of that history warrants attention here: the methods employed by skeptics four decades ago. A book by Heidi Dulay, Marina Burt and Stephen Krashen published in 1982 marks, it can be argued, the high-water mark in the tide of skepticism. Much of their case against transfer relied on studies that compared speakers of quite different languages, such as Chinese and Spanish, on their success (or lack of success) in using grammatical morphemes such as plural inflections, definite and indefinite articles, and the possessive on English nouns as in *the child's stories*. Dulay *et al.* (1982) claimed that the developmental path for acquiring such morphemes did not vary significantly for speakers of any L1 background, and therefore speakers of a language such as Spanish would have no advantage with articles or plurals despite the presence of quite similar structures in their L1. Several developmental studies in addition to those of Dulay *et al.* (1982) seemed to provide convincing evidence (which, however, some contemporaries disputed). Nevertheless, in the last three decades, the counterevidence to the claims of Dulay *et al.* (1982) has increased steadily. Luk and Shirai (2009), for example, have reviewed several studies looking at speakers of Chinese, Japanese and Korean and conclude that articles and plural morphemes prove consistently more difficult for speakers of these languages (which do not have articles or plurals) in comparison with speakers of languages such as Spanish. Furthermore, the same research indicates that the possessive morpheme of English proves easier for speakers of the three East Asian languages (all of which have similar possessive structures) when compared with speakers of Spanish (a language with no close parallel to English in this area).

Findings such as those of Luk and Shirai do not discredit all developmental analyses, but the method of comparing at least two distinct L1 groups has been used effectively to demonstrate transfer in many instances, as in the study by Helms-Park (2003) cited above, where speakers of Vietnamese were compared with speakers of Hindi and Urdu (two closely related Indic languages). The comparison showed that only speakers of Vietnamese were at all prone to producing serial verb constructions such as *She has managed to rise the kite fly over the tallest building*. Since Vietnamese has serial verb constructions, whereas Hindi and Urdu do not, the conclusion of Helms-Park that transfer explains the intergroup difference is hard to refute. In an earlier study, Helms-Park (2001) used the same comparative method to demonstrate positive transfer in causative verb patterns that are sometimes similar between Vietnamese and English and, crucially, not similar between Hindi/Urdu and English. So-called periphrastic causative constructions, such as *The man made the lion jump through the hoop*, proved relatively easy for speakers of Vietnamese to use but not for speakers of Hindi/Urdu.

Such comparative studies are not the only way to make a strong case for transfer. Selinker (1969), for example, used a different approach in comparing the placement of adverbs by native speakers of Hebrew, native speakers of English and learners of EFL with Hebrew as their L1. He found a greater statistical similarity of the EFL patterns to those of the L1 Hebrew than to those of the L1 English group. An especially powerful method of verification comes, however, from combining the two methods, that is, by considering both the differences between native and non-native speakers and the differences between L1 groups, as Jarvis (2000) has demonstrated. In effect, his approach relies on five databases, one each for native speakers of Finnish and Swedish writing in their native languages, one each for speakers of these languages writing in EFL and one for native speakers of the target language (English). Not many SLA researchers may be in a position to collect so much data or to compare such closely matched groups as the Finnish and Swedish participants in the work of Jarvis, and less extensive data collection can still result in persuasive demonstrations of transfer. Even so, the approach advocated by Jarvis offers an especially strong methodology to forestall many of the conceivable counterarguments against transfer analyses.

The first use of such a method relying on five corpora (i.e. databases of text) involved lexis (Jarvis, 1998), but the usefulness of the method for morphosyntactic structures such as articles and prepositional phrases is also evident (e.g. Jarvis, 2002; Jarvis & Odlin, 2000; Odlin, 2012a). Lexical research remains, however, an important source of methodological advances. Jarvis and colleagues have refined a technology to study corpora gathered from speakers of several languages, including Finnish, Swedish, Spanish, Portuguese and Danish (Jarvis & Crossley, 2012). In one sense, however, the technological refinements evident in the Jarvis and Crossley volume still suggest continuity with earlier demonstrations of lexical transfer (e.g. Ard & Homburg, 1993) since in both the recent and the earlier investigations, the focus has been on intergroup differences.

Although English remains the most widely studied target language in regard to cross-linguistic influence, researchers have also looked at transfer in the acquisition of other target languages and have recognized the methodological significance of intergroup differences. Convincing evidence for transfer is indeed available in work on the acquisition of Arabic (Alhawary, 2009), Chichewa (Orr, 1987), Danish (Cadierno, 2010), Dutch (Sabourin et al., 2006), Finnish (Kaivapalu & Martin, 2007), French (Sleman, 2004), Hebrew (Olshtain, 1983), Japanese (Nakahama, 2011), Spanish (Montrul, 2000) and Swedish (Hyltenstam, 1984), to mention just some of the available studies.

What is the Place of Language Transfer in Theories of SLA?

Virtually every model of how learners acquire an L2 (or L3, L4, etc.) discusses transfer. Even skeptics such as Dulay et al. (1982) conceded that it had some role although, as discussed above, their overall position on transfer is now discredited. In the last three decades, cross-linguistic influence has been ascribed a greater role in theories of acquisition such as the competition model (e.g. MacWhinney, 2008), processability theory (PT; Pienemann *et al.*, 2005) and universal grammar (UG; White, 2003). A detailed summary of the perspectives on transfer in each of those models is beyond the scope of this chapter. However, it is important to note that each approach has its own emphases with regard to transfer, with varying amounts of attention to concerns such as linguistic typology, the frequency of particular structures in the source language(s) and the target, and the readiness of learners to acquire a particular target language structure. Along with the wider-ranging theoretical frameworks just cited, some approaches focus on more specific theoretical issues such as linguistic relativity in the approach known as thinking for speaking (e.g. Han, 2010; Slobin, 1996; Yu, 1996), while others have developed models that examine specific dimensions of transfer such as the implications of the differences between L1 writing systems (e.g. Wang *et al.*, 2003) and the implications of only partial lexical correspondences as where, for instance, German *Tasche* can translate into English as either *bag* or *pocket* (Elston-Güttler & Williams, 2008).

No single theory really attempts to model the full complexity of the phenomenon of cross-linguistic influence. The limited reach of theory building with regard to transfer is not surprising, given that the myriad concerns in complex domains (for example, discourse analysis) overlap only partially with the immediate concerns of transfer research. For those whose primary aim is to understand the multifaceted phenomenon of cross-linguistic influence, it is important to consider any empirical findings not only with regard to the theories invoked by researchers responsible for the findings but also with regard to alternative analyses. Two recent studies of transfer in grammatical gender can illustrate the potential value of considering alternative analyses. Sabourin *et al.* (2006) and Alhawary (2009) came to similar conclusions that when speakers of a language with grammatical gender (e.g. French) attempt to acquire one that also has grammatical gender (e.g. Arabic), these learners will have an advantage over speakers of a language (e.g. English) that does not have grammatical gender. Apart from the focus on transfer, however, the theoretical concerns in the two studies were quite different: UG in the study of Sabourin *et al.* and PT in the study of Alhawary (who is actually skeptical about PT as opposed to UG). Yet, while the issues foregrounded in UG and PT are important, neither model speaks directly to the questions of why any language has grammatical gender in the first place or why French learners, for example, might try to use their L1 knowledge to deal with the challenges of grammatical gender in a new language. Although UG and PT have virtually nothing to say on the possible communicative motivations for grammatical gender, linguists using other theoretical approaches have offered explanations that may prove helpful (e.g. Corbett, 1999; Senft, 2007). Corbett (1999: 17), for instance, has viewed gender as a subtype of an agreement system and, in general, the usefulness of such systems lies 'in allowing the speaker to keep track of referents in a discourse by means of the agreement categories'. There does not yet seem to be much SLA research focusing on this specific claim, but clearly such work could build on transfer research that has looked closely at how speakers with different L1 backgrounds try to maintain topic continuity in discourse (e.g. Jarvis, 2002).

Can Linguists Predict when Transfer will Occur?

Several decades ago, contrastive analysts such as Lado (1957: v) confidently assumed that 'we can predict and describe the patterns that will cause difficulty in learning, and those that will not cause difficulty, by comparing systematically the language and culture to be learned with the native language and culture of the student'. However, the skepticism about contrastive analysis in the succeeding years resulted in very different – and widely accepted – assessments such as the following:

Ideally, the psychological aspect of the Contrastive Analysis Hypothesis[3] should deal with the conditions under which interference takes place. That is, it should account for instances when linguistic differences between the first and second languages lead to transfer errors and instances when they do not. It is because it is not possible to predict or explain the presence of transfer errors solely in terms of linguistic differences between the first and second languages that a psychological explanation is necessary. What are the non-linguistic variables that help determine whether and when interference occurs? (Ellis, 1985: 24)

Like many others, Ellis doubted that linguists could make good predictions of the kind that Lado envisioned (and like many others, Ellis emphasized negative transfer – 'interference' – over positive transfer in his assessment). However, in the three decades since, two significant changes have occurred. First, a large number of SLA studies that compare different L1 groups, as in the case of studies of articles, offer evidence that L1 groups having a native language with articles (e.g. Swedish) normally have an advantage over groups having a native language without articles (e.g. Finnish). Second, many linguists (both SLA specialists and researchers in other fields) now try to include a 'psychological explanation', as Ellis phrased it, in their analyses. Accordingly, predictions that build not only on earlier transfer research (e.g. on articles and gender) but also on psychological explanations (e.g. reference tracking) may prove to be very robust. For example, while there does not yet appear to be any empirical validation of it, the following prediction seems quite plausible: Speakers of Finnish as a group will have greater difficulty with the articles of Portuguese than will speakers of Swedish as a group (Odlin, 2014). It also seems reasonable to predict that Swedish learners as a group will do better with Portuguese articles than will English speakers because, unlike English, Swedish has grammatical gender (even though English speakers would probably outperform Finnish speakers in at least supplying articles).

There might be, of course, individual exceptions to the group tendency in the prediction if some Finns happen to be more successful than some Swedes. Yet, the focus on group tendencies allows for statistical inferences if tests such as an analysis of variance (ANOVA) are employed. When such measures do indicate group differences, it becomes hard to deny that positive transfer plays an important role. Even so, individual differences still matter and, as Jarvis and Pavlenko (2008: 33) observe, it is also necessary 'to uncover as many specifics as possible about how CLI [cross-linguistic influence] manifests itself in the language and cognition of real individuals'. Even in groups, of course, it is always an individual who is making a (necessarily) subjective assessment about the similarity of something in the source and something in the target languages. One example of where such individual assessments matter involves the transferability of idioms. Kellerman (1977) found that Dutch students often seemed skeptical that certain phrases such as *dyed-in-the-wool* were genuine English idioms, and the reason for their skepticism appears to have been that the sayings have close equivalents in Dutch – in other words, the resemblance seemed to many students to be too good to be true. Even so, the graphs and figures in Kellerman's (e.g. 1977: 119) study indicate considerable individual variation: while some learners seemed quite skeptical about the transferability of Dutch idioms, some seemed more inclined to view such idioms as transferable. The finding about learner skepticism is indeed significant, but it would be mistaken to conclude, as some readers of Kellerman's study have done, that there is some absolute 'constraint' on the transferability of idioms.

Discussions of transfer have often considered the issue of constraints of one kind or another, including alleged constraints on the transfer of word order, bound morphology and article systems. However, counterexamples to the claimed constraints are relatively easy to find in the literature on language contact and SLA (Odlin, 2003, 2006), and so predicting when a structure will *not* transfer is, if anything, more perilous than making predictions about when transfer will occur. Predictions about supposed 'processing constraints' on transfer (e.g. Pienemann *et al.*, 2005) are likewise questionable since there exist individual exceptions to deterministic models of acquisition that posit strict developmental sequences (Odlin, 2013). Such facts do not rule out the possibility of constraints, however. As with predictions such as the one about Portuguese articles, it may prove viable to specify what is less likely to transfer in large groups as long as any predicted constraint acknowledges that at least a few individuals might depart from the group tendency. The importance of individual variation also urges caution in how statistics are reported. When the stated results focus mainly on differences in group means, as in ANOVA and other inferential statistics, such reporting may invite the conclusion that individual differences are trivial, when in fact they may be crucial to understand the entire range of possibilities for the ways that cross-linguistic influence can work. Research in other areas of SLA (e.g. Dewaele, 2009: 639–640) has noted the need for more care about inferences from statistical results, and the need is no less great in transfer research.

Aims and Focus of the Book

Any serious attempt to understand SLA requires close attention to cross-linguistic influence. Naturally, sound insights about transfer in SLA and multilingualism can aid teachers and program designers in their efforts to improve instruction, and the study of transfer is also important in its own right, as it offers unique perspectives on human cognition. As Jarvis and Pavlenko (2008: 11) put it, the ultimate goal of transfer research is 'the explanation of how the languages a person knows interact in the mind'.

The purpose of this volume is threefold: (i) to bring together several data-based studies presenting new findings on language transfer; (ii) to offer new theoretical perspectives on transfer, some in the empirical studies and some in other chapters; and (iii) to provide an in-depth look at transfer phenomena in a one language-contact setting, namely, China: six of the chapters in the volume examine either L1 Chinese influence on the acquisition of L2 English or (in Chapter 8) L1 English influence on L2 Chinese. Among the theoretical issues addressed are the interaction of transfer with comprehension and production processes, the interaction of the age of the learner and the influence of the L1, the role of social contexts in acquisition, the structure of the L2 lexicon, the relationship between transfer and perceptions of acceptability and the use of transfer research today to shed light on language contact situations in the past.

The volume consists of four sections considering lexical, syntactic, phonological and cognitive perspectives, and summaries at the beginning of each section will help readers to note the similarities and differences in the chapters. In addition, two other chapters offer overviews of transfer beyond this introduction: Chapter 13 (by Terence Odlin) provides a retrospective look at the other chapters in the volume, and Chapter 2 (by Scott Jarvis) addresses problems of transfer relevant to all four sections as well as to problems considered only briefly in this introduction. Jarvis focuses on the following concerns: empirical discoveries, theoretical advances, methodological tools and argumentation heuristics.

Notes

(1)   Here and in other parts of the chapter, we follow the convention of historical linguists in employing angled brackets to refer to orthographic symbols and slashes to refer to phonemes. Thus, a <k> represents the letter in the alphabet while a /k/ represents the voiceless velar stop.

(2)   The examples of English used by Finnish- and Swedish-speaking students (including the earlier example with *crass*) come from a database compiled by Jarvis (1998). Some details about the corpus are also given in Chapter 11 of this volume.

(3)   Many SLA specialists along with Ellis have used the term *contrastive analysis hypothesis*, but definitions of the so-called hypothesis vary to the point of making the term quite nebulous (Odlin, 2012b).

References

Alhawary, M. (2009) Speech processing prerequisite or language transfer? Evidence from English and French L2 learners of Arabic. *Foreign Language Annals* 42, 367–390.

Ard, J. and Homburg, T. (1993) Verification of language transfer. In S. Gass and L. Selinker (eds) *Language Transfer in Language Learning* (pp. 47–70). Amsterdam: John Benjamins.

Bloch, J. and Chi, L. (1995) A comparison of the use of citations in Chinese and English academic discourse. In D. Belcher and G. Braine (eds) *Academic Writing in a Second Language: Essays on Research and Pedagogy* (pp. 231–274). Norwood, NJ: Ablex.

Blum-Kulka, S. (1982) Learning to say what you mean: A study of speech act performance of learners of Hebrew as a second language. *Applied Linguistics* 3, 29–59.

Brown, A. (2007) Cross-linguistic influence in first and second languages: Convergence in speech and gesture. Unpublished PhD dissertation, Boston University.

Cadierno, T. (2010) Motion in Danish as a second language: Does the learner's L1 make a difference? In Z. Han and T. Cadierno (eds) *Linguistic Relativity in Second Language Acquisition: Evidence of First Language Thinking for Speaking* (pp. 1–33). Bristol: Multilingual Matters.

Corbett, G. (1999) Agreement. In J. Miller (ed.) *Concise Encyclopedia of Grammatical Categories* (pp. 12–18). Amsterdam: Elsevier.

Corder, S. (1983) A role for the mother tongue. In S. Gass and L. Selinker (eds) *Language Transfer in Language Learning* (pp. 85–97). Rowley, MA: Newbury House.

De Angelis, G. (2007) *Third or Additional Language Acquisition.* Clevedon: Multilingual Matters.

De Angelis, G. and Dewaele, J.-M. (eds) (2011) *New Trends in Cross-Linguistic Influence and Multilingualism Research.* Bristol: Multilingual Matters.

Dechert, H. (2006) On the ambiguity of the notion 'transfer'. In J. Arabski (ed.) *Cross-Linguistic Influence in the Second Language Lexicon* (pp. 3–11). Clevedon: Multilingual Matters.

Dewaele, J-M. (2009) Individual differences in second language acquisition. In W. Ritchie and T. Bhatia (eds) *The New Handbook of Second Language Acquisition* (pp. 623–646). Bingley: Emerald.

Dulay, H., Burt, M. and Krashen, S. (1982) *Language Two.* New York: Oxford University Press.

Elliott, A. (1885) Review of Schuchardt (1884). *American Journal of Philology* 89–94.

Elliott, A. (1886) Speech mixture in French Canada, Indian and French. *Transactions and Proceedings of the Modern Language Association of America* 2, 158–186.

Ellis, R. (1985) *Understanding Second Language Acquisition.* Oxford: Oxford University Press.

Elston-Güttler, K. and Williams, J. (2008) L1 polysemy affects L2 meaning interpretation: Evidence for L1 concepts active during L2 reading. *Second Language Research* 24, 167–187.

Filppula, M., Klemola, J. and Paulasto, H. (2008) *English and Celtic in Contact*. New York: Routledge.

Gabryś-Barker, D. (ed.) (2012) *Cross-Linguistic Influences in Multilingual Language Acquisition, Second Language Learning and Teaching*. Berlin: Springer.

Gullberg, M. (2008) Gestures and second language acquisition. In P. Robinson and N. Ellis (eds) *Handbook of Cognitive Linguistics and Second Language Acquisition* (pp. 276–305). New York: Routledge.

Gullberg, M. (2011) Language-specific coding of placements in gestures. In J. Bohnemeyyer and E. Pederson (eds) *Event Representation in Language and Cognition* (pp. 166–188). Cambridge: Cambridge University Press.

Hammarberg, B. (2009) *Processes in Third Language Acquisition*. Edinburgh: Edinburgh University Press.

Han, Z. (2010) Grammatical inadequacy as a function of linguistic relativity: A longitudinal case study. In Z. Han and T. Cadierno (eds) *Linguistic Relativity in Second Language Acquisition: Evidence of First Language Thinking for Speaking* (pp. 154–182). Bristol: Multilingual Matters.

Helms-Park, R. (2001) Evidence of lexical transfer in learner syntax: The acquisition of English causatives by speakers of Hindi-Urdu and Vietnamese. *Studies in Second Language Acquisition* 23, 71–102.

Helms-Park, R. (2003) Transfer in SLA and creoles: The implications of causative serial verbs in the interlanguage of Vietnamese ESL learners. *Studies in Second Language Acquisition* 25, 211–244.

Humboldt, W. von ([1836] 1960) *Über die Verschiedenheit des menschlichen Sprachbaues und ihren Einfluss auf die geistige Entwickelung des Menschengeschlechts* [*On the Diversity of Human Language Construction and Its Influence on Human Mental Development*]. Bonn: Dümmler.

Hyltenstam, K. (1984) The use of typological markedness conditions as predictors in second language acquisition. In R. Andersen (ed.) *Second Languages: A Cross-Linguistic Perspective* (pp. 39–58). Rowley, MA: Newbury House.

Isurin, L., Winford, D. and de Bot, K. (eds) (2009) *Multidisciplinary Approaches to Code-Switching*. Amsterdam: John Benjamins.

Jarvis, S. (1998) *Conceptual Transfer in the Interlanguage Lexicon*. Bloomington, IN: IULC Publications.

Jarvis, S. (2000) Methodological rigor in the study of transfer: Identifying L1 influence in the interlanguage lexicon. *Language Learning* 50, 245–309.

Jarvis, S. (2002) Topic continuity in L2 English article use. *Studies in Second Language Acquisition* 24, 387–418.

Jarvis, S. and Odlin, T. (2000) Morphological type, spatial reference, and language transfer. *Studies in Second Language Acquisition* 22, 535–556.

Jarvis, S. and Pavlenko, A. (2008) *Cross-Linguistic Influence in Language and Cognition*. New York: Routledge.

Jarvis, S. and Crossley, S. (eds) (2012) *Approaching Language Transfer Through Text Classification*. Bristol: Multilingual Matters.

Jespersen, O. (1922) *Language: Its Nature, Development, and Origin*. London: Allen and Unwin.

Kaivapalu, A. and Martin, M. (2007) Morphology in transition: Plural inflection of Finnish nouns by Estonian and Russian learners. *Acta Linguistica Hangarica* 54 (2), 129–156.

Klee, C. and Ocampo, A. (1995) The expression of past reference in Spanish narratives of Spanish–Quechua bilingual speakers. In C. Silva-Corvalán (ed.) *Spanish in Four Continents* (pp. 52–70). Washington, DC: Georgetown University Press.

Lado, R. (1957) *Linguistics Across Cultures*. Ann Arbor, MI: University of Michigan Press.

Lakoff, G. and Johnson, M. (1980) *Metaphors We Live By*. Chicago, IL: University of Chicago Press.

Lakoff, G. and Johnson, M. (1999) *Philosophy in the Flesh: The Embodied Mind and Its Challenge to Western Thought*. New York: Basic Books.

Larsen-Freeman, D. and Long, M. (1991) *An Introduction to Second Language Acquisition Research*. London: Longman.

Luk, Z. and Shirai, Y. (2009) Is the acquisition order of grammatical morphemes impervious to L1 knowledge? Evidence from the acquisition of plural -s, articles, and possessive 's. *Language Learning* 59, 721–754.

MacWhinney, B. (2008) A unified model. In P. Robinson and N. Ellis (eds) *Handbook of Cognitive Linguistics and Second Language Acquisition* (pp. 341–371). New York: Routledge.

Master, P. (1987) A cross-linguistic interlanguage analysis of the acquisition of the English article system. Unpublished PhD dissertation, University of California at Los Angeles.

Migge, B. (2003) *Creole Formation as Language Contact*. Amsterdam: Benjamins.

Montrul, S. (2000) Transitivity alternations in L2 acquisition: Toward a modular view of transfer. *Studies in Second Language Acquisition* 22, 229–273.

Mufwene, S. (2010) SLA and the emergence of creoles. *Studies in Second Language Acquisition* 32, 1–42.

Nakahama, Y. (2011) *Referent Markings in L2 Narratives: Effects of Task Complexity, Learners' L1, and Proficiency Level*. Tokyo: Hituzi Syobo.

Nash, R. (1979) Cognate transfer in Puerto Rican English. In R. Andersen (ed.) *The Acquisition and Use of Spanish and English as First and Second Languages* (pp. 33–42). Washington, DC: Teachers of English to Speakers of Other Languages.

Odlin, T. (1989) *Language Transfer: Cross-Linguistic Influence in Language Learning*. Cambridge: Cambridge University Press.

Odlin, T. (2003) Cross-linguistic influence. In C. Doughty and M. Long (eds) *Handbook of Second Language Acquisition* (pp. 436–486). Oxford: Blackwell.

Odlin, T. (2006) Could a contrastive analysis ever be complete? In J. Arabski (ed.) *Cross-Linguistic Influences in the Second Language Lexicon* (pp. 22–35). Clevedon: Multilingual Matters.

Odlin, T. (2008) Conceptual transfer and meaning extensions. In P. Robinson and N. Ellis (eds) *Handbook of Cognitive Linguistics and Second Language Acquisition* (pp. 306–340). New York: Routledge.

Odlin, T. (2012a) Nothing will come of nothing. In B. Kortmann and B. Szmrecsanyi (eds) *Linguistic Complexity in Interlanguage Varieties, L2 Varieties, and Contact Languages* (pp. 62–89). Berlin: de Gruyter.

Odlin, T. (2012b) The contrastive analysis hypothesis. In P. Robinson (ed.) *The Routledge Encyclopedia of Second Language Acquisition* (pp. 129–131). New York: Routledge.

Odlin, T. (2013) Accelerator or inhibitor? On the role of substrate influence in interlanguage development. In D. Schreier and M. Hundt (eds) *English as a Contact Language* (pp. 298–313). Cambridge: Cambridge University Press.

Odlin, T. (2014) Rediscovering prediction. In Z. Han and E. Tarone (eds) *Interlanguage 40 Years Later* (pp. 27–45). Amsterdam: Benjamins.

Oller, J. and Redding, E. (1971) Article usage and other language skills. *Language Learning* 20, 183–189.

Olshtain, E. (1983) Sociocultural competence and language transfer: The case of apology. In S. Gass and L. Selinker (eds) *Language Transfer in Language Learning* (pp. 232–249). Rowley, MA: Newbury House.

Orr, G. (1987) Aspects of the second language acquisition of Chichewa noun class morphology. Unpublished PhD dissertation, University of California at Los Angeles.

Osgood, C. (1949) The similarity paradox in human learning: A resolution. *Psychological Review* 36, 132–143.

Pavlenko, A. (2003) 'I feel clumsy speaking Russian': L2 influence on L1 in narratives of Russian L2 users of English. In V. Cook (ed.) *Effects of the Second Language on the First* (pp. 32–61). Clevedon: Multilingual Matters.

Pienemann, M., Di Biase, B., Kawaguchi, S. and Håkansson, G. (2005) Processing constraints on L1 transfer. In J.F. Kroll and A.M.B. de Groot (eds) *Handbook of Bilingualism: Psycholinguistic Approaches* (pp. 128–153). Oxford, New York: Oxford University Press.

Porte, G. (2003) English from a distance: Code-mixing and blending in the L1 output of long-term resident overseas EFL teachers. In V. Cook (ed.) *Effects of the Second Language on the First* (pp. 103–119). Clevedon: Multilingual Matters.

Reddy, M. (1979) The conduit metaphor: A case of frame conflict in our language about language. In A. Ortony (ed.) *Metaphor and Thought* (pp. 284–324). Cambridge: Cambridge University Press.

Ringbom, H. (1987) *The Role of the First Language in Foreign Language Learning*. Clevedon: Multilingual Matters.

Ringbom, H. (2007) *Cross-Linguistic Similarity in Foreign Language Learning*. Clevedon: Multilingual Matters.

Rocca, S. (2007) *Child Second Language Acquisition*. Amsterdam: Benjamins.

Sabourin, L., Stowe, L. and de Haan, G. (2006) Transfer effects in learning a second language grammatical gender system. *Second Language Research* 22, 1–29.

Sapir, E. (1921) *Language*. New York: Harcourt, Brace, Jovanovich.

Schuchardt, H. ([1884] 1971) *Slawo-deutsches und Slawo-italiensches*. Munich: Wilhem Fink.

Selinker, L. (1969) Language transfer. *General Linguistics* 9, 67–92.

Selinker, L. (2006) Afterword: Fossilization or 'does your mind mind'? In Z-H. Han and T. Odlin (eds) *Studies of Fossilization in Second Language Acquisition* (pp. 201–210). Clevedon: Multilingual Matters.

Senft, G. (2007) Nominal classification. In D. Geeraerts and H. Guyckens (eds) *The Oxford Handbook of Cognitive Linguistics* (pp. 676–696). Oxford: Oxford University Press.

Siegel, J. (2012) Accounting for analyticity in creoles. In B. Kortmann and B. Szmrecsanyi (eds) *Linguistic Complexity in Interlanguage Varieties, L2 Varieties, and Contact Languages* (pp. 35–61). Berlin: de Gruyter.

Sleman, P. (2004) The acquisition of definiteness distinctions by L2 learners of French. *Linguistics in the Netherlands* 21, 158–168.

Slobin, D. (1996) From 'thought and language' to 'thinking for speaking'. In J. Gumperz and S. Levinson (eds) *Rethinking Linguistic Relativity* (pp. 97–114). Cambridge: Cambridge University Press.

Vervaeke, J. and Kennedy, J. (2004) Conceptual metaphor and abstract thought. *Metaphor and Symbol* 19, 213–231.

Wang, M., Koda, K. and Perfetti, C. (2003) Alphabetic and nonalphabetic L1 effects in English word identification: A comparison of Korean and Chinese English L2 learners. *Cognition* 87, 129–149.

Weinreich, U. (1953) *Languages in Contact*. The Hague: Mouton.

White, L. (2003) On the nature of interlanguage representation: Universal Grammar in the second language, In C. Doughty and M. Long (eds) *Handbook of Second Language Acquisition* (pp. 19–42). Oxford: Blackwell.

Whitney, W. (1881) On mixture in language. *Transactions of the American Philological Association* 12, 5–26.

Yu, L. (1996) The role of cross-linguistic lexical similarity in the use of motion verbs in English by Chinese and Japanese learners. Unpublished EdD dissertation, University of Toronto.

2 The Scope of Transfer Research

Scott Jarvis

Defining the Scope

Transfer is a phenomenon that has been recognized since time immemorial. The ancient Greeks were certainly aware of it, as can be found in the writing of Homer, Herodutus and Flavius Philostratus (see Adams *et al.*, 2002; Janse, 2002). Probably just about all people who have ever learned a language beyond their native one have been aware to some degree of how their knowledge of one language has affected their knowledge and use of another. Historically, transfer has, of course, been seen mainly as an obstacle. When it became an object of scholarly interest in the 1800s (e.g. von Humboldt, 1963; Whitney, 1881) and the 1900s (e.g. Fries, 1945; Haugen, 1953; Lado, 1957; Weinreich, 1953), it was investigated mainly as a factor that interferes with what were seen as bigger, more important phenomena, such as knowledge of or performance in another language.

In other words, transfer was historically treated essentially as an independent variable that affects a more important dependent variable (see Figure 2.1). Up to a few decades ago, it was seen as the main independent variable – or the main obstacle to learning a second language (L2) (e.g. Lado, 1957: 59). However, as the results of empirical studies involving contrastive analysis and error analysis emerged in the 1960s and 1970s (e.g. Dušková, 1969; Richards, 1971; Selinker, 1969), the importance of other independent variables was recognized, and the impact of transfer was subsequently downplayed and even treated as negligible by researchers such

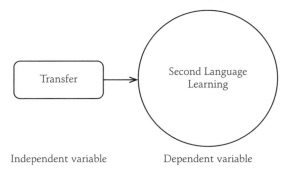

Independent variable   Dependent variable

Figure 2.1 Transfer viewed as an independent variable

as Heidi Dulay, Marina Burt and Stephen Krashen (e.g. Bailey *et al.*, 1974; Dulay & Burt, 1973; Krashen, 1983).

I have often heard it said that in the late 1960s and throughout the 1970s, transfer research was shunned and even abandoned in the United States. There is some truth to this, though many American researchers, such as Andersen (1977), Schachter (1974), Selinker (1972) and Taylor (1975), clearly did keep pushing transfer research forward during this time. It is nevertheless equally clear that they did so in a climate that did not place a very high value on such research (cf. Andersen, 1983: 177; Gass & Selinker, 1983: 6). During this same period of time in Europe, transfer research appears to have flourished, and it even underwent what I consider to have been a fundamental transformation. Many researchers contributed to this transformation, and certainly Ringbom (1976, 1978) and Kellerman (1977, 1978) deserve a great deal of the credit. The transformation was this: Transfer went from being treated as an independent variable, to becoming a dependent variable worthy of investigation in its own right, with its own set of independent variables (see Figure 2.2). Transfer research changed from a preoccupation with the proportion of errors that it accounts for, to the pursuit of questions about what causes transfer to occur, and what constraints keep it from happening when it does not occur (see e.g. Andersen [1983] and Kellerman [1983] for detailed discussions of these issues). Transfer research also changed its emphasis from questions about how strong an effect cross-linguistic influence (CLI) (=transfer) has on L2 learning to questions about what its specific effects are (see Odlin [1989] and Ringbom [1987] for comprehensive reviews of the relevant literature).

In Jarvis and Pavlenko (2008), we characterized the life course of transfer research as progressing through four general phases. The phases are abstractions of the types of emphases that can be found at different time periods as the field has matured. According to our explanation, the life course of transfer research began with an emphasis on *the identification and quantification of transfer effects*, from which it progressed into a broader *exploration of the causes of and constraints on transfer*. Exploratory research has

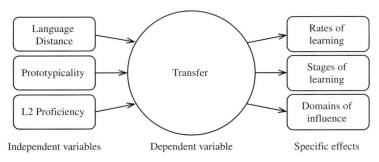

Figure 2.2 A transformed view of transfer

Table 2.1 Old and new paradigms of transfer research in relation to the four general phases

Old paradigm	Phase 1	Identification and quantification of transfer effects
New paradigm	Phase 2	Exploration of the causes of and constraints on transfer
	Phase 3	Development of theoretical explanations
	Phase 4	Description of how transfer takes place in the brain

increasingly given way to hypothesis-driven research, which is a prominent emphasis of the current phase of transfer research; the third and current phase is characterized by the *development of theoretical explanations* of CLI and its relationship with other constructs. A fourth phase, which is beginning to emerge (see below), will give increasing priority to the *description of how transfer takes place in the brain*. This will require advanced brain-imaging technologies beyond what are currently available. A fuller discussion of these phases can be found in Jarvis and Pavlenko (2008: 4–8). The important point for now is that the fundamental transformation of transfer research can be thought of as a paradigm shift that took place between Phases 1 and 2 in the life course of transfer research (see Table 2.1). This was a paradigm shift that, in my view, changed the meaning, objectives and ultimately the scope of transfer research.

Phases 2 through 4 are all part of the new paradigm – or the current era of transfer research. Even though we can distinguish consecutive phases in the developments and discoveries that have taken place in the current era, all phases of the new paradigm represent a progression toward the same ultimate goal, which can be described as follows: 'The ultimate goal of transfer research [is] the explanation of how the languages a person knows interact in the mind' (Jarvis & Pavlenko, 2008: 111). There are, of course, other ways of describing the ultimate goal of transfer research, but regardless of how it is described, it is clear that the fullest account of CLI will involve an explanation of how it takes place through the internal mechanisms of the mind and by means of mental representations of language and of the contexts in which it is embedded. These representations are formed, stored, accessed, modified and combined with other representations in the minds of individuals, and it is the mental interaction between an individual's representations of two or more languages that ultimately needs to be explained.

Even though most transfer research does not contribute directly to the ultimate goal, most studies do contribute more or less directly to what can be described as enabling goals, which are intermediate steps toward the ultimate goal. The enabling goals involve work in discovering more about the nature of CLI and its causes and consequences, and in developing better tools and protocols for studying it. Beyond the enabling goals, transfer research also includes a few side goals, which are not necessarily intended to lead to the ultimate goal, but are rather pursued in an attempt to derive applications and other types of practical benefits from the developments and discoveries made vis-à-vis the enabling goals. The side goals involve practical applications directed particularly toward the enhancement of language learning, language teaching and language diagnosis and assessment, and various types of fact-finding purposes that fall within the domain of forensic linguistics (see e.g. Jarvis & Crossley, 2012).

As illustrated in Figure 2.3, the enabling goals of transfer research include (a) the pursuit of *empirical discoveries* that expand our pool of knowledge regarding the nature of this phenomenon, its subsystems, its domains of influence, its impetuses and its specific outcomes; (b) *theoretical advances* that account for these empirical discoveries and which offer further, empirically testable hypotheses concerning the nature of CLI, what its impetuses and constraints are, how it operates in the mind and brain, what its specific consequences are and how it interacts with other factors and influences; (c) ongoing efforts to develop new and relevant *methodological tools*, instruments and procedures for testing those hypotheses, for disambiguating cases where cross-linguistic effects are uncertain and for pushing the envelope into new domains of discovery that were previously beyond the bounds of inquiry due to methodological and conceptual limitations; and finally (d) developing and refining a coherent set of *argumentation heuristics* that serve as standards for what counts as valid evidence for or against the presence of transfer, and which clarify the criteria for achieving methodological (or argumentative) rigor in one's analysis and interpretations. These four enabling goals are part of a cycle wherein advancements in the pursuit of one goal can lead to simultaneous or future progress in another. These goals also overlap in such a way that

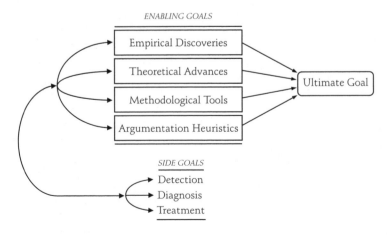

Figure 2.3 The scope of transfer research in terms of its main goals

a single study might contribute to more than one at the same time. This point should become clearer in the following sections of this chapter.

The side goals include the ways in which we are able to gain practical benefits from the empirical, theoretical and methodological advances in transfer research. Broadly speaking, the side goals include the *detection* of cross-linguistic effects, which might be used for forensic purposes; the *diagnosis* of cross-linguistic effects in learners' language performance, which could be used for pedagogical purposes; and the development of *treatment* interventions designed to minimize the negative effects of transfer in language learners or language communities and to take maximum advantage of its positive consequences. As implied in Figure 2.3, advances in the side goals can result from progress in the enabling goals, but the inherited benefits can also work in the opposite direction. In practice, what often happens is that scholarly work on CLI advances both enabling and side goals at the same time (see e.g. Jarvis & Crossley, 2012).

The scope of transfer research encompasses its ultimate goal together with its enabling and side goals. This is a scope that is rich in both its breadth and depth. In my career as a transfer researcher, I have attempted to contribute to each of the four enabling goals; perhaps more importantly, I have also attempted to lay the necessary groundwork for other researchers in order to help them to properly situate their own contributions within the overall scope of this area of research so as to give those contributions greater clarity, relevance and value. An important part of the necessary groundwork is a clear explanation of the scope of transfer research, its primary components and how they fit together. This is the purpose of the present chapter. In the remaining sections of this chapter, I will attempt to illustrate in some detail the progress that has been made in relation to each of the four enabling goals, what the current and emerging trends are and how the four enabling goals overlap and feed into one another. Where relevant, I will use examples from my own research and from areas of research that I am particularly interested in. I acknowledge, however, that the existing major contributions to each of the four enabling goals extend far beyond the narrow range of issues dealt with in this chapter. An adequate synthesis of even just the major discoveries and developments in each area would, of course, require a book-length treatment. Such book-length syntheses of transfer research can be found, among other places, in Jarvis and Pavlenko (2008), Odlin (1989) and Ringbom (1987, 2007).

Empirical Discoveries

The first enabling goal centers on empirical discoveries, and it is directed toward increasing what the field knows about CLI. Work on this goal can be thought of as an ongoing endeavor to add to the pool of empirically documented and confirmed facts about the nature of CLI and its relationship with other constructs. Among other things, the goal is to discover as much as possible about the domains of language use in which transfer can occur, under which conditions it will occur, how it will manifest itself and which other factors it interacts with and what their specific effects on transfer are.

Landmark findings

A great deal of progress has already been made in relation to this goal. It includes, first of all, the eight landmark findings on transfer discussed by Jarvis and Pavlenko (2008), which are summarized in Table 2.2. Although some of the sources I have listed in Table 2.2 are quite recent, all eight of these landmark findings were first observed before 1990 (cf. Odlin, 1989). In the years since then, the field's understanding of these principles has become ever more refined in terms of both the contexts in which such effects have been found and the theoretical explanations that have been offered to account for them. Further on, I will describe some theoretical explanations, but for now I will simply note that empirical discoveries and theoretical explanations link into each other in the form of an ongoing cycle through which findings such as those listed in Table 2.2 often begin as observations (=empirical discoveries), for which researchers later attempt to find or formulate theoretical explanations; those theoretical explanations then generate new hypotheses, and the testing of those hypotheses leads to new empirical discoveries and so forth, in a perpetual cycle.

Dispelling myths

The eight landmark findings listed in Table 2.2 are but a small sampling of the existing empirical discoveries. Some of the recent research that I find particularly interesting has focused on the discovery of transfer effects in areas of language knowledge and acquisition where transfer has previously been claimed not to occur, or to be relatively rare. This includes transfer involving overt inflectional morphology, the order in which grammatical morphemes are acquired, the acquisition of tense and aspect and the emergence of word-order rules.

Concerning overt inflectional morphology, Eubank (1993/1994) cited Weinreich (1953) as having indicated that bound morphology (e.g. plural suffixes) tends not to transfer from one language to another. Eubank also referenced the work of Dulay and Burt (1973, 1974) as showing that inflectional morphemes that represent functional heads (i.e. plural, possessive, tense and person/number agreement) are not susceptible to transfer effects in relation to the order in which they are acquired. A few years later, Eubank et al. (1997: 176) made similar claims, saying that 'overt inflectional morphology generally does not transfer from [L1] to L2'. It is somewhat surprising that Eubank and his colleagues made this claim given that prior research (of which they were perhaps unaware) had shown

Table 2.2 Eight landmark findings concerning transfer

Finding	Explanation	Relevant literature
(1) Positive effects	CLI does not always result in errors. Most cross-linguistic effects may in fact be positive and advantageous for a language learner.	Kecskes and Papp (2000); Ringbom (1987)
(2) Rate and route	CLI can affect both how quickly a learner acquires the language and the stages and sequences he/she will go through.	Master (1997); Ringbom (2007)
(3) Similarities	Most cases of transfer appear to derive not from cross-linguistic differences per se, but rather from the learner's assumptions about which features of the native language and the target language are similar.	Andersen (1983); Kellerman (1995); Ringbom and Jarvis (2009)
(4) Non-linear changes	Transfer effects do not steadily decrease over time. In some areas, they may fluctuate and even increase with advancing L2 proficiency.	Jarvis (2000); Zobl (1984)
(5) Directions	CLI does not work solely from the L1 to an L2. It can also operate from an L2 to an L3, an L3 to an L2 and even an L2 to the L1.	Cenoz *et al.* (2001); Cook (2003)
(6) Transferability	Not all features of a language are equally likely to show cross-linguistic effects. Learners' intuitions about which features are universal versus language-specific have an important impact on the cross-linguistic associations they make.	Eckman (1977); Kellerman (1978, 1983)
(7) Meaning	CLI involves not only forms and structures, but also the meanings and functions that underlie those forms and structures.	Graham and Belnap (1986); Odlin (2008); Pavlenko (2011); Ringbom (1987)
(8) Individual differences	No two learners will be identical in terms of motivation, language aptitude, language experience (both L1 and L2), reliance on implicit versus explicit knowledge or ultimately the types of assumptions they make about how the target language works. Such differences can and do give rise to differing patterns of transfer.	Hakuta (1976); Jarvis and Pavlenko (2008); Odlin (1989)

that bound, overt inflectional morphology – even morphemes representing functional heads such as past tense and plural markers – does indeed transfer, and that such transfer is not at all rare when the first language (L1) and L2 are closely related, as for example Czech and Russian are (see Selinker & Lakshamanan, 1992). More recent research has unambiguously confirmed this finding with other combinations of closely related languages, such as Spanish and Italian (De Angelis & Selinker, 2001), Spanish, French and Italian (De Angelis, 2005) and Estonian and Finnish (Kaivapalu & Martin, 2007). Additionally, as pointed out by Jarvis and Odlin (2000), transfer involving bound inflectional morphology extends beyond the direct usage of overt L1 inflections on L2 words; like other domains of transfer, it very often involves the use of L2 forms to express L1 meanings and functions (see also Meriläinen, 2010).

As mentioned, Eubank's claims were based partially on the results of Dulay and Burt (1973, 1974), which were interpreted as suggesting that essentially all L2 learners of English, regardless of their L1 background, acquire English grammatical morphemes in the same order. This claim was also adopted by Krashen (1977) and formalized as part of his monitor model in the form of the natural order hypothesis. The natural order hypothesis has been very influential in L2 research, not only because of the large number of studies that have found support for it (see e.g. Gass & Selinker, 2008: 126–135), but also because L2 acquisition (SLA) textbooks tend to highlight the studies that have found support for it while overlooking a number of studies that disconfirm it. A recent study by Luk and Shirai (2009) reviews the findings of many relevant studies that have been overlooked. These studies examine morpheme acquisition (or accuracy) orders among Chinese-, Korean- and Japanese-speaking learners of English, and they indicate that learners' L1s do indeed substantially affect their acquisition of articles as well as plural and possessive markers (i.e. even functional heads). The aggregated results of these studies further show that learners tend to have little difficulty with L2 grammatical morphemes that (a) have functional counterparts in their L1 and (b) are structured similarly (e.g. with respect to word order) to their L1 counterparts. Learners correspondingly have more difficulty with L2 morphemes that fail to meet one or both of these criteria. These empirical discoveries regarding the effects of the L1 on the acquisition of L2 grammatical morphemes are of immense value to the field in dispelling a myth that has been perpetuated for far too long.

Tense and aspect is another area where the role of CLI has been downplayed. In her book-length review of prior research on the SLA of tense and aspect, Bardovi-Harlig (2000: 411) noted that 'no significant L1 effect has been identified in the longitudinal studies of the acquisition of temporal expression' and that 'comparisons across studies have also revealed little first language influence'. She also pointed out, however, that future analyses that give more attention to the details of what learners do in their expression of tense and aspect might very well be able to identify L1 effects. Indeed, this has occurred. Studies by Collins (2002) and Ayoun and Salaberry (2008), for example, have shown that French-speaking learners of English overuse the perfect aspect with telic verbs (e.g. 'Mary has read the book') because of the formal similarity between French past tense *passé composé* and the English perfect aspect. L1 influence in learners' use of tense and aspect is not limited to the forms they use to express these notions, however. Graduate research conducted by some of my former students has shown that Russian-speaking learners of English are significantly affected by L1 aspectual distinctions in their choice of tense and aspect markers in English (Polunenko, 2004), and Bulgarian-speaking learners often make a categorical distinction between the Bulgarian notions of witnessed and non-witnessed in their use of English tense and aspectual morphology (Dragiev, 2004).

Regarding the emergence of word-order rules, Pienemann (1998) has theorized that, although L1 influence does occur in learners' L2 syntax, there are certain processability constraints that prevent this from occurring during the earliest stages of acquisition. That is, until learners' ability to process the L2 develops beyond the initial stages, they rely on a universal canonical word order, which Pienemann believes is subject-verb-object (SVO). SVO happens to be the predominant word order for English sentences and clauses, and it is also a common word order in other Germanic languages, such as German and Swedish. German and Swedish nevertheless adhere to a verb-second (V2) rule, which results in subject-verb inversion when an adverbial phrase (A) is placed at the beginning of the sentence. Table 2.3 illustrates the V2 rule in two sample sentences from Swedish, one with subject-verb-object-adverb (SVOA) word order, and the other with fronted and inverted AVSO word order (i.e. adverbial-verb-subject-object). In both cases, the V2 rule is in effect.

Even though German and Swedish are subject to the same V2 constraint, Pienemann's model predicts that Swedish-speaking learners of German (or vice versa) will, in their earliest stages of sentence formation, rely on the canonical SVO word order even when adverbial structures are

Table 2.3 Examples of the verb-second rule in Swedish

Example 1:	Vi	Köpte	en	bok	igår.
	We	*bought*	*a*	*book*	*yesterday*
	S	V		O	A
Example 2:	Igår	köpte	vi	en	bok.
	yesterday	*bought*	*we*	*a*	*book*
	A	V	S		O

placed at the beginning of the sentence. Håkansson *et al.* (2002: 258) set out to test this prediction, and their results indeed show that Swedish-speaking learners in their first two years of German study at school 'do not transfer the verb-second structure from their L1 to the L2, even though the structure is identical in both languages and is contained in the learning input', and even though the learners' failure to transfer the V2 rule results in ASVO structures that are 'ungrammatical in the L1 and in the L2'. The data therefore appear to support the theoretical assumption that the SVO word order is a universal canonical word order for the early stages of L2 syntax. One problem with this interpretation, however, is that the learners in this study had actually learned English before they began German, so there is a possibility that they were simply transferring the SVO word order from English rather than from a universal canonical base. The researchers acknowledged this possibility, but quickly dismissed it as untestable. Yet, as pointed out by Bohnacker (2006), it is testable when one compares the results of Håkansson *et al.* with those of Swedish-speaking learners of German who have not yet learned English. This is precisely what Bohnacker did, and she found that such learners adhere fully to the V2 constraint from the earliest stages of German learning. Her results therefore seem to disconfirm the predictions of Pienemann's theory while at the same time confirming transfer not only in her own results, but also in those of Håkansson *et al.* (2002): L1 transfer from Swedish in the former case and L2 transfer from English in the latter case. This and the other recent discoveries described in this section have been invaluable in dispelling myths about transfer, even myths that have gained theoretical status.

Discovering hidden effects

Some of the additional promising empirical discoveries about transfer relate to cross-linguistic effects that have tended to go unnoticed until recently. In some cases, they have been discovered because a researcher was insightful enough to look for transfer effects in places where others had not yet thought to look. A good example of this is the study by Odlin (this volume), in which he examines how often and how accurately Finnish speakers versus Swedish speakers make use of available L2 input when producing written descriptions of a silent film in English. I collected the data in Finland in 1995, and Terence Odlin and I have used the data in several studies since then (e.g. Jarvis, 2000, 2002; Jarvis & Odlin, 2000; Odlin & Jarvis, 2004). The prompt for the learners' narratives was an eight-minute segment of the Chaplin film *Modern Times*. The film does not include any spoken dialog, but it does contain a few titles, which are short written quotations of what a character is saying. To illustrate, in one scene, a baker is shown accusing a woman of stealing a loaf of bread from the back of his bakery truck. Immediately after showing the baker speaking (but without having an audio track that allows the viewer to hear him speak), the screen turns blank and then shows the words 'She stole a loaf of bread'. In my own analyses of the data, I have always avoided learners' use of words and syntactic structures from titles because of the strong possibility that their use of such words and structures might simply reflect their memory of the language they were exposed to during the task rather than being generated from their own knowledge of the target language (TL). Odlin (this volume), however, has recognized that memory is one of the domains in which learners' knowledge of one language can affect their learning and use of another. Odlin shows that Swedish speakers, whose L1 is very similar to English, appear to be able to remember the titles from the film better than the Finnish speakers, whose L1 is unrelated to English. This finding is fully in line with what Ringbom (2007) has said about how cross-linguistic similarity enhances comprehension, and with what Gass (1997) has said about how learners' prior language knowledge has an effect on how well they are able to analyze and make use of L2 input. I will return to a discussion of the relationship between transfer and memory in the section on theoretical advances.

Another fascinating transfer-related discovery brought to light in recent years – which is also an outcome of looking where no one else thought to look – is the finding that speakers of certain languages are far more likely to refer to the end points of events than are speakers of other languages (e.g. von Stutterheim, 2003; von Stutterheim & Nüse, 2003). For example, when German speakers and English speakers are asked to describe brief film clips of motion events where the end point of the action is not shown and is also not easily inferable, German speakers tend to mention the end point anyway (e.g. *Two nuns are walking to a church*; *The boy is building a sandcastle*), whereas English speakers tend not to (e.g. *Two nuns are walking down a road, The boy is playing in the sand*). Von Stutterheim (2003) showed that this is true of German speakers and English speakers regardless of whether they perform the task in their L1 or L2. Von Stutterheim and her colleagues have explained this finding in relation to whether the learners' L1 contains a grammaticalized progressive aspect (which English does but German does not). They have also explored whether this phenomenon can be found in the L1 and L2 use of speakers of many other languages. Additionally, they have investigated whether the people who tend to mention end points also spend more time looking at those end points, and whether they are also better able to recall details about the potential end points that they have seen (for summaries of this line of inquiry, see e.g. Bylund [2011], Flecken [2010] and Schmiedtová *et al.* [2011]). Importantly, this line of research shows a solid interplay between empirical discovery and theoretical advances, as well as between theoretical advances and the development or appropriation of the methodological tools (e.g. eye-tracking equipment) necessary to test the theories.

The increasing availability of new technologies and new methodological tools also expands the horizon for exploratory work on transfer. New tools bring to our attention new places to look for transfer, and they also allow us to look more thoroughly through places we have already searched. Concerning the latter, although essays written by learners have already been scoured for evidence of transfer for decades if not centuries, what we have not been able to do very well until recently is to identify within them complex language-use patterns that are characteristic of specific language backgrounds. By analogy, I might say that we have already searched the evening sky for all of the stars that might reflect particular language backgrounds, but we have not yet searched for all of the possible constellations that might reflect those backgrounds. This work has recently begun, however, and it relies on the use of computer-based classification tools, some of which are not new to science per se, but which are at least new to transfer research. The first study to use computer-based classification of learner texts by L1 background appears to have been Mayfield Tomokiyo and Jones (2001), and the most recent studies can be found in a collected volume edited by Jarvis and Crossley (2012). The collected volume consists of five empirical studies that use computer classification techniques with learner essays to discover the constellations of words, multiword sequences, textual indices and error types that are most predictive of learners' L1 backgrounds. The results are quite revealing, and they have important consequences not just in terms of their value as empirical discoveries (the first enabling goal), but also in terms of the contributions they make to the third and fourth enabling goals (i.e. the development of methodological tools and argumentation heuristics). I will return to this point later on.

Theoretical Advances

The second enabling goal involves theoretical advances, and I begin this section by reiterating that theoretical advances both drive and are driven by empirical discoveries. There is a necessary relationship between the two, just as there is a necessary relationship between language assessment and theories about language. Assessment involves the empirical measurement of constructs, whereas theories explain what those constructs are and how they relate to one another (see e.g. Fulcher & Davidson, 2007: 8–10). Neither empirical work nor theorizing can reach its full potential without the other.

In accordance with the observations just noted, theoretical work on CLI will need to define and explain the theoretical construct of transfer as well as theoretical constructs of the factors and processes believed to interact with it. In relation to the ultimate goal of transfer research, theoretical advances need to achieve a level of depth and precision in describing how these constructs are related, both in the mind and in the brain. Theoretical explanations of transfer also need to take into account the linguistic, social and situational contexts in which languages are learned and used. Such explanations can be expected to begin as attempts to account for previous empirical observations, but they also need to push beyond the observed facts in order to offer a fuller explanation of the sources and causes of transfer, the mechanisms through which it operates, the factors that constrain it and the domains in which its effects can be detected. A useful theoretical explanation will also generate coherent and empirically testable hypotheses concerning the predictable, measurable or otherwise documentable consequences of transfer. These will then lead to the empirical testing of such hypotheses, which will give rise to new questions to explore, and will bring about refinements to existing theories as well as the impetus to develop new ones.

Although a full theory of transfer has not yet been attempted, most theories of bilingualism, multilingualism and SLA give at least some attention to transfer, and include it as one among many phenomena that can affect a person's acquisition, competence or performance in the TL (see e.g. Gass & Selinker, 2008). Some of the relatively recent hypotheses and theoretical models that deal more directly with transfer are the full transfer/full access model from the universal grammar framework (Schwartz & Sprouse, 1996), the multicompetence model (Cook, 2002), the thinking for speaking and conceptual transfer frameworks (Han & Cadierno, 2010; Jarvis, 2011a; Jarvis & Pavlenko, 2008; Pavlenko, 2011; von Stutterheim & Nüse, 2003) and models of inhibitory control, cross-linguistic interaction and activation and resonance (Flege, 1995; Green, 1998; MacWhinney, 2005). Space does not allow me to elaborate on all of these models, but I will deal briefly with the inhibitory control model (ICM) including some of the promising theoretical advances currently taking place with respect to the relationship between transfer and memory. This relationship has interesting implications for research on input and output. Before turning to those sections, let me point out that (a) all of the hypotheses and models just mentioned – as well as many others – represent important theoretical advances for transfer research, and (b) a necessary challenge for the future will be to draw these advances together into a single framework to show how they relate to one another and whether they are fully complementary.

Transfer and memory in the processing of target language input

In order to contribute to the ultimate goal of transfer research, efforts related to the third enabling goal need to be directed toward accounting for how CLI affects a learner's comprehension of and ability to process the TL input, his/her ability to create mental representations of the form-function and form-meaning mappings found within the input, his/her ability to relate those representations to his/her prior language knowledge and to integrate and store the new representations permanently within that system of knowledge, and his/her ability to access that knowledge later and encode it back into language. Ringbom (2007) refers to these processes as comprehension, learning and production, and he discusses at length how the types and degrees of similarity between the learner's L1 and L2 have substantial effects on each of these processes. Nowhere is this clearer than in the studies that have compared Finnish speakers with Swedish speakers in their learning and use of English. Studies reviewed by Ringbom show that Swedish speakers, whose L1 is closely related to English, comprehend a great deal more of the TL in the early stages of acquisition than do Finnish speakers, whose L1 is unrelated to English. Swedish speakers also tend to learn English at substantially faster rates than Finnish speakers do, and they tend to produce far fewer errors (see also Jarvis, 2002; Ringbom, 1987). As Terence Odlin's chapter in this volume suggests, some of these effects can probably be understood in relation to memory. That is, because of the similarities between Swedish and English, Swedish speakers are able to retain a good deal more of the TL input in memory than are Finnish speakers.

Odlin is careful not to make strong claims about whether the effects of cross-linguistic similarity are to be understood more in terms of short-term memory, working memory or long-term memory, and he also questions whether these categories of memory are even the most useful for understanding the relationship between CLI and memory. Even so, it is worth exploring the relationship between transfer and each of these constructs of memory. The large amount of attention that working memory has been receiving in the field of SLA recently (e.g. Goo, 2010; Kormos & Sáfár, 2008; Trude & Tokowicz, 2011) makes this a good place to start. Together with some colleagues and students of mine, I have recently initiated a theory-driven research project designed to investigate the possible relationships among working memory capacity (WMC), cross-linguistic similarity and TL proficiency in terms of the effects that these factors have on how efficiently learners can process TL input for comprehension, and also on how much of the TL input they can accurately retain and recall.

Our data collection process is still in its early stages, but in keeping with the topic of this section, I will briefly discuss the theoretical underpinnings of the project. They rely on theoretical explanations of both SLA and working memory. The former can perhaps be described most clearly in relation to Gass' (1988, 1997) framework for understanding how TL input is processed by the mind, how it becomes integrated into learners' developing knowledge of the TL and how this knowledge forms the basis of learners' output. The model shows several progressive stages through which the TL input must be processed in order to eventually become integrated into the learner's developing knowledge of the TL. These stages include (a) registering (or apperceiving) the input, (b) comprehending its meaning, (c) converting it into intake (i.e. creating a mapping between the form and meaning of the input) and (d) integrating the intake into the learner's TL knowledge system. The model also shows a subsequent stage where output is generated from the TL knowledge system. I will return to this final stage a little later. The main point for now is that, even though Gass has not (to my knowledge) described these stages in relation to working memory versus long-term memory, it seems quite clear that stages (a)–(c) entail working memory, whereas stage (d) implies long-term memory, as depicted in Figure 2.4.

The full, expanded version of Gass's (1997) model indicates that many important factors determine whether TL input will be apperceived, whether apperceived input will be comprehended, whether comprehended input will become intake and so forth. One of the prominent factors at work between each of these stages is learners' prior language knowledge, which includes their knowledge of the L1 as well as what they have already acquired in the TL. Based on the points raised and the research reviewed by Ringbom (2007), we can assume that the progression of input to comprehension and then onward to intake is greatly enhanced when the TL input closely resembles the learner's L1 knowledge. We also know that learners with higher levels of TL proficiency are better able to process and retain TL input.

So, cross-linguistic similarity and TL proficiency are known to affect how efficiently and effectively a learner can process and retain TL input in his/her working memory. Recent research shows that WMC also produces these effects (e.g. Goo, 2010; Kormos & Sáfár, 2008; Rai *et al.*, 2011). The fact that all three factors have been noted to produce similar effects raises questions about (a) whether all three factors really do produce independent effects, (b) whether or to what degree these factors might modulate one another's effects and (c) whether the effects of these factors and their

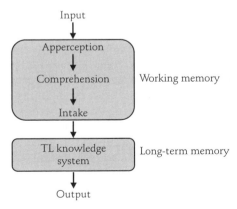

Figure 2.4 A simplified version of Gass's (1997) model shown in relation to working memory and long-term memory

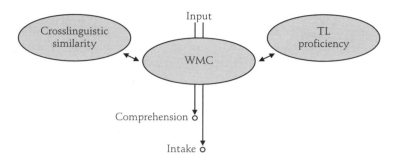

Figure 2.5 Current aims of the Ohio University project on the relationship between cross-linguistic similarity, working memory capacity and TL proficiency

relationship with one another change over time as the learner's knowledge of the TL develops.

In order to test the predictions and address the questions just presented, it is necessary to rely on theories of working memory. Current theories of working memory, such as Baddeley's (2007) model, generally assume that working memory includes both a processing component and a storage component. Baddeley refers to the processing component as the *central executive*, which is responsible for the speed and efficiency of the system in terms of how it manages the allocation of mental resources to all of the many tasks the mind may be attempting to regulate at the same time. The storage component is what we normally think of as short-term memory. It stores information very briefly unless that information is mentally rehearsed (by the central executive). In accordance with these theoretical assumptions, the testing of WMC can involve tests of mental processing efficiency (e.g. speed, latencies, reaction times) and/or tests of how much information a person can retain accurately while performing parallel mental tasks. In the project I am involved in at Ohio University, we are using the latter type of task as a measurement of learners' WMC, and are investigating how well this factor, together with learners' current level of TL proficiency and the degree of similarity between the L1 and the TL input, predicts how quickly they can process the input for comprehension and how much of the input is retained as intake (see Figure 2.5). These and related questions are important questions about transfer that, to our knowledge, have not yet been addressed in prior research, but which are now possible to address due to theoretical (and also methodological) advances in both SLA and psychology.

Transfer and memory in the production of target language output

Although Gass's (1988, 1997) model does not show any stages between the TL knowledge system and learners' language output (cf. Figure 2.4), we know

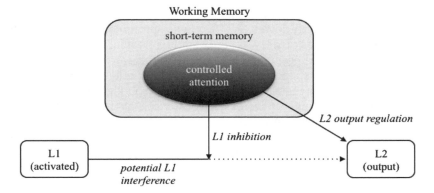

Figure 2.6 The role of controlled attention in inhibiting L1 interference and regulating L2 output

that working memory mediates not just between input and TL knowledge, but also between TL knowledge and output. Working memory is where both semantic and linguistic content is called up from long-term memory and is segmented, organized, and structured for expression (for a comprehensive explanation of how this works, see Levelt [1989]; see also von Stutterheim & Nüse [2003]). As described by Trude and Tokowicz (2011), working memory is used to regulate the learner's output, and this has consequences for both the speed with which he/she is able to produce output (cf. e.g. Guion *et al.*, 2000) and also the accuracy (and presumably complexity) of his/her output. Learners with higher WMCs will therefore presumably produce output more quickly and accurately than those with lower WMCs.

The story is even more complex than this, however. According to Green's (1998) ICM, stimuli often activate information that is not relevant to the current task. In particular, when a learner or bilingual is performing a task in the less-dominant language, words and other structures from the more dominant language can become activated. This means that the learner will have to use his/her mental resources not just for constructing a message, but also for inhibiting task-irrelevant information (such as words and other structures from the L1) from interfering with his/her TL output. According to Trude and Tokowicz (2011), the component of working memory that is responsible for inhibiting task-irrelevant information is what Kane and Engle (2003) describe as *controlled attention*, and this corresponds with what Baddeley (2007) calls the *central executive* (as mentioned earlier). This is not the storage component of working memory, but rather the component that manages and regulates where attention is directed and how mental resources are allocated. Figure 2.6 illustrates what the ICM predicts in relation to the functions of controlled attention (a component of working memory) in both inhibiting L1 interference and regulating TL output.

In order to test this theory, Trude and Tokowicz (2011) examined whether learners with lower WMCs, who presumably have reduced abilities to inhibit task-irrelevant information, would produce a greater number of L1-induced pronunciation errors. The researchers recruited two groups of participants, both of which consisted of adult English speakers who were taught Portuguese sound–letter correspondences so that they could pronounce Portuguese words correctly. None of the participants had any prior learning experience with Portuguese, but one of the groups had had at least four semesters of Spanish at university level. The other group had not previously studied any Romance language. After administering the Portuguese pronunciation tutorial, the researchers then tested the participants' WMCs using an operation span task. This task required the participants to remember sets of words in which the presentation of each consecutive word in a set was interrupted with a math problem that the participants had to solve. Their WMC was measured as both the set size for which they could remember all words in a set in at least two trials, and as the overall number of words they could remember across all trials. The operation span task was thus designed in such a way as to test not just the ability to store information temporarily (i.e. short-term memory), but also the ability to regulate both the storing and processing of information. Finally, after testing the participants' WMCs, the researchers tested their ability to read aloud (i.e. pronounce) a series of Portuguese words that were different from those used during the earlier tutorial. This was done to examine how well the participants could make use of the principles of Portuguese pronunciation they had learned previously.

The results showed that participants with higher WMCs were indeed able to pronounce the test words with higher levels of pronunciation accuracy than the participants with lower WMCs. Thus, the hypothesis that WMC aids in L1 inhibition was supported. An unexpected result, however, was that participants with higher WMCs showed elevated levels of interference from Spanish. The researchers suggested that this latter result did not contradict the theory, which gives the L1 a different status from non-target L2s. Perhaps an alternative explanation is that the very close similarities between Spanish and Portuguese made it more difficult for the participants to differentiate between these two languages than between English and Portuguese (cf. Ringbom, 2007) independently of WMC effects. Whichever interpretation is more plausible, the results of this study demonstrate how sophisticated theoretical models can provide the impetus for intriguing studies like this, and how the results of the study reciprocally indicate which assumptions of the theory are validated and which are in need of further refinement. All of the work described in this section also indicates that there is plenty more work to be done on the relationship between transfer and memory. On one level, for example, we need to know more about the nature of cross-linguistic similarity and of how it is perceived by the mind. We also need to know more about the interface between working memory and long-term memory and how it is that constructs such as prior knowledge – which is by definition stored in long-term memory – can affect processes of working memory (see e.g. Ericsson *et al.*, 1993; Unsworth & Engle, 2007). Similarly, we need to learn more about whether a learner's performance on a WMC task is tied to the language of the task, and also whether WMC might increase with advancing TL proficiency (van den Noort *et al.*, 2006).

Methodological Tools

The third enabling goal involves the discovery, development and use of new methodological tools that promote both empirical discoveries and theoretical advances. In some cases, the new tools involve new ways of collecting data without the need for new technologies. This can be seen, for example, in recent work on conceptual transfer, thinking for speaking and linguistic relativity that uses carefully compiled pictures or film clips to investigate whether learners from different language backgrounds differ in how they perceive and categorize qualities, substances and objects (e.g. Athanasopoulos, 2009; Cook *et al.*, 2006; Pavlenko & Malt, 2011), and in how they construe events (e.g. Bylund & Jarvis, 2011; Flecken, 2010; von Stutterheim & Nüse, 2003). New methodological tools also involve new, sophisticated ways of analyzing data, which has been a hallmark of transfer-related work carried out under the framework of thinking for speaking, which includes work on learners' use of speech-accompanying gestures (see the volumes edited by Han & Cadierno [2010] and Pavlenko [2011]). Such work can, of course, also be enhanced with new technologies, such as eye-tracking equipment used in combination with pictures or films, in order to gain a clearer understanding of what learners mentally attend to as they prepare their thoughts for verbalization (e.g. Flecken, 2010).

In most cases, these new technologies, procedures and other types of tools are adopted from other disciplines; nevertheless, researchers in our field often need to adjust the parameters for these tools and develop context-appropriate protocols for their use. Nowhere is this clearer than in the case of computer-based text classification tools used recently in a series of L1 identification studies compiled by Jarvis and Crossley (2012). As mentioned earlier, the purpose of these studies was to determine how reliably certain constellations of words, multiword sequences, error categories and textual indices could identify L2 texts with the L1 backgrounds of the learners who wrote those texts. One of the initial challenges the researchers faced was deciding which computer-based classifier to use, given that there are literally dozens of available classifiers to choose from (see e.g. Jarvis, 2011b; Kotsiantis, 2007). In order to determine which classifier would be the most effective for the purposes of the four studies in Jarvis and Crossley (2012) that rely on data from the *International Corpus of Learner English* (ICLE; Granger *et al.*, 2009), I conducted a pilot study (Jarvis, 2011b) in which I compared 20 of the most prominent classifiers in relation to their ability to identify the L1 affiliations of ICLE texts written by speakers from 12 different L1 backgrounds. The classifiers classified texts by L1 background by relying on the frequencies of various words and multiword sequences found in the data. Obtaining optimal results for each classifier required me to adjust its parameters and to use different feature-selection protocols. In the end, the best cross-validated results from each classifier were compared against one another, and they showed that the linear discriminant analysis classifier was the most effective for this particular classification task. On the basis of these results, and in order to maintain a certain degree of methodological consistency across studies, all five of the empirical studies in Jarvis and Crossley (2012) relied on the linear discriminant analysis classifier. Even though this is a widely available tool, and can be found in popular statistical applications such as R, SAS and SPSS, we learned from the literature of other disciplines (e.g. Lecocke & Hess, 2006) that these statistical applications do not have built-in means for performing the most reliable forms of cross-validation. The authors of the studies in Jarvis and Crossley (2012) were therefore not able to rely solely on the available tools, such as SPSS, but had to add some of their own programming and manual analysis to the analysis protocol. In perhaps most areas of transfer research where tools are adopted from other disciplines, certain modifications will be necessary.

As mentioned earlier, the increasing availability of new technologies expands the horizon for exploratory work on transfer. As the detection research shows, new tools allow us to find previously undiscovered cross-linguistic effects in data (such as the ICLE) that have been examined many times before. New technologies – or the new availability of technologies that were previously inaccessible to researchers – also give us new places to look for transfer. In the remainder of this section, I will describe how the increasing availability of brain-imaging technologies to researchers is enhancing our understanding of the mechanisms through which transfer occurs in the brain. The relevant research relates both to brain structures and brain functions. The tool of choice for investigating brain structures appears to be (structural) magnetic resonance imaging (MRI). MRI provides fairly clear and detailed images of the brain, and can also do so at different depth dimensions. Additionally, MRI can indicate the density of brain tissue. A paper by Green *et al.* (2007) reviews previous research that shows that vocabulary knowledge is associated with the density of brain tissue in an area of the brain referred to as the posterior supramarginal gyrus. The previous research shows that, with increasing vocabulary knowledge in their L1, native English speakers show increasing tissue density in this area. The research also indicates that Italian speakers show increasing tissue density in this same area as their vocabulary knowledge increases in both their L1 and in L2 English. So far, there does not seem to be anything language-specific about the relationship between vocabulary knowledge and brain tissue density. However, Green *et al.* conducted their own investigation of participants who knew Chinese either as an L1 or L2; in both groups, the researchers found significantly enhanced tissue densities in areas of the left and right hemispheres where English monolinguals and Italian–English bilinguals do not show such densities. Follow-up work is clearly needed here, but the tentative conclusion is that the specific languages a person knows has an effect on which specific areas of the brain become most developed. Presumably, this will also have observable consequences for language performance and expression.

Concerning brain functions, these can be examined either in relation to blood flow or electrical activity, and a paper by Kotz (2009) reviews the relevant literature related to both. The tool of choice for examining blood flow appears to be functional MRI (fMRI), whereas the tool of choice for examining electrical activity is electroencephalography (EEG), which uses a series of electrodes placed around the scalp, and which measures electrical activity in the form of event-related potentials (ERP) – or voltage fluctuations. The main finding from data collected with both technologies is that cross-linguistic similarity between the L1 and L2 plays an important role in terms of both blood flow and electrical activity. As described by Kotz (2009), research with native speakers shows that language stimuli that are ungrammatical, ambiguous or complex result in higher levels of blood flow to certain parts of the brain and also higher voltage fluctuations. The question is whether this also happens with language learners. Regarding blood flow, studies by Jeong and colleagues show that Korean speakers who are equally proficient in Japanese and English show more blood flow to certain areas of the brain when processing English sentences than when processing equivalent sentences in Korean or Japanese, but Chinese speakers who are equally proficient in Japanese and English show increased blood flow with Japanese sentences in comparison with both Chinese and English sentences. Crucially, the sentences in question show the highest structural congruity between Korean and Japanese, and between Chinese and English, suggesting that language differences do indeed have neurophysiological consequences for learners (Jeong *et al.*, 2007a, 2007b).

Not all cross-linguistic differences are equal, however. As described by Ringbom (2007: 5–9), differences between languages can involve either a contrast relation or a zero relation. 'In a contrast relation... the learner perceives a TL item or pattern as in important ways different from an L1 form or pattern, though there is also an underlying similarity between the two', whereas in a zero relation, 'items and patterns in the TL at early stages of learning appear to have little or no perceptible relation to the L1 or any other language the learner knows' (Ringbom, 2007: 6). The question for now is whether these two types of differences have different physiological consequences for learners. A study by Tokowicz and MacWhinney (2005) has addressed this question with university-level, English-speaking learners of Spanish. They were given a task where they were asked to read a number of sentences, some of which were grammatical and some ungrammatical. While reading the sentences on the computer, where they saw only one word at a time, their electrical brain activity was measured. Also, after reading each sentence, the participants indicated whether the sentence was grammatical or ungrammatical. Whereas English speakers tend to show large voltage fluctuations when encountering an ungrammatical form, the researchers in this study found that the learners' voltage fluctuations with ungrammatical sentences occurred mainly with structures that are similar between English and Spanish (e.g. a progressive construction) and with structures that have a zero relation (e.g. grammatical gender), but not with structures that represent a contrast relation (e.g. determiners). In other words, the learners' electrical brain activity indicated that they were developing native-like intuitions with similar and zero relations, but not with contrast relations. Another fascinating dimension of the results is that they showed that learners' intuitions (as measured by their electrical brain activity) did not always accord with their judgments of whether the sentences were grammatical. Clearly, this is a finding worth following up on. It also demonstrates the value of combining new technologies with traditional forms of data collection.

Argumentation Heuristics

The fourth and final enabling goal deals with argumentation heuristics, which come into play not just during the interpretation of a study's results, but also earlier when the design of the study is being considered. The purpose of argumentation heuristics is to detail the types of evidence and the conditions necessary to reach a firm conclusion about whether cross-linguistic effects either are or are not present in a particular set of data. Before going further, I should point out that the value of a study is not always determined by whether it produces firm conclusions. The results of a particular study can, in many cases, push the field forward and provide the impetus for future promising work even if the study's results have multiple interpretations. The lack of a firm conclusion is not nearly as severe a shortcoming as an over-interpretation of the results, by which I mean a case where a conclusion is stated as if it were well supported by the results but in fact is not. The firmest, most justified conclusion is where all of the available evidence points to one and only one possible interpretation. A somewhat less firm but still fully justified conclusion involves cases where the same results could be accounted for by multiple explanations, but where one explanation is incontrovertibly far more plausible than all others. *Argumentative rigor* – or what I have previously called *methodological rigor* (Jarvis, 2000; Jarvis & Pavlenko, 2008) – is achieved under both of these conditions. In principle, argumentative rigor could be achieved with a single piece of evidence as long as that evidence points to only one plausible interpretation. However, because language performance is subject to such an array of forces, in practice it is often difficult if not impossible to achieve argumentative rigor on the basis of a single piece of evidence alone. For this reason, in my past discussions of transfer methodology (Jarvis, 2000, 2010, 2012; Jarvis & Pavlenko, 2008), I have emphasized the need to consider multiple types of evidence when making claims about whether cross-linguistic effects are present.

In courts of law involving criminal trials, the attorneys representing both the defendant(s) and the plaintiff(s) present all available evidence in order to make the strongest case possible. However, making a strong case is not just a matter of presenting evidence; it also requires organizing that evidence into certain threads (or premises) that cohere together in relation to a particular argument. The strength of an argument is determined by whether the evidence on which it is based leads to a single interpretation, and the strength of a case is related to the strength and number of arguments on which it rests. Figure 2.7, which comes from Jarvis (2012: 4), illustrates how pieces of evidence combine to form premises, which in turn combine to form arguments, which themselves combine to form a case.

In Jarvis (2000), I described three types of evidence that are critical to investigations of L1 influence. These include what I called *intra-L1-group homogeneity*, *inter-L1-group heterogeneity* and intra-L1-group congruity between L1 and TL performance. This last one can also be referred to more simply as *cross-language congruity*. The first two types of evidence are obtained through within-*group* and between-*group* comparisons, whereas the third type of evidence is obtained through a between-*language* comparison – that is, through a comparison of similarities between learners' performance in the TL and their performance on a comparable task in the L1. More recently, I have recognized a fourth type of evidence that is also valuable to transfer research (see Jarvis, 2010). Like the third type of evidence, it relies

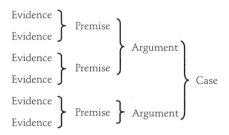

Figure 2.7 Argumentation hierarchy

on a language-based instead of a group-based comparison, but unlike the third type of evidence, it involves a within-language instead of a between-language comparison. The fourth type of evidence is what I call *intralingual contrasts*, and it can be derived through comparisons of features of the TL that differ with respect to how (closely) related they are to features of the L1. An example of a study that has done this is the Trude and Tokowicz (2011) study mentioned earlier, which compared learners' performance on TL structures that are either similar or different or show no relationship between the L1 and TL. These four types of evidence represent two separate premises (i.e. group based vs. source language based), but both premises support the same argument concerning whether a particular pattern of behavior in the TL is representative of learners from a particular source language background. Together, they form what I call the *comparison-based argument* for transfer, as illustrated in Figure 2.8 (from Jarvis, 2012: 5).

There are potentially many types of arguments that could be made for transfer, each with its own set of evidence and premises. For example, teachers and researchers have occasionally suggested that learners' introspections could be used as a type of evidence for transfer. This is certainly true on an individual level, where a learner may be fully aware of many of the specific instances where he/she has made an interlingual identification between a feature of the TL and a feature of a previously learned language, as well as of instances where he/she has relied on a previously learned language to compensate for a lack of relevant knowledge of the TL (cf. Williams & Hammarberg, 1998). When it comes to making generalizations across groups of learners, however, introspection and any other form of evidence that applies to a single individual will need to be embedded within the types of evidence that lead to a generalizable argument, such as the comparison-based argument.

There is, however, at least one other type of argument for transfer that is generalizable. It relies on two of the same types of evidence as are used in the comparison-based argument, but it uses them as the basis for a different premise. The argument is what I call the *detection-based argument*, and it underlies the L1 detection research referred to previously. The evidence on which it is based includes intragroup homogeneity and intergroup heterogeneity, but these types of evidence are actually part of the method (for building an L1 classification model) rather than serving

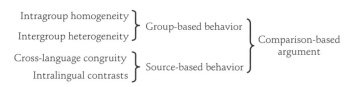

Figure 2.8 The comparison-based argument

Intragroup homogeneity ⎤
                          ⎬ Detection accuracy ⎫ Detection-based
Intergroup heterogeneity ⎦   ⎬   argument

Figure 2.9 The detection-based argument

as primary evidence for transfer. The primary evidence is essentially the premise they enable, which is the degree of accuracy with which language samples can be classified according to the language backgrounds of the people who produced them. The strength of the argument rests on the level of cross-validated detection accuracy that can be achieved. If high levels of detection accuracy can be achieved, then this will leave little doubt that transfer is present *as long as there are no other reliable differences between the groups* (e.g. age, TL proficiency, years of instruction, context of learning, types and amounts of TL exposure) besides their language backgrounds (which also include other languages they may have learned previously). An illustration of the detection-based argument is shown in Figure 2.9 (from Jarvis, 2012: 6).

It is critical to emphasize that the strength of either the comparison-based or the detection-based argument does not depend solely on the strength and number of types of evidence it is based on, but it also depends heavily on whether other possible influences on the data have been eliminated, restricted, equally balanced across groups or adequately randomized. Critically, argumentative rigor (or methodological rigor) is achieved only when alternative explanations have been ruled out, and this requires not just evidence indicative of transfer, but also the researcher to demonstrate convincingly that the patterns found in the data could not have been caused by any other factor independently of transfer.

Let me emphasize that the conditions surrounding any particular study might make it impossible to present an entire argument for transfer, let alone a complete case involving more than one argument. What we can strive for, however, is to collect as many types of evidence as are available to us, to control as many of the potentially intervening variables as possible and to interpret our results honestly in terms of whether we have achieved full argumentative rigor or whether there exist plausible alternative explanations for our results. When putting together a comparison-based argument, it might not be feasible to collect all four types of evidence. It might also not be necessary to do so. This depends on how much evidence is needed to rule out alternative explanations. Generally speaking, however, the more types of evidence one has for transfer, the fewer alternative explanations there will be; likewise, the more external factors have been controlled, the fewer types of evidence will be needed to achieve argumentative rigor. Again, though, argumentative rigor need not be the goal of every study. Some studies will of course focus more on exploration and discovery than on drawing conclusions, but here, too, the comparison- and detection-based frameworks can offer valuable tools and heuristics (see Jarvis, 2012: 2–10).

Returning for a moment to the important interrelationship between the four enabling goals of transfer research, it is noteworthy that my recognition of the detection-based argument came about largely as a result of my encounters with authorship attribution research (e.g. Holmes, 1998), in which computer-based classifiers have been used to identify the specific authors of texts whose authorship was previously unknown or disputed. Becoming familiar with the tools used in a related discipline and considering how they could be applied to transfer research, and then considering whether the types of evidence for transfer that these tools could provide were already accounted for by the methodological framework I proposed in Jarvis (2000), is ultimately what led me to discover the detection-based argument. In hindsight, though, I now recognize that the essence of the detection-based argument had already received some attention by Ioup (1984) and Odlin (1996).

Concluding Thoughts

In this chapter, I have attempted to show that the scope of transfer research is broad and multifaceted, with new, sophisticated and fascinating discoveries continuing in relation to each of the four enabling goals, and with advances in one area leading to simultaneous discoveries and advances in other areas. Although I have merely scratched the surface regarding the work that has been done and is currently underway in the current era of transfer research, I hope I have successfully illustrated what the main objectives of this area of research are, and how its pieces fit together. An understanding of these purposes and principles can greatly enhance a researcher's ability to make valuable contributions and find satisfaction while conducting work in this intriguing and ever-expanding area of scholarly inquiry.

References

Adams, J., Janse, M. and Swain, S. (eds) (2002) *Bilingualism in Ancient Society: Language Contact and the Written Word*. Oxford: Oxford University Press.

Andersen, R. (1977) The impoverished state of cross-sectional morpheme acquisition/accuracy methodology. *Working Papers on Bilingualism* 14, 47–82.

Andersen, R. (1983) Transfer to somewhere. In S. Gass and L. Selinker (eds) *Language Transfer in Language Learning* (pp. 177–201). Rowley, MA: Newbury House.

Athanasopoulos, P. (2009) Cognitive representation of colour in bilinguals: The case of Greek blues. *Bilingualism: Language and Cognition* 12, 83–95.

Ayoun, D. and Salaberry, M.R. (2008) Acquisition of English tense-aspect morphology by advanced French instructed learners. *Language Learning* 58 (3), 555–595.

Baddeley, A.D. (2007) *Working Memory, Thought, and Action*. Oxford: Oxford University Press.

Bailey, N., Madden, C. and Krashen, S. (1974) Is there a "natural sequence" in adult second language learning? *Language Learning* 24, 235–243.

Bardovi-Harlig, K. (2000) Tense and aspect in second language acquisition: Form, meaning, and use. *Language Learning* 50 (supplement 1), xi–491.

Bohnacker, U. (2006) When Swedes begin to learn German: From V2 to V2. *Second Language Research* 22 (4), 443–486.

Bylund, E. (2011) Language-specific patterns in event conceptualization: Insights from bilingualism. In A. Pavlenko (ed.) *Thinking and Speaking in Two Languages* (pp. 108–142). Bristol: Multilingual Matters.

Bylund, E. and Jarvis, S. (2011) L2 effects on L1 event conceptualization. *Bilingualism: Language and Cognition* 14 (1), 47–59.

Cenoz, J., Hufeisen, B. and Jessner, U. (eds) (2001) *Cross-Linguistic Influence in Third Language Acquisition: Psycholinguistic Perspectives*. Clevedon: Multilingual Matters.

Collins, L. (2002) The roles of L1 influence and lexical aspect in the acquisition of temporal morphology. *Language Learning* 52 (1), 43–94.

Cook, V. (ed.) (2002) *Portraits of the L2 User*. Clevedon: Multilingual Matters.

Cook, V. (ed.) (2003) *Effects of the Second Language on the First*. Clevedon: Multilingual Matters.

Cook, V., Bassetti, B., Kasai, C., Sasaki, M. and Takahashi, J.A. (2006) Do bilinguals have different concepts? The case of shape and material in Japanese L2 users of English. *International Journal of Bilingualism* 10, 137–152.

De Angelis, G. (2005) Interlanguage transfer of function words. *Language Learning* 55 (3), 379–414.

De Angelis, G. and Selinker, L. (2001) Interlanguage transfer and competing linguistic systems in the multilingual mind. In J. Cenoz, B. Hufeisen and U. Jessner (eds) *Cross-Linguistic Influence in Third Language Acquisition: Psycholinguistic Perspectives* (pp. 42–58). Clevedon: Multilingual Matters.

Dragiev, K. (2004) Influence of an L1 grammaticized concept on the L2 acquisition of English by Bulgarian learners. Unpublished MA thesis, Ohio University.

Dulay, H. and Burt, M. (1973) Should we teach children syntax? *Language Learning* 23, 245–258.

Dulay, H. and Burt, M. (1974) Natural sequences in child second language acquisition. *Language Learning* 24, 37–53.

Dušková, L. (1969) On sources of errors in foreign language teaching. *IRAL: International Review of Applied Linguistics* 7, 11–36.

Eckman, F.R. (1977) Markedness and the contrastive analysis hypothesis. *Language Learning* 27, 315–330.

Ericsson, K.A., Krampe, R.T. and Tesch-Römer, C. (1993) The role of deliberate practice in the acquisition of expert performance. *Psychological Review* 100 (3), 363–406.

Eubank, L. (1993/1994) On the transfer of parametric values in L2 development. *Language Acquisition* 3 (3), 183–208.

Eubank, L., Bischof, J., Huffstutler, A., Leek, P. and West, C. (1997) "Tom eats slowly cooked eggs": Thematic-verb raising in L2 knowledge. *Language Acquisition* 6 (3), 171–199.

Flecken, M. (2010) Event conceptualization in language production of early bilinguals. PhD thesis, Heidelberg University and Radboud University, Nijmegen.

Flege, J.E. (1995) Second-language speech learning: Theory, findings, and problems. In W. Strange (ed.) *Speech Perception and Linguistic Experience: Theoretical and Methodological Issues* (pp. 233–273). Timonium, MD: York Press.

Fries, C. (1945) *Teaching and Learning English as a Foreign Language*. Ann Arbor, MI: University of Michigan Press.

Fulcher, G. and Davidson, F. (2007) *Language Testing and Assessment: An Advanced Resource Book*. New York/London: Routledge.

Gass, S.M. (1988) Integrating research areas: A framework for second language studies. *Applied Linguistics* 9, 198–217.

Gass, S.M. (1997) *Input, Interaction, and the Second Language Learner*. Mahwah, NJ: Erlbaum.

Gass, S.M. and Selinker, L. (eds) (1983) *Language Transfer in Language Learning*. Rowley, MA: Newbury House.

Gass, S.M. and Selinker, L. (2008) *Second Language Acquisition: An Introductory Course* (3rd edn). New York/London: Routledge.

Goo, J. (2010) Working memory and reactivity. *Language Learning* 60 (4), 712–752.

Graham, R. and Belnap, K. (1986) The acquisition of lexical boundaries in English by native speakers of Spanish. *International Review of Applied Linguistics in Language Teaching* 24, 275–286.

Granger, S., Dagneaux, E., Meunier, F. and Paquot, M. (2009) *The International Corpus of Learner English. Handbook and CD-ROM (Version 2)*. Louvain-la-Neuve: Presses Universitaires de Louvain.

Green, D. (1998) Mental control of the bilingual lexico-semantic system. *Bilingualism: Language and Cognition* 1, 67–81.

Green, D.W., Crinion, J. and Price, C.J. (2007) Exploring cross-linguistic vocabulary effects on brain structures using voxel-based morphometry. *Bilingualism: Language and Cognition* 10 (2), 189–199.

Guion, S.G., Flege, J.E., Liu, S.H. and Yeni-Komshian, G.H. (2000) Age of learning effects on the duration of sentences produced in a second language. *Applied Psycholinguistics* 21, 205–228.

Hakuta, K. (1976) A case study of a Japanese child learning English as a second language. *Language Learning* 26, 321–351.

Han, Z. and Cadierno, T. (eds) (2010) *Linguistic Relativity in SLA: Thinking for Speaking*. Bristol: Multilingual Matters.

Haugen, E. (1953) *The Norwegian Language in America*. Philadelphia, PA: University of Pennsylvania Press.

Holmes, D.I. (1998) The evolution of stylometry in humanities scholarship. *Literary and Linguistic Computing* 13, 111–117.

von Humboldt, W. (1963) *Humanist Without Portfolio: An Anthology of the Writings of Wilhelm von Humboldt* (M. Cowan, trans.). Detroit, MI: Wayne State University Press.

Håkansson, G., Pienemann, M. and Sayehli, S. (2002) Transfer and typological proximity in the context of second language processing. *Second Language Research* 18 (3), 250–273.

Ioup, G. (1984) Is there a structural foreign accent? A comparison of syntactic and phonological errors in second language acquisition. *Language Learning* 34, 1–17.

Janse, M. (2002) Aspects of bilingualism in the history of the Greek language. In J. Adams, M. Janse and S. Swain (eds) *Bilingualism in Ancient Society: Language Contact and the Written Text* (pp. 332–390). Oxford: Oxford University Press.

Jarvis, S. (2000) Methodological rigor in the study of transfer: Identifying L1 influence in the interlanguage lexicon. *Language Learning* 50 (2), 245–309.

Jarvis, S. (2002) Topic continuity in L2 English article use. *Studies in Second Language Acquisition* 24 (3), 387–418.

Jarvis, S. (2010) Comparison-based and detection-based approaches to transfer research. *EUROSLA Yearbook* 10, 169–192.

Jarvis, S. (2011a) Conceptual transfer: Crosslinguistic effects in categorization and construal. *Bilingualism: Language and Cognition* 14 (1), 1–8.

Jarvis, S. (2011b) Data mining with learner corpora: Choosing classifiers for L1 detection. In F. Meunier, S. De Cock, G. Giquin and M. Paquot (eds) *A Taste for Corpora. In Honour of Sylviane Granger* (pp. 127–154). Amsterdam: Benjamins.

Jarvis, S. (2012) The detection-based approach: An overview. In S. Jarvis and S.A. Crossley (eds) *Approaching Language Transfer Through Text Classification: Explorations in the Detection-Based Approach* (pp. 1–33). Bristol: Multilingual Matters.

Jarvis, S. and Odlin, T. (2000) Morphological type, spatial reference, and language transfer. *Studies in Second Language Acquisition* 22 (4), 535–556.

Jarvis, S. and Pavlenko, A. (2008) *Crosslinguistic Influence in Language and Cognition*. New York/London: Routledge.

Jarvis, S. and Crossley, S.A. (eds.) (2012) *Approaching Language Transfer Through Text Classification: Explorations in the Detection-Based Approach*. Bristol: Multilingual Matters.

Jeong, H., Sugiura, M., Sassa, Y., Haji, T., Usui, N., Taira, M., Horie, K., Sato, S. and Kawashima, R. (2007a) Effect of syntactic similarity on cortical activation during second language processing: A comparison of English and Japanese among native Korean trilinguals. *Human Brain Mapping* 28 (3), 194–204.

Jeong, H., Sugiura, M., Sassa, Y., Yokoyama, S., Horie, K., Sato, S., Taira, M. and Kawashima, R. (2007b) Cross-linguistic influence on brain activation during second language processing: An fMRI study. *Bilingualism: Language and Cognition* 10 (2), 175–187.

Kaivapalu, A. and Martin, M. (2007) Morphology in transition: Plural inflection of Finnish nouns by Estonian and Russian learners. *Acta Linguistica Hungarica* 54 (2), 129–156.

Kane, M. and Engle, R.W. (2003) Working-memory capacity and the control of attention: The contributions of goal neglect, response competition, and task set to Stroop interference. *Journal of Experimental Psychology: General* 132, 47–70.

Kecskes, I. and Papp, T. (2000) *Foreign Language and Mother Tongue*. Mahwah, NJ: Erlbaum.

Kellerman, E. (1977) Toward a characterization of the strategy of transfer in second language learning. *Interlanguage Studies Bulletin* 2, 58–145.

Kellerman, E. (1978) Giving learners a break: Native language intuitions as a source of predictions about transferability. *Working Papers on Bilingualism* 15, 59–92.

Kellerman, E. (1983) Now you see it, now you don't. In S. Gass and L. Selinker (eds) *Language Transfer in Language Learning* (pp. 112–134). Rowley, MA: Newbury House.

Kellerman, E. (1995) Crosslinguistic influence: Transfer to nowhere? *Annual Review of Applied Linguistics* 15, 125–150.

Kormos, J. and Sáfár, A. (2008) Phonological short-term memory, working memory and foreign language performance in intensive language learning. *Bilingualism: Language and Cognition* 11 (2), 261–271.

Kotsiantis, S.B. (2007) Supervised machine learning: A review of classification techniques. *Informatica Journal* 31, 249–268.

Kotz, S. (2009) A critical review of ERP and fMRI evidence on L2 syntactic processing. *Brain and Language* 109 (2–3), 68–74.

Krashen, S. (1977) Some issues relating to the monitor model. In H. Brown, C. Yorio and R. Crymes (eds) *On TESOL '77: Teaching and Learning English as a Second Language: Trends in Research and Practice* (pp. 144–158). Washington, DC: TESOL.

Krashen, S. (1983) Newmark's "Ignorance Hypothesis" and current second language acquisition theory. In S. Gass and L. Selinker (eds) *Language Transfer in Language Learning* (pp. 135–153). Rowley, MA: Newbury House.

Lado, R. (1957) *Linguistics Across Cultures*. Ann Arbor, MI: University of Michigan Press.

Lecocke, M. and Hess, K. (2006) An empirical study of univariate and genetic algorithm-based feature selection in binary classification with microarray data. *Cancer Informatics* 2, 313–327.

Levelt, W. (1989) *Speaking: From Intention to Articulation*. Cambridge, MA: MIT Press.

Luk, Z.P. and Shirai, Y. (2009) Is the acquisition order of grammatical morphemes impervious to L1 knowledge? Evidence from the acquisition of plural -s, articles, and possessive 's. *Language Learning* 59 (4), 721–754.

MacWhinney, B. (2005) A unified model of language acquisition. In J. Kroll and A.M.B. De Groot (eds) *Handbook of Bilingualism: Psycholinguistic Approaches* (pp. 49–67). Oxford: Oxford University Press.

Master, P. (1997) The English article system: Acquisition, function, and pedagogy. *System* 25, 215–232.

Mayfield Tomokiyo, L. and Jones, R. (2001) You're not from 'round here, are you? Naive Bayes detection of non-native utterance text. *Proceedings of the Second Meeting of the North American Chapter of the Association for Computational Linguistics (NAACL '01)* (unpaginated electronic document). Cambridge, MA: The Association for Computational Linguistics.

Meriläinen, L. (2010) *Language Transfer in the Written English of Finnish Students*. Joensuu: University of Eastern Finland.

van den Noort, M.W.M.L., Bosch, P. and Hugdahl, K. (2006) Foreign language proficiency and working memory capacity. *European Psychologist* 11 (4), 289–296.

Odlin, T. (1989) *Language Transfer: Cross-Linguistic Influence in Language Learning*. Cambridge: Cambridge University Press.

Odlin, T. (1996) On the recognition of transfer errors. *Language Awareness* 5, 166–178.

Odlin, T. (2008) Conceptual transfer and meaning extensions. In P. Robinson (ed.) *Handbook of Cognitive Linguistics and Second Language Acquisition* (pp. 306–340). New York/London: Routledge.

Odlin, T. and Jarvis, S. (2004) Same source, different outcomes: A study of Swedish influence on the acquisition of English in Finland. *International Journal of Multilingualism* 1 (2), 123–140.

Pavlenko, A. (ed.) (2011) *Thinking and Speaking in Two Languages*. Bristol: Multilingual Matters.

Pavlenko, A. and Malt, B.C. (2011) Kitchen Russian: Cross-linguistic differences and first-language object naming by Russian-English bilinguals. *Bilingualism: Language and Cognition* 14 (1), 19–46.

Pienemann, M. (1998) *Language Processing and Second Language Development: Processability Theory*. Amsterdam: Benjamins.

Polunenko, A. (2004) English past tense forms in Russian speakers' oral and written production. Unpublished departmental MA thesis, Ohio University.

Rai, M.K., Loschky, L.C., Harris, R.J., Peck, N.R. and Cook, L.G. (2011) Effects of stress and working memory capacity on foreign language readers' inferential processing during comprehension. *Language Learning* 61 (1), 187–218.

Richards, J. (1971) A noncontrastive approach to error analysis. *English Language Teaching* 25, 204–219.

Ringbom, H. (1976) What differences are there between Finns and Swedish-speaking Finns learning English? In H. Ringbom and R. Palmberg (eds) *Errors Made by Finns and Swedish-Speaking Finns in the Learning of English* (pp. 1–13). Åbo: Åbo Akademi University.

Ringbom, H. (1978) The influence of the mother tongue on the translation of lexical items. *Interlanguage Studies Bulletin* 3, 80–101.

Ringbom, H. (1987) *The Role of the First Language in Foreign Language Learning*. Clevedon: Multilingual Matters.

Ringbom, H. (2007) *Cross-Linguistic Similarity in Foreign Language Learning*. Clevedon: Multilingual Matters.

Ringbom, H. and Jarvis, S. (2009) The importance of cross-linguistic similarity in foreign language learning. In M.H. Long and C.J. Doughty (eds) *Handbook of Language Teaching* (pp. 106–118). Chichester: Wiley-Blackwell.

Schachter, J. (1974) An error in error analysis. *Language Learning* 24, 205–214.

Schmiedtová, B., von Stutterheim, C. and Carroll, M. (2011) Language-specific patterns in event construal of advanced second language speakers. In A. Pavlenko (ed.) *Thinking and Speaking in Two Languages* (pp. 66–107). Bristol: Multilingual Matters.

Schwartz, B. and Sprouse, R. (1996) L2 cognitive states and the full transfer/full access model. *Second Language Research* 12, 40–72.

Selinker, L. (1969) Language transfer. *General Linguistics* 9, 67–92.

Selinker, L. (1972) Interlanguage. *IRAL: International Review of Applied Linguistics* 10, 209–231.

Selinker, L. and Lakshamanan, U. (1992) Language transfer and fossilization: The Multiple Effects Principle. In S. Gass and L. Selinker (eds) *Language Transfer in Language Learning* (pp. 197–216). Amsterdam: Benjamins.

von Stutterheim, C. (2003) Linguistic structure and information organization: The case of very advanced learners. *EUROSLA Yearbook* 3, 183–206.

von Stutterheim, C. and Nüse, R. (2003) Processes of conceptualization in language production: Language-specific perspectives and event construal. *Linguistics* 41, 851–881.

Taylor, B. (1975) The use of overgeneralization and transfer learning strategies by elementary and intermediate students of ESL. *Language Learning* 25, 73–107.

Tokowicz, N. and MacWhinney, B. (2005) Implicit and explicit measures of sensitivity to violations in second language grammar: An event-related potential investigation. *Studies in Second Language Acquisition* 27, 173–204.

Trude, A.M. and Tokowicz, N. (2011) Negative transfer from Spanish and English to Portuguese pronunciation: The roles of inhibition and working memory. *Language Learning* 61 (1), 259–280.

Unsworth, N. and Engle, R.W. (2007) The nature of individual differences in working memory capacity: Active maintenance in primary memory and controlled search from secondary memory. *Psychological Review* 114 (1), 104–132.

Weinreich, U. (1953) *Languages in Contact*. The Hague: Mouton.

Whitney, W. (1881) On mixture in language. *Transactions of the American Philological Association* 12, 5–26.

Williams, S. and Hammarberg, B. (1998) Language switches in L3 production: Implications for a polyglot speaking model. *Applied Linguistics* 19, 295–333.

Zobl, H. (1984) Cross-language generalizations and the contrastive dimension of the interlanguage hypothesis. In A. Davies, C. Criper and A. Howatt (eds) *Interlanguage* (pp. 79–97). Edinburgh: Edinburgh University Press.

Part 1

Lexical Perspectives

Lexical transfer involves many problems of both word forms and word meanings, and the studies in this section offer diverse perspectives on a number of those problems. Chapter 3 by David Singleton considers how lexical knowledge is organized in bilingual and multilingual minds and how the organization has implications for the study of transfer. According to some researchers, lexical knowledge of one language is quite separate from knowledge of another, yet for other researchers the knowledge of two systems is highly interdependent. Still other researchers go so far as to claim that there are no real boundaries between languages and question the assumption that languages actually exist as distinct entities: for adherents of this position, linguistic systems blur to the point where there can only be a unitary lexicon. Singleton rejects the notion of a blurred unitary system, but he also stakes out a theoretical middle ground between those who view lexical knowledge as quite distinct and those who view the systems as more or less unitary. Some of the evidence that he discusses comes from a previous study of his own of a multilingual individual whose patterns of lexical transfer draw on some languages much more than on others. Singleton also considers the type of transfer evident in sentences such as *I could not find a parking* which, when said by French speakers, will suggest the influence of the way the French language has adapted this English loanword so that *parking* means a place to park. Similar evidence comes from studies of Japanese and Korean, two languages that have adapted many more English loanwords than French has. If learners often show the influence of semantic adaptations frequently found in loanwords or the influence of second language (L2) words in third language (L3) acquisition, learners' metalinguistic awareness indicates, as Singleton argues, distinct yet interdependent lexical systems.

The chapter by Jia Li and Jinting Cai focuses on semantic transfer in spatial expressions. Languages can vary in how their speakers construe relations in space, as where speakers of English tend to view the location of someone near a waterfall as *above* it or *below* it (with the italicized prepositions denoting vertical polarity) whereas speakers of Chinese tend to construe the same relation as simply one of distance. Languages can likewise vary in how specific the spatial terms are that express spatial relations. The English prepositions *below* and *under* both denote negative vertical polarity, yet only the latter would be normal in a sentence such as *There is a pillow _____ her head*. Li and Cai observe that Chinese does not routinely provide information about contact or non-contact in the same context. Using a fill-in-the-blank format in a test accompanied by pictures, Li and Cai show systematic group differences between Chinese English as a foreign language (EFL) students and native speakers of English in their responses on the test. Retrospective interviews with EFL students provide further insights, and the overall results suggest language-specific effects in how spatial relations are construed, effects that are often similar in the native language and in the interlanguage because of transfer.

While the study of Li and Cai considers the interaction of word meanings and visual arrays, Chapter 5 by T. Sima Paribakht and Marjorie Bingham Wesche focuses on how learners infer word meanings through a wide range of linguistic as well as non-linguistic clues. Any word itself may have morphological or other grammatical information that can help, for example, in deciding whether the unknown lexical item denotes a human being or whether a verb involves both a causer and a causee (which is typically the case with a transitive verb). Beyond clues in the target word itself, the context of the sentence can sometimes aid, as can the larger textual domain (perhaps along with non-linguistic or cultural contexts). These types of help in inferring the meaning of a new word may exist in the target language itself or in similar domains in the native language (or perhaps some other previously acquired language). Paribakht and Wesche administered a number of different vocabulary tests to two groups of L2 English learners: native speakers of Persian (aka Farsi) and native speakers of French. (Paribakht and Wesche call their research a 'trilingual study', but it should be kept in mind that theirs is an investigation of L2, not L3, acquisition.) The authors found both similarities and differences in learners' reliance on various kinds of contextual clues along with similarities and differences in the inference patterns of a control group of native speakers of English. All groups, which also included native speakers of French and Persian reading in their native languages, relied heavily on sentence contexts to infer meanings of unfamiliar forms, though the degree of reliance varied somewhat among groups. In contrast to such relative homogeneity at the sentence level, the reliance on the larger discourse context proved to be far greater among the Persian speakers than the French speakers when reading in English (Paribakht and Wesche call these groups L2 Persian and L2 French, respectively, but the target language for both groups was English). The greater reliance of the Persian speakers on discourse context instead of on morphology suggests very different processing routines so that, as the authors assert, the transfer patterns involve the influence of L1 procedural knowledge along with L1 structural influences. The processing difference seems to involve, as the authors maintain, a number of causes, one being the different degrees of exposure to English linguistic and cultural patterns, and another being the frequent (though not total) absence of vowels in the Persian alphabet.

3 Cross-Lexical Interaction and the Structure of the Mental Lexicon

David Singleton

Introduction

This chapter begins with a brief historical overview of the notion of cross-linguistic influence. It goes on to discuss the application of this notion to the lexical domain, and attempts to derive from this review some thoughts on what cross-lexical interaction does and does not imply with regard to the organization of the mental lexicon.

The Notion of Cross-Linguistic Influence: A Brief Historical Sketch

Traditionally, cross-linguistic influence has been represented as something negative – to be avoided, resisted or remedied (cf. Singleton, 1987a). One can cite in this connection a number of tales of caution dating from the First World War recounted by Postgate in a book on translation published in 1922.

> ... on one occasion the mild [French] expression *demander une explication* ['to ask for an explanation'] gave dire offence to the Government of the United States because it looked like 'to demand an explanation', while the English translation of the Allied Note answering Germany's first offer of peace in January 1917, renders *prétendu* as 'pretended' where it clearly means, as generally, 'alleged'. (Postgate, 1922: 48ff.)

In the same place, Postgate tells the story of an English bishop 'who concluded an address to French soldiers with the prayer "Que Dieu vous blesse" ["May God wound you"]'.

A negative aura continued to surround discussion of cross-linguistic influence through the period during which contrastive analysis dominated applied linguistics. At this time, contrastive analysis drew heavily, of course, on the psychological theory of behaviorism. Behaviorists fully recognized that transfer could be either negative or positive, and so, in principle, did applied linguists working within the contrastive analysis paradigm, as the following quotation from Lado makes clear:

> We assume that the student who comes in contact with a foreign language will find some features of it quite easy and others extremely difficult. Those elements that are similar to his native language will be simple, and those elements that are different will be difficult. (Lado, 1957: 2)

On the other hand, the predominant focus of contrastive analysis, as its name clearly indicates, was on points of conflict between languages, which were taken to be the sole or chief source of second language (L2) learners' difficulty and error (cf. James, 1971: 54ff.). Accordingly, during this time, its profile tended to be associated with problematicity, and this profile continued for similar reasons through the heyday of error analysis.

Much of the seminal discussion of error analysis originated in Corder's (1967, 1971) work, which noted that the predictions of contrastive analysis were very frequently not borne out in L2 learners' errors and that many of such errors were in fact of the same kind as forms produced by child learners in their first language (L1). In his elaboration of a hypothesis-testing model of L2 acquisition (SLA), however, Corder was very clear that for him, one of the hypotheses to be put under scrutiny by the learner was whether his/her L2 was the same as or different from his/her L1 and that the testing of this hypothesis would manifest itself in L1-influenced errors.

Other researchers – under what became known as the creative constructionist banner – at one point interpreted the occurrence of L1-like developmental forms in L2 production as evidence that the process of learning an L2 is actually *the same* as that of learning an L1, involving the same developmental sequences and the same developmental departures from the target language norms (e.g. Dulay & Burt, 1974, 1977). This line of thinking patently left little room for the idea of cross-linguistic influence, and it was indeed accompanied by a fierce critique of all approaches to SLA attributing any real importance to cross-linguistic factors, so that these latter tended for a while to have a rather shadowy profile in some quarters of the SLA literature.

However, learners' experience of cross-linguistic influence was so widespread, and the evidence of cross-linguistic influence emerging from empirical SLA research was so overwhelming that the phenomenon could no longer be de-emphasized or denied, and it swiftly became rehabilitated as a respectable object of study in the SLA research enterprise. Thus, Kasper wrote in 1984:

The research question as it puts itself today ... is no more 'is transfer a relevant phenomenon in L2 acquisition and use or is it not?' The generally shared assumption is that it is... (Kasper, 1984: 4)

Moreover, recent research explorations of cross-linguistic influence have exorcised some of its perceived demons, focusing on facilitatory as well as interfering aspects of cross-linguistic interaction (cf. Ringbom, 2007).

Cross-Lexical Operations and the Mental Lexicon

The (re-)establishment of the assumption that knowledge of L1 interacted with knowledge of L2 was itself based on the assumption that the L1 knowledge and the L2 knowledge were similar in nature – an idea that was in fact shared by behaviorists, error analysts and creative constructionists, even if their respective conceptions of the knowledge in question differed. Some widely cited early research on the L2 mental lexicon called this latter assumption into question, however. Researchers such as Meara (1984) and Laufer (1989) advanced the view that there was a qualitative difference between L1 and L2 lexical knowledge, postulating that 'while in the native speaker's mental lexicon there are strong semantic links between the words, the connections between words in additional languages are primarily phonological' (Laufer, 1989: 17). This standpoint, let it be said, was based on what many researchers saw as a misinterpretation of evidence (see e.g. Singleton, 1999: 130ff.). By implication, it cast doubt on the possibility of a substantial interplay between the L1 mental lexicon and the L2 mental lexicon, since it posited a very radical divergence between these two entities.

As in the case of the earlier questioning of the existence or extent of cross-linguistic influence, the matter was in the end resolved by evidence (see e.g. Singleton, 1999; Singleton & Little, 1991; Wolter, 1991). Some of the data emerging from the Trinity College Dublin Modern Languages Research Project, for example, were specifically scrutinized with a view to gauging the deniability of cross-lexical interaction. The data in question were items recognized as L1–L2 blends, coinages which existed in the form given in neither the L1 nor the L2, but which had clearly emerged from the consultation of both. The following are cases in point – anglophones' attempts at French expressions, drawn from C-test, word association and translation data.

volcanos   (C-test stimulus *vol-*, required word *volcans*, cf. English *volcanoes*)

lionesse   (word-association test stimulus *lion* ['lion'], cf. English *lioness*)

harnesses   (expression to be translated *seat belts*, cf. English *harness*)

(Cited in Singleton, 1996: 248; cf. also Hammarberg, 2009: 140ff.)

Arguments against the idea of a qualitative difference between the L1 mental lexicon and the L2 mental lexicon have more recently gone to the opposite extreme. Thus, for example, Cook's (1992) notion of 'holistic multicompetence' argues for a very high degree of integration of language competence, including lexical competence, across languages, and Dijkstra (e.g. 2003) takes the position that the mental lexicon is fully integrated and 'fundamentally nonselective', no matter how many languages are involved.

Cook's (1992) exposition and defence of his multicompetence model contain reference to the following evidence of cross-lexical interaction:

- reaction time to a word in one language is related to the frequency of its cognate in another known language (Caramazza & Brones, 1979);
- morphemic similarities between two known languages influence translation performance (Cristoffanini *et al.*, 1986);
- when processing an interlingual homograph, bilinguals access its meanings in both their languages rather than just the meaning specific to the language being used (Beauvillain & Grainger, 1987).

This and similar evidence cited by Cook strongly suggests extremely high levels of connectivity between the L1 and L2 mental lexicon. Dijkstra's (2003) perspective, for its part, rests on findings from a range of experimental studies, including his own, indicating that when a particular word form is activated, similar word forms known to the individual in question are activated also, whatever the language affiliation of the words in question (at least beyond a certain proficiency level). Such cross-lingual activation once again points to a very high level of connectivity between the lexicons associated with the different languages concerned.

Although their argumentation seems sometimes to come close to claiming cross-linguistic unitariness for lexical operations, both Cook and Dijkstra draw back from such a conclusion. Cook (2003: 7f.) in the end takes the line that while 'total separation is impossible since both languages are in the same mind', it is also the case that 'total integration is impossible since L2 users can keep the languages apart', going on to claim that 'between these two extremes and probably untenable positions of total separation and total integration, there are many different degrees and types of interconnection'. As for Dijkstra (2003), he accepts that individual languages as sets can be at different levels of activation, and, indeed, he proposes a model in which 'language nodes' are operative, thus recognizing that the lexical items and processes associated with each of the languages known to an individual may be activated and/or deactivated as a set.

All of a Blur?

A very much more radical point of view is put before us by 'integrational linguistics'. Its founder and advocate Harris (1998) claims that both within the individual and within the community the continuum of variation is such that it makes no sense to talk about clear demarcations, and that languages blur into each other in myriad ways. Toolan (2008: 4), espousing broadly the same point of view, rejects the notion that concepts of separate languages are 'objectively grounded in linguistic facts'. This kind of position would presumably interpret cross-linguistic influence as evidence of the general blur assumed to characterize the entirety of language.

One kind of evidence that might support the 'blur' conception of things would be any evidence suggesting that language users confuse the languages they are using. We have noted Cook's remark to the effect that language users generally keep their languages apart, but cross-lexical effects do not seem to fit this pattern. This may seem particularly to be the case when the language user in question seems unsure where the lexical expression deployed actually comes from.

An instance of this is to be found in an early study of my own (Singleton, 1987b), involving Philip, an English-speaking learner of French who also had formal school knowledge of Latin and Irish plus conversational knowledge of Spanish deriving from an extended stay in Spain. When trying to use French, Philip drew on and 'Frenchified' a large number of Spanish lexical items. For instance, when trying to express 'although' on one occasion he came out with a 'Frenchified' version of the Spanish expression for 'although' *aunque,* which he pronounced [a'ɔ̃ke]. In Philip's introspections on his use of this form, it emerged that he did not know whether he had borrowed it from Spanish or Latin. On the other hand, in general, Philip seemed, from his introspective comments elsewhere, fairly focused about his borrowing from Spanish. He declared that he knew Spanish and French to be historically related, both being descended from Latin, and he reported deliberately making use of Spanish expressions – with appropriate phonological adjustment – to fill gaps in his French. Indeed, it turned out that Spanish was the privileged source of transferred expressions in his French, which appears to reveal a very well-motivated transfer strategy, whether or not this was always conscious, since of the languages he knew, Spanish was the 'best bet' as far as expanding his resources in French was concerned. In other words, Philip was not so much confused as exploiting his linguistic resources intelligently. As for not knowing whether *aunque* was Latin or Spanish, given his rather limited command of Spanish and his only vestigial knowledge of Latin, we should surely not make too much of this – especially since Latin and Spanish have many words and indeed phrases in common, so that, for example, 'I love you' is expressed as *te amo* in both.

Another cross-linguistic phenomenon of relevance for our present discussion is the existence of cognateness effects. De Groot (1995: 173), for instance, notes that '[c]ognates are translated faster, more often (fewer omissions), and more often correctly that noncognates'. She concludes that cognates are less segregated by language than non-cognates. Kirsner *et al.* (1993: 228), looking at a similar range of evidence, go further, suggesting that 'some fraction of the second language vocabulary is represented and stored as variants of the first language vocabulary', the size of this fraction depending on 'the extent to which the two vocabularies involve reference to a shared set of roots or stems'. Kirsner *et al.* appear here to be proposing an absence of boundaries between the L1 mental lexicon and the L2 mental lexicon for at least a portion of the L2 vocabulary. It should be immediately noted that suggesting cross-language integration for a very specific set of lexical items on the basis of formal similarity is an entirely different proposition from that of the notion of a global commingling of the two lexicons. Moreover, we need to be careful how we interpret Kirsner *et al.*'s words, and to focus, in particular, on the term *variant*. The suggestion seems to be that, e.g. anglophone learners of French store French *table* as a 'variant' of English *table*. Presumably, *variant* implies that the French version is stored with its specifically French pronunciation and also that it is tagged to be deployed whenever the active language is French. This obviously implies selectivity rather than full integration and the dissolution of all frontiers. In sum, Kirsner *et al.*'s position is far from favoring the notion of a blurring of languages. Their version of integration is founded on the specific motivation of formal near-identity and semantic proximity, and they tacitly accept the idea that the integration is far from complete, the L2 items retaining their distinctiveness as variants. This is in fact not very different from the notion, favored by Dijkstra and others, that words are 'tagged' for language affiliation.

More complex is the case of cognates – in a broader sense than that sanctioned traditionally in historical linguistics – which owe their existence to their entry into a language of items from another language, which change their sense in the process, and which are then used in the original source language by L2 learners of that language who have been exposed to the items in question in their own language. For example, when a French-speaking learner of English excuses his/her late arrival with the words 'I could not find a parking' what he/she means is 'I couldn't find anywhere to park'. The English word *parking* has been imported into French with the meaning *car park*, so that when a French speaker uses it in English in that sense, he/she is drawing on his/her French mental lexicon, even if the word was originally borrowed from English. This kind of situation may at first give the impression of languages blurring into each other, and it is actually not an especially unusual situation.

In Japanese, for example, as Daulton (2008: 1) notes, there are very large numbers of loanwords from English in Japanese, the scale of this influx of English being 'virtually unparalleled in the world'. Loanwords from the West (*gairaigo*) are recognizable in writing, since they have a particular syllable-based script devoted to them – *katakana* – which coexists with *kanji* (Chinese characters used for content words) and *hiragana* (a syllabary used mostly for Japanese grammatical elements). Some Western loanwords are also written in Roman script (Daulton, 2008: 12ff.). By and large, English loanwords are pronounced in a Japanese fashion, although, interestingly, there has been a recent tendency for such pronunciations to move closer to the original English sound shapes; thus *nyuusu* (from *news*) is increasingly pronounced as *nyuuzu* (Daulton, 2008: 17). With regard to semantics (Daulton, 2008: 87ff.), English loanwords in Japanese may retain meanings more or less identical with those (or some of those) of the source items (e.g. *hoomushikku* – which means 'homesick'), or not too far removed from the English meanings (e.g. *saabisu*, from *service*, meaning 'free of charge'), but may also be semantically quite distant from the original expressions (e.g. *mentaritii*, from *mentality*, meaning 'intelligence'). Daulton's (2008, 72ff.) conclusion from an investigation of the English language production of Japanese learners of English is that the effect of their knowledge of English loanwords in Japanese in this connection is copious and on the whole positive. This is to say, the evidence seems to be that Japanese learners of English systematically expand their resources in English by exploiting their familiarity with English loanwords in Japanese.

This is far from evidence of confusion, however. On the contrary, it bespeaks a high degree of language awareness and a rather sophisticated use of such awareness. Nor is the basic fact of loanwords – which are felt still to have a 'foreign' aura – a denial of boundaries between languages. Thus, the English word *restaurant* – imported from French – still has a French enough profile to have retained a French nasal vowel in its final syllable, and English learners of French are probably on the whole aware that they can use the word in question in French. However, it is worth noting that they may also try it out when attempting to communicate in other languages – German, Polish, Chinese, etc.; if they do so, they are undoubtedly deploying an L1-based communication strategy, or at least a strategy that draws on knowledge of both English and French. To return to the case of Japanese learners, they are no doubt cognizant of the English language origins of many of the English loanwords they use in Japanese, on the basis of the phonological shapes of the words in question, on the basis of their written *katakana* forms, on the basis of having encountered their counterparts in English and/or on the basis of general knowledge. When they exploit their familiarity with such words in their use of English, therefore, they are not mixing or conflating languages, rather they are quite simply making very sensible use of their knowledge, or perhaps even only their suspicion, that

Japanese borrowed the items in question from the language they are trying to get to grips with.

Another language featuring large numbers of English loanwords that has recently been investigated in an English language learning perspective is Korean. English language elements are widely and deeply embedded in Korean, and they have in many instances taken on a distinctly Korean flavor in terms of meaning and usage. There is indeed even a term, *Konglish*, for borrowed English expressions that have been thus Koreanized. Examples are the use of Koreanized versions of *skin*, *talent* and *hostess* to denote, respectively, 'after-shave', 'TV actor/actress' and 'prostitute'. Other English expressions that have entered Korean have, as in the Japanese case, remained closer in meaning to their source items – examples being *lip gloss*, *stapler* and *van*.

Nam's (2009) recent study of Konglish explores this phenomenon in an English language learning perspective. That is to say, she investigates the extent to which Korean English language learners draw on Konglish and other borrowings from English in their use of English, and she attempts to elucidate the nature of the process involved when Koreans use loan expressions from English which have become established in Korean in their endeavors to produce English. She adduces evidence that certain loan expressions were used by her participants both in the initial L1 version and in the subsequent L2 version of a picture-naming task and concludes that in those cases the items have to be seen as entries in the Korean learners' L1. She also shows that reliance on Konglish was in inverse proportion to proficiency levels, the quantity and quality of the target language exposure and the richness of the instructional environment, and that awareness of influence from Korean grew in parallel with these factors. She infers that avoidance of Konglish and self-correction in this area are related to language awareness derived from longer and more meaningful engagement with English. Finally, Nam reports a finding that English learners were aware that a particular usage was Konglish and not likely to be appropriate.

Unlike Daulton, who explores the facilitative dimensions of English loan expressions in Japanese, Nam focuses on the more negative impact of English loan expressions. As we have seen, her study mostly concerns the impact of Konglish on the use of English by Korean learners. Nevertheless, the conclusion that flows from Nam's study is, as in the case of Daulton's study, that the loan expressions investigated have been assimilated into her subjects' L1 lexicon and that their deployment in English is to be seen as L1 lexical transfer with rather particular features. The features in question resemble those applying in Daulton's data. Korean borrowings from Western languages are not, unlike Western borrowings in Japanese, marked out by a particular script, but there does seem to be a general – if not complete – awareness of their foreign, Western origins. Nam claims that some English loanwords are not in fact recognized as loanwords at all.

It is certainly the case that some loanwords from other Western languages are assumed to be from English. An example of this latter phenomenon is that of *aijen* ('crampon') from German *Eisen* ('iron'). However, the factors of the distinctiveness of English loanwords' sound shapes, of encounters with English and of general knowledge apply in the Korean as in the Japanese situation. What Nam finds is that as proficiency in English increases and as awareness of the non-English meanings of certain Konglish expressions grows, the assumption that Konglish is recyclable as English diminishes. This confirms both that the expressions in question are sourced in the L1 mental lexicon and also that even in naïve learners there is a vague awareness that they have something to do with English.

The main point for the present discussion is that the use of Konglish in English is not a question of language confusion; it is a question of learners' drawing on their L1 lexical resources on the basis of a (perhaps informed) hunch that these resources might be of help to them in English. This is really no different from the case of an English-speaking learner of French 'Frenchifying' an English word like *admiration* to /admirasjɔ̃/ on the basis that other English -*ation* words have /-asjɔ̃/ 'versions' in French. In the instance of English and French, one can clearly talk about a psychotypological factor, since at the lexical level the two languages are close and are perceived to be close. However, it may well be that in languages like Japanese and Korean, the English loanword dimension is now so enormous that, given also the widespread presence of English in the relevant countries, intuitions about how to convert English loanwords into 'real' English words are developing in the same way that intuitions about converting Romance words in English into French words have developed among English speakers.

Mention of psychotypologically motivated cross-lexical interaction between English and French brings me to the final research project that I wish to refer to. This comprised a series of studies carried out in Ireland (Ó Laoire & Singleton, 2009; Singleton & Ó Laoire, 2006a, 2006b). The first two of these studies involved teenaged learners of French who were native speakers of English, and who had extensive knowledge of Irish, whether as an L2 or as a second L1. The languages under scrutiny in these studies all belong to different language families. English is a Germanic language, Irish a Celtic language and French a Romance language. However, the languages are not equidistant from each other. The lexical consequences of the Norman invasion of England in the 11th century and of the continuing close relations between England and France during the Middle Ages mean that the French and English lexicons have thousands of cognates (cf. Claiborne, 1990; McArthur & Gachelin, 1992; Pei, 1967; Robertson, 1954; Van Roey *et al.*, 1988). The Romance component of the Irish lexicon is significantly more restricted. Following the Christianization of Ireland, some loanwords from ecclesiastical Latin were borrowed into Irish. It should be noted, though, that apart from being few in number, these words have become assimilated to the point where their resemblance to forms in contemporary Romance languages is barely discernible. With regard to French influence, after the arrival of the Anglo-Normans in Ireland in the 12th century, French became one of the major languages of medieval Ireland together with Irish, English and Latin (cf. Picard, 2003), and French influence can be seen in the fact that some hundreds of Irish lexical borrowings from French have been identified (see e.g. Risk, 1969). However, more precisely the point is that French loanwords in Irish are counted in the hundreds, whereas in English they are counted in the thousands.

On the basis of the foregoing, it is clear that in lexical terms the distance between English and French is considerably less than that between Irish and French. Moreover, it is also obvious from the experience of generations of teachers of French working with English speakers and teachers of English working with French speakers that the cognates shared by English and French are rapidly noticed by L2 learners. Hence, the perceived need for dictionaries of French–English 'false friends' (see e.g. Kirk-Greene, 1981; Thody & Evans, 1985; Van Roey et al., 1988). The hypothesis in the studies, therefore, was that, faced with a task in French which posed lexical gaps for them, the participants would resort to English rather than Irish to expand their resources. This indeed was the result that emerged, not only from the words actually produced but also from the participants' introspective commentaries on the manner in which they went about trying to find appropriate expressions in French. Such choice of the most promising source available for expressions that could be put to work in French bespeaks a high degree of linguistic sophistication and – since choice implies separability and separation – it runs counter to the notion that cross-lexical interplay is simply a matter of blurred boundaries between languages.

Conclusion

We have noted in the foregoing that with the exception of a very brief period in the 1970s, cross-linguistic influence has been a major and perennial focal topic of research on SLA and use. With regard to the lexical dimension of such research, however, we have also seen that this was at one point in time and in some quarters predicated on the proposition that the L2 mental lexicon is qualitatively different from that of the L1, and by implication not closely connected to it. It has been suggested here that the relevant evidence, properly interpreted, runs counter to this viewpoint, and it has been shown, indeed, that some researchers have been tempted by the evidence in the exact opposite direction, toying with (but in the end rejecting) the proposition that the lexicon is radically unitary no matter how many languages are involved.

The final part of the chapter has addressed the notion propounded by Harris and his followers that languages blur into each other. The conclusion which emerges from a review of some of the evidence from cross-lexical research, which at first sight appears to support the 'blur' conception in respect of cross-linguistic interaction, is that, at least in the instances examined here, what seems in fact to be operative is a highly sophisticated set of processes based on experience-driven language awareness which takes language differences fully into account.

References

Beauvillain, C. and Grainger, J. (1987) Accessing interlexical homographs: Some limitations of a language-selective access. *Journal of Memory and Language* 26 (6), 658–672.

Caramazza, A. and Brones, I. (1979) Lexical access in bilinguals. *Bulletin of the Psychonomic Society* 13, 212–214.

Claiborne, R. (1990) *The Life and Times of the English Language*. London: Bloomsbury.

Cook, V. (1992) Evidence for multicompetence. *Language Learning* 42, 557–591.

Cook, V. (2003) Introduction: The changing L1 in the L2 user's mind. In V. Cook (ed.) *Effects of the Second Language on the First* (pp. 1–18). Clevedon: Multilingual Matters.

Corder, S.P. (1967) The significance of learners' errors. *International Review of Applied Linguistics* 5, 161–170.

Corder, S.P. (1971) Idiosyncratic dialects and error analysis. *International Review of Applied Linguistics* 9, 147–159.

Cristoffanini, P., Kirsner, K. and Milech, D. (1986) Bilingual lexical representation: The status of Spanish-English cognates. *Quarterly Journal of Experimental Psychology* 38A, 367–393.

Daulton, F.E. (2008) *Japan's Built-in Lexicon of English-based Loanwords*. Clevedon: Multilingual Matters.

De Groot, A. (1995) Determinants of bilingual lexicosemantic organization. *Computer Assisted Language Learning* 8, 151–180.

Dijkstra, T. (2003) Lexical processing in bilinguals and multilinguals. In J. Cenoz, B. Hufeisen and U. Jessner (eds) *The Multilingual Lexicon* (pp. 11–26). Dordrecht: Kluwer.

Dulay, H.C. and Burt, M.K. (1974) You can't learn without goofing: An analysis of children's second language errors. In J.C. Richards (ed.) *Error Analysis: Perspectives on Second Language Acquisition* (pp. 95–123). London: Longman.

Dulay, H.C. and Burt, M.K. (1977) Remarks on creativity in language acquisition. In H. Dulay and M. Finocchiaro (eds) *Viewpoints on English as a Second Language* (pp. 95–126). New York: Regents.

Hammarberg, B. (2009) The factor 'perceived crosslinguistic similarity' in third language production: How does it work? In B. Hammarberg (ed.) *Processes in Third Language Acquisition* (pp. 127–153). Edinburgh: Edinburgh University Press.

Harris, R. (1998) *Introduction to Integrational Linguistics*. Oxford: Pergamon.

James, C. (1971) The exculpation of contrastive linguistics. In G. Nickel (ed.) *Papers in Contrastive Linguistics* (pp. 53–68). Cambridge: Cambridge University Press.

Kasper, G. (1984) Perspectives on language transfer. *BAAL Newsletter* 22, 3–23.

Kirk-Greene, C.W.E. (1981) *French False Friends*. London: Routledge and Kegan Paul.

Kirsner, K., Lalor, E. and Hird, K. (1993) The bilingual lexicon: Exercise, meaning and morphology. In R. Schreuder and B. Weltens (eds) *The Bilingual Lexicon* (pp. 215–248). Amsterdam: John Benjamins.

Lado, R. (1957) *Linguistics Across Cultures*. Ann Arbor, MI: University of Michigan Press.

Laufer, B. (1989) A factor of difficulty in vocabulary learning: Deceptive transparency. *AILA Review* 6, 10–20.

McArthur, T. and Gachelin, J.-M. (1992) Romance. In T. McArthur (ed.) *The Oxford Companion to the English Language* (pp. 872–74). London: BCA/Oxford University Press.

Meara, P. (1984) The study of lexis in interlanguage. In A. Davies, C. Criper and P.R. Howatt (eds) *Interlanguage* (pp. 225–235). Edinburgh: Edinburgh University Press.

Nam, N. (2009) Exploring Konglish: Cross-linguistic lexical issues with reference to Korean learners of English. PhD thesis, Trinity College Dublin.

Ó Laoire, M. and Singleton, D. (2009) The role of prior knowledge in L3 learning and use: Further evidence of psychotypological dimensions. In L. Aronin and B. Hufeisen (eds) *The Exploration of Multilingualism: Development of Research on L3, Multilingualism and Multiple Language Acquisition* (pp. 79–102). Amsterdam: John Benjamins.

Pei, M. (1967) *The Story of the English Language*. London: George Allen and Unwin.

Picard, J.M. (2003) The French language in medieval Ireland. In M. Cronin and C. Ó Cuilleanáin (eds) *The Languages of Ireland* (pp. 57–77). Dublin: Four Courts Press.

Postgate, J.P. (1922) *Translation and Translations: Theory and Practice*. London: Bell.

Ringbom, H. (2007) *Cross-Linguistic Similarity in Foreign Language Learning*. Clevedon: Multilingual Matters.

Risk, H (1969) French loan-words in Irish. *Études Celtiques* 12, 585–655.

Robertson, S. (1954) *Development of Modern English*. New York: Prentice-Hall.

Singleton, D. (1987a) The fall and rise of language transfer. In J.A. Coleman and R. Towell (eds) *The Advanced Language Learner* (pp. 27–53). London: CILT.

Singleton, D. (1987b) Mother and other tongue influences on learner French. *Studies in Second Language Acquisition* 9, 327–345.

Singleton, D. (1996) Crosslinguistic lexical operations and the L2 mental lexicon. In T. Hickey and J. Williams (eds) *Language, Education and Society* (pp. 246–252). Clevedon: IRAAL/Multilingual Matters.

Singleton, D. (1999) *Exploring the Second Language Mental Lexicon*. Cambridge: Cambridge University Press; Beijing: Beijing World Publishing.

Singleton, D. and Little, D. (1991) The second language lexicon: Some evidence from university-level learners of French and German. *Second Language Research* 7, 61–82.

Singleton, D. and Ó Laoire, M. (2006a) Psychotypologie et facteur L2 dans l'influence translexicale. Une analyse de l'influence de l'anglais et de l'irlandais sur le français L3 de l'apprenant, *Acquisition et Interaction en Langue Étrangère* 24, 101–117.

Singleton, D. and Ó Laoire, M. (2006b) Psychotypology and the 'L2 factor' in cross-lexical interaction: An analysis of English and Irish influence in learner French. In M. Bendtsen, M. Björklund, C. Fant and L. Forsman (eds) *Språk, Lärande och Utbildning i Sikte* (pp. 191–205). Vasa: Faculty of Education, Åbo Akademi.

Thody, P. and Evans, H. (1985) *Faux Amis and Key Words – A Dictionary-Guide to French Language, Culture and Society through Lookalikes and Confusables*. London: The Athlone Press.

Toolan, M. (2008) Introduction: Language teaching and integrational linguistics. In M. Toolan (ed.) *Language Teaching: Integrational Linguistic Approaches* (pp. 1–23). London: Routledge.

Van Roey, J., Granger, S. and Swallow, H. (1988) Introduction générale. *Dictionnaire des faux amis français–anglais*. Paris-Gembloux: Duculot.

Wolter, B. (2001) Comparing the L1 and L2 mental lexicon: A depth of individual word knowledge model. *Studies in Second Language Acquisition* 23, 41–69.

4 L1 Transfer in Chinese Learners' Use of Spatial Prepositions in EFL

Jia Li and Jinting Cai

Introduction

Space is obviously a fundamental reality of human existence, but its expression can vary from language to language quite radically, thus posing a real challenge for second language (L2) learners. Prepositions, whether their meanings involve space, time or other concepts, are 'notoriously difficult' for L2 learners of English, as stated by Celce-Murcia and Larsen-Freeman (1999: 401) among others. Indeed, prepositions continue to pose problems for learners even at the very advanced level (Lennon, 1991). While considerable research has investigated transfer in spatial expressions (e.g. Coventry & Guijarro-Fuentes, 2008), relatively few studies have focused on transfer in the use of English spatial prepositions by Chinese English as a foreign language (EFL) learners. The present study accordingly focuses on this area, with special attention to four prepositions that denote vertical polarity: *above, over, under* and *below*.

Literature Review

Cognitive linguistics has proved helpful for investigations of the acquisition of spatial meanings in a new language, and certain cognitivist concerns about meaning inform our investigation. One such concern is the non-arbitrary relation between the forms and meanings that denote spatial concepts. A number of cognitive theorists (e.g. Lakoff, 1987; Lakoff & Johnson, 1980, 1999; Langacker, 2008) have argued that a good deal more systematicity exists in the semantics of English prepositions than has traditionally been assumed. The non-arbitrary nature of the English spatial system is evident in, for example, metaphoric extensions that relate space to more abstract phenomena such as purposes, as seen in the metaphoric equation between purposes and destinations. Statements such as *We're behind schedule in the project* link a spatial concept (denoted by *behind*) with a plan (the schedule), and while the example uses a prepositional phrase, other structures can also realize the same metaphoric equation: e.g. *Let's keep moving forward* and *We're backsliding* (Lakoff & Johnson, 1999: 191). In further analyses of metaphoric relations, Tyler and Evans (2001, 2003) propose a theoretical framework called the principled polysemy network, stating that many of the multiple uses associated with a preposition are related in relatively straightforward, systematic ways.

The cognitivist emphasis on *construals* also offers useful insights. What may be construed can vary in terms of what is specified, what is salient, what is profiled or in terms of what the speaker's perspective is (Langacker, 2008). Construals often involve subtle as well as transparent meanings as in an example given by Langacker: *It is pretty through the valley*. As Langacker (2008: 80) notes, although there is no verb of motion, a preposition suggesting motion (i.e. *through*) occurs, and the construction 'evokes the conception of someone traveling through the valley and observing its appearance'.

Recent transfer research has shown increasing attention to a wide range of cognitive processes. Among the distinctions that Jarvis and Pavlenko (2008: 115) propose in their study of cross-linguistic influence is one between linguistic transfer and conceptual transfer, and the present study will also differentiate semantic transfer and conceptual transfer. Indeed, several relevant studies of spatial cognition in relation to second language acquisition (SLA) and transfer have appeared in the last few decades (e.g. Carroll, 2000; Coventry & Guijarro-Fuentes, 2008; Harley, 1989; Ijaz, 1986; Jarvis & Odlin, 2000; Pavesi, 1987; Schumann, 1986). Although the methods in these studies vary considerably, they all suggest, to some degree, that language transfer affects the acquisition and use of spatial expressions in an L2. For example, Ijaz (1986) found that Urdu and German influenced native speakers of those languages in their choice of English spatial prepositions, though in contrast to Jarvis and Pavlenko, she seemed to equate meaning transfer with conceptual transfer. Schumann (1986) found that while speakers of Chinese, Japanese and Spanish all omitted English prepositions, the Spanish speakers, whose first language (L1) has prepositions formally and functionally more similar to those of English, omitted prepositions far less frequently than did Chinese or Japanese speakers. Similarly, Jarvis and Odlin (2000) investigated the transferability of bound morphology in relation to transfer in the spatial expressions of Finnish-speaking and Swedish-speaking adolescent learners of English. Jarvis and Odlin found that the morphology and semantics of the L1 Finnish and Swedish spatial systems influenced the use of L2 English prepositions and also omissions (the latter coming almost always from speakers of Finnish, whose spatial reference system has few prepositions).

A Study of Transfer of Spatial Meanings

Given the evidence of transfer in previous research with other L1 groups, the present study investigates semantic transfer in the use of spatial prepositions by Chinese EFL learners. Evidence for such transfer comes from the results of a test in which participants had to complete sentences. Before our discussion of the test, however, a contrastive analysis of spatial constructions in Chinese and English is necessary.

Spatial contrasts in Chinese and English

Chinese and English differ considerably in how they express spatial concepts, including differences in formal patterns. While English is clearly a prepositional language, Chinese uses both prepositions and postpositions (Li & Thompson, 1978). The semantic differences between the two languages are, at least in some cases, even more striking. Prominent among such contrasts are the differences between the Chinese words *shang* and *xia* and four corresponding English spatial prepositions: *above, over, below* and *under*. *Shang* denotes positive vertical polarity and thus can translate as either *above* or *over*, while *xia* can be translated with the negative polarity words *under* and *below*. The semantics of the English forms have been studied extensively (e.g. Tyler & Evans, 2001, 2003), but as will be seen, rather different descriptions are required for the corresponding Chinese forms. The positive/ negative polarity in *shang/xia* does of course overlap with the polarity relations of *above/below* and *over/under*. However, there are clear differences since the *shang/xia* contrast is less fine-grained. In order to analyze the semantic differences in detail, we searched the Center for Chinese Linguistics (CCL) corpus and Chinese–English parallel corpora with *shang* ('above/below') and *xia* as keywords to sort out all sentences containing these keywords.[1]

In considering cross-linguistic correspondences in spatial reference between English and Korean, Bowerman (1996: 393–402) identified the following three types of cross-linguistic contrast that may have implications for language-mediated differences in cognition. Those differences will be discussed here with regard to their relevance for English and Chinese.

Type 1. Languages differ in what is treated as a vertical relationship. What English construes as a vertical polarity relation is often construed simply as a distance relation in Chinese. Thus, in Example (1), the waterfall is described in English as being located vertically (with the preposition *above*) in relation to the bridge, whereas the Chinese version uses the word *juli*, which can be translated as *from*:

(1) *zui jin- de   qiaoliang   juli   pubu   you   jiangjin   ban yingli.*
    Nearest-NOM   bridge   from   fall   exist   close to   half mile
    The nearest bridge is about half a mile above the fall.
    (NOM = nominalizer[2])

Type 2. Languages differ in how much information they conventionally evoke. In comparison with Chinese, the English spatial terms investigated here convey more information: *over* and *under* contrast with *above* and *below* with regard to information about contact between objects. For instance, the English translation of the Chinese sentence in Example (2) allows for the use of *over*, but not for *above*, since the latter preposition would imply that the truck was somehow not on the surface of the road. In contrast, Chinese *shang* ('on') is neutral as to whether or not the objects are in contact, and such information has to be inferred from the context.

(2) | *yi- liang* | *kache* | *zai* | *shanqiu* | *shang* | *chuxian*. |
     |-------------|---------|-------|-----------|---------|-----------|
     | One-CL | truck | at | hill | on | appear |

A truck appears over the hill.

(CL = classifier)

Type 3. Languages differ in how their users conventionally construe objects in space (see also Coventry, 1998). This typological contrast is similar to the Type 1 contrast, but it is not restricted to construals involving vertical polarity. Thus, for instance, referents often construed in English as being somehow within a container are viewed in Chinese as being located on a plane, as evident in the difference in spatial words in Example (3), with English *in* contrasting with Chinese *shang* ('on').

(3) | *Ta-de* | *maozi* | *shang* | *cha-zhe* | *yigen* | *yumao* |
     |---------|---------|---------|-----------|---------|---------|
     | his | hat | on | insert | one | feather |

He has a feather in his hat.

The research question

To investigate L1 transfer in the acquisition of English *over*, *above*, *under* and *below* by Chinese EFL learners, we formulated the following research question. Do the differences between spatial words in Chinese and English result in L1 → L2 semantic transfer?

Participants

In total, 60 Chinese learners of English and 15 native speakers of English volunteered for the study. Among the 60 EFL learners, 30 were undergraduate intermediate English majors in their second year of study at a foreign language university in Central China, and their ages ranged from 19 to 21, with an average of 19.4 years. All were native speakers of Chinese who had received English training for at least seven years. The other 30 learners were postgraduate advanced English majors who had been studying English for at least 11 years and who had passed the Test for English Majors,

Band 8. The 15 native speakers of English were all adult students studying in a management program at a university in the UK; they were born in the UK and were living there at the time of the present study.

The group of intermediate level L2 learners will hereafter be referred to as Group 1 (G1), the postgraduate L2 learners as Group 2 (G2) and the group of native speakers of English as Group 3 (G3).

Instrument

A sentence-completion task (SCT) was developed to elicit the participants' use of English prepositions, especially the four polarity words *above, over, below* and *under.* The test consisted of nine sentences with one blank space in each for the subjects to fill in with an appropriate preposition. Pictures accompanying SCT items came from a variety of sources including MS Word 2003 Clip Art and drawings of our own, with examples of some of the illustrations used appearing below in the discussion of participants' answers.

Data collection and analysis

Instructions were explained to the EFL subjects in Chinese to clarify the requirements and avoid misunderstanding, and Chinese explanations were given for every possible new word. The native speakers of English read the instructions in their mother tongue, and they did not take part in the retrospective interviews described below.

The data collection consisted of two sessions:

(1) The SCT. Participants were asked to complete nine sentences in the task with appropriate English prepositions. They were allowed to use any preposition more than once.
(2) The introspective interview. In order to get a sense of what the subjects were thinking about as they supplied particular prepositions in the SCT, an interview with nine questions was conducted with a random sample of Chinese participants, as explained below in the discussion of the results. During the interview, the questions were asked by the researchers and the answers were given by the students in spoken English. The interviews normally lasted about three minutes, with the researchers writing down details of the participants' answers.

Results

Evidence involving Type 1 differences

The first type of cross-linguistic contrast discussed above focuses on the fact that languages differ in what is treated as a vertical relationship.

Three items on the SCT (1, 3 and 7) offer insights about the significance of this contrast between English and Chinese.

Item 1: He stood about a mile _____ the fall.
Item 3: The nearest bridge is about half a mile _____ the falls.
Item 7: The hydroelectric station is five miles _____ the dam.

The first item was accompanied by a picture of a waterfall, whereas the others were accompanied by drawings such as the one used for Item 7.

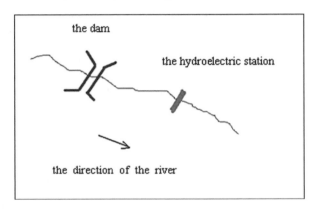

Table 4.1 shows the distribution of responses in the items for this type of difference.

For all three items there are striking group tendencies. In the case of the first SCT item, 13 out of 15 (86.7%) native speakers (G3) chose the preposition *below*, while only two of them (13.3%) chose *from*, whereas in the two L1 Chinese groups (G1 and G2), the response pattern showed *from* overwhelmingly preferred over *below*. Only 3 out of 30 (10%) learners from G1 and 4 out of 30 (13.3%) from G2 gave *below* as responses, while 19 out of 30 (63.3%) learners from G1 and 22 out of 30 (73.3%) from G2 used *from* as their responses. Taken as a whole, only 11.7% of the Chinese learners used *below*, and the responses with *from* constituted the overwhelmingly favored choice (68.3%).

Although Item 1 shows hardly any difference between the G1 and G2 groups, the choices in Items 3 and 7 suggest a possible effect of increased exposure to the target language. G2 participants showed a stronger preference for *above* (Item 3) and *below* (Item 7) than did their G1 counterparts, while the native speakers of English overwhelmingly preferred the vertical polarity choices instead of *from* on both items. At the same time, fewer G2 participants used other responses than did their G1 counterparts, such responses never being the choices of the G3 group.

Among the nine questions in the retrospective interview, two of them involve the Type 1 contrast. For Question 1, we randomly chose two subjects from each of the two EFL groups who used *from* in Items 1, 3 and 7.

Table 4.1 Distribution of responses in the items for Type 1 differences

Item Choices	LG*	n	Above	Below	From	Other
1	G1	30		3 (10.0%)	19 (63.3%)	8 (16.7%)
	G2	30		4 (13.3%)	22 (73.3%)	4 (13.3%)
	G1 + G2	60		7 (11.7%)	41 (68.3%)	12 (20.0%)
	G3	15		13 (86.7%)	2 (13.3%)	
3	G1	30	5 (16.7%)		11 (36.7%)	14 (46.7%)
	G2	30	12 (40.0%)		13 (43.3%)	5 (16.7%)
	G1 + G2	60	17 (28.3%)		24 (40.0%)	19 (31.7%)
	G3	15	14 (93.3%)		1 (6.7%)	
7	G1	30		5 (16.7%)	16 (53.3%)	9 (30.0%)
	G2	30		10 (33.3%)	13 (43.3%)	7 (23.3%)
	G1 + G2	60		19 (31.7%)	25 (41.7%)	16 (26.7%)
	G3	15		13 (86.7%)	2 (13.3%)	

*LG=language group

Likewise, for Question 2, another four subjects who chose *above/below* were selected randomly from G1 and G2.

Question 1: Why did you use *from* in Items 1, 3 and 7? Do you think the word *below* or *above* or other prepositions are correctly used when they are put in these sentences? Why or why not?

Question 2: Why did you use *above/below* in Items 1, 3 and 7? How do you understand the sense of these two words in these sentences? And are you sure about your choice?

All the subjects who had chosen *from* mentioned their knowledge of Chinese, as in the following cases:

Subject 1 from G1: The reason why I have used the preposition *from* is that this word can denote the sense of distance, whose Chinese equivalence is *juli* [from]. And all ... I think we cannot use *above/below* in these sentences, because their senses are all about spatial relations, something like *up/down*.

Subject 2 from G2: The word *from* can express the sense of distance, so I used this word... I am not sure whether we can use *above/below* here. I don't know.

None of the four subjects who chose *above/below* could explain why they had used these prepositions of vertical polarity. Again, two sample answers are given here:

Subject 3 from G1: (laugh) I don't know why I used *above/below*. And now, I think that my answers are wrong.

Subject 3 from G2: I chose the word just because of my own feeling. I am really not sure whether my choice is right or wrong.

Evidence involving Type 2 differences

The second type of cross-linguistic contrast involves, it will be recalled, how much information languages conventionally evoke in a spatial description. As with the first type of contrast, the relevance of Type 2 to transfer seems evident in the differences between several responses of L1 Chinese speakers and those of L1 English speakers on the SCT.

Items 4, 5 and 9 provided contexts to study the sensitivity of L2 learners to the semantic contrasts between *over* and *above* and between *under* and *below*.

Item 4: The little boy hid his key _____ the carpet.
Item 5: There is a pillow _____ her head.
Item 9: A man appeared _____ the hill.

The picture used with Item 5 appears below. The one used with Item 9 showed a man at the summit of a hill. For Item 4, no picture was used.

Table 4.2 shows the distribution of responses for the four vertical polarity words given in separate columns along with the combined figures for other choices.

On Item 4, the vast majority of the G1 and almost all of the G2 participants selected *under*, which was the unanimous choice of the L1 English speakers. Item 5 likewise elicited a unanimous choice among the L1 English speakers (again choosing the preposition *under*). However, while the majority of the G1 and G2 participants made the same choice, sizeable percentages opted for *below* (26.7% of the G1 and 20% of the G2 students). A similar pattern obtained for Item 9, with a unanimous choice of *over* among the L1 English speakers and sizeable majorities of the G1 and G2 groups making the same choice, yet with several individuals opting instead for *above* or other choices.

In the retrospective interviews, the same method of randomly choosing two individuals each from the G1 and G2 groups was used as in the case of the Type 1 inquiries. Sample answers follow each of the three questions pertinent to Type 2 contrasts. As the answers indicate, Chinese learners of

Table 4.2 Distribution of responses in the items for Type 2 difference by three LGs

Item	LG	n	Under	Over	Above	Below	Other choices
4	G1	30	23 (76.7%)			1 (3.3%)	6 (20.0%)
	G2	30	28 (93.3%)			1 (3.3%)	1 (3.3%)
	G1 + G2	60	51 (85.0%)			2 (3.3%)	7 (11.7%)
	G3	15	15 (100.0%)				
5	G1	30	21 (70.0%)			8 (26.7%)	1 (3.3%)
	G2	30	24 (80.0%)			6 (20.0%)	
	G1 + G2	60	45 (75.0%)			14 (23.3%)	1 (1.7%)
	G3	15	15 (100.0%)				
9	G1	30		24 (80.0%)	4 (13.3%)		2 (6.7%)
	G2	30		26 (86.7%)	3 (10.0%)		1 (3.3%)
	G1 + G2	60		50 (83.3%)	7 (11.7%)		3 (5.0%)
	G3	15		15(100.0%)			

English had become familiar with the contact/non-contact distinction in *under* and *below*, even though they did not always keep the distinction in mind when selecting their SCT answer:

Question 3: Why did you use *under* rather than *below* in Item 5? Do you think your answer is correct? If not, which word should be used?

Subject 6 from G1: I think the pillow is in contact with her head, so I used *under* rather than *below*. I have once met this kind of questions before when I did exercise. My answer should be correct.

Subject 5 from G2: The difference between *under* and *below* is that the former one can denote the sense of contact while the last [latter] one cannot. In this sentence, the woman's head is definitely in contact with the pillow, so I used the word *under*. My answer is correct.

Question 4: Why did you use *below* rather than *under* in Item 5? Do you think your answer is correct? If not, which word should be used?

Subject 7 from G2: My answer is incorrect. The word *under* should be used. These two words are different in that *under* can express the sense of contact while the word *below* cannot.

Question 5: Why did you use *over* rather than *above* in Item 9? Do you think your answer is correct? If not, which word should be used?

Subject 8 from G1: If we say A is above B, then we mean that A is higher than B and A is in the middle air [aloft]. However, in this sentence the man is not in middle air [aloft]. So I used *over* rather than *above*. I think my answer is correct.

Evidence involving Type 3 differences

The third type of cross-linguistic contrast considered in this chapter is the variation in how people describe locations that can be construed as involving containers, planes and other relations. This type is related, of course, to Type 1 (which focuses on vertical relationships) and Type 2 (which focuses on the specificity of the spatial information); however, as noted earlier, Type 3 looks at a somewhat wider range of meanings. Items 2, 6 and 8 in the SCT were designed to investigate the effect of Type 3 contrasts between Chinese and English. Item 2 was accompanied by a picture showing buildings just below a mountain and Item 4 came with a picture of a man with a hat with a feather. The picture used for Item 8 appears below.

Item 2: The houses are _____ the foot of the mountain.
Item 6: There is a feather _____ his hat.
Item 8: There is red ink _____ the nib.

Table 4.3 shows the response patterns for each of the three items.

Table 4.3 Distribution of responses in the items for Type 3 difference by three LGs

Item	LG	n	At	In	Under	On
2	G1	30	26 (86.7%)		4 (13.3%)	
	G2	30	29 (96.7%)		1 (3.3)	
	G1 + G2	60	55 (91.7%)		5 (8.3%)	
	G3	15	15 (100.0%)			
6	G1	30		5 (16.7%)		25 (83.3%)
	G2	30		8 (26.7%)		22 (73.3%)
	G1 + G2	60		13 (21.7%)		47 (78.3%)
	G3	15		15 (100.0%)		
8	G1	30	8 (26.7%)			22 (73.3%)
	G2	30	10 (33.3%)			20 (66.7%)
	G1 + G2	60	18 (30.0%)			42 (70.0%)
	G3	15	15 (100.0%)			

On Items 6 and 8, both EFL groups (G1 and G2) differed considerably from the native speakers of English (G3). Item 6 showed an especially strong divergence, with the vast majority of G1 and G2 participants choosing *on* over *in*. Item 2, however, showed a more complicated response pattern. Large percentages of EFL learners, 86.7% of G1 and 96.7% of G2 (or 91.7% of G1 and G2 taken together), did make the same choice of *at* as did all participants in the G3 group. Even so, five Chinese learners did chose *under*, which suggests influence from the L1 Chinese postposition *xia*. The reason for the more frequent selection of the target-like *at* is probably that most learners had apparently become quite familiar with such usage in the course of their study, which thus forestalled negative transfer. This interpretation is supported by what we learned in retrospective interviews.

Once again, two individuals from each of the learner groups were randomly selected. Questions 6 and 7 focused on Item 2 and Questions 8 and 9 focused on Items 6 and 8:

Question 6: Can you translate Item 2 into Chinese?
Question 7: Why did you use *at* in Item 2? You know the word *at* is completely different from *zai...xia* ('under').
Question 8: Can you translate Items 6 and 8 into Chinese?
Question 9: Why did you use *on* in Items 6 and 8?

As in the other interviews, our informants' answers often confirmed the likelihood of Chinese influence. For example, the translations that the participants provided suggest that the postposition *xia* was the source for the use of *under* by some individuals as the answer for SCT Item 2. The translation template for these individuals was thus:

(4)	*Fangzi*	*wei yu*	*shan*	*jiao*	*xia.*
	house	lie at	mountain	foot	under

The house is at the foot of the mountain.

Conclusion

Based on the quantitative and qualitative analyses of the data, we obtained evidence for negative L1 transfer in Chinese learners' acquisition of semantic networks of English spatial prepositions. All three types of cross-linguistic differences seemed to influence the results, even though some test items (e.g. Item 2) showed in only a few cases of interference. Most intriguing of all the results is arguably the Type 1 contrast, where speakers of English typically construe certain locations in terms of vertical polarity while speakers of Chinese construe the same locations simply in terms of distance. Perhaps such differences in construal are associated with differences involving non-linguistic cognition. In any case, the results regarding some learners' metalinguistic awareness also indicate that negative transfer can often be forestalled by effective EFL teaching.

Acknowledgments

This chapter is part of a project on L1 transfer supported by the National Social Sciences Fund in China (Project No. 11CYY021). The authors express their deep gratitude to Professor Liming Yu and Professor Terence Odlin for their insightful comments on and attention to earlier drafts of the chapter.

Notes

(1) The CCL corpus and the parallel corpora, designed by Xiamen University, are available at http://www.luweixmu.com/ec-corpus/query.asp.
(2) Sentences 1a and 1b through 5a and 5b are from the Chinese–English parallel corpora.

References

Bowerman, M. (1996) Learning how to structure space for language: A crosslinguistic perspective. In P. Bloom, M.A. Peterson, L. Nadel and M.F. Garrett (eds) *Language and Space* (pp. 385–436). Cambridge, MA and London: MIT Press.
Carroll, M. (2000) The relevance of information organization to second language acquisitions studies: The descriptive discourse of advanced adult learners of German. *Studies in Second Language Acquisition* 22 (3), 441–466.
Celce-Murcia, M. and Larsen-Freeman, D. (1999) *The Grammar Book: An ESL/EFL Teacher's Course*. Boston, MA: Heinle and Heinle.
Coventry, K.R. (1998) Spatial prepositions, functional relations, and lexical specification. In P. Olivier and K.P. Gapp (eds) *Representation and Processing of Spatial Expressions* (pp. 247–262). Mahwah, NJ: Lawrence Erlbaum Associates.
Coventry, K.R. and Guijarro-Fuentes, P. (2008) Spatial language learning and the functional geometric framework. In P. Robinson and N. Ellis (eds) *Handbook of Cognitive Linguistics and Second Language Acquisition* (pp. 114–138). New York and London: Routledge.
Harley, B. (1989) Transfer in the written compositions of French immersion students. In H. Dechert and M. Raupach (eds) *Transfer in Language Production* (pp. 3–19). Norwood, NJ: Ablex.
Ijaz, I.H. (1986) Linguistic and cognitive determinants of lexical acquisition in a second language. *Language Learning* 36 (4), 401–451.
Jarvis, S. and Odlin, T. (2000) Morphological type, spatial reference, and language transfer. *Studies in Second Language Acquisition* 22 (4), 535–556.
Jarvis, S. and Pavlenko, A. (2008) *Cross-Linguistic Influence in Language and Cognition*. New York: Routledge.
Lakoff, G. (1987) *Woman, Fire, and Dangerous Things: What Categories Reveal about the Mind*. London: The University of Chicago Press.
Lakoff, G. and Johnson, M. (1980) *Metaphors We Live By*. Chicago, IL: The University of Chicago Press.

Lakoff, G. and Johnson, M. (1999) *Philosophy in the Flesh: The Embodied Mind and its Challenge to Western Thought*. New York: Basic Books.

Langacker, R. (2008) Cognitive grammar as a basis for language acquisition. In P. Robinson and N. Ellis (eds) *Handbook of Cognitive Linguistics and Second Language Acquisition* (pp. 66–88). New York: Routledge.

Lennon, P. (1991) Error and the very advanced learner. *IRAL* 29 (1), 31–44.

Li, C. and Thomson, S. (1978) An exploration of Mandarin Chinese. In W. Lehmann (ed.) *Syntactic Typology: Studies in the Phenomenology of Language* (pp. 223–266). Austin, TX: University of Texas Press.

Pavesi, M. (1987) Variability and systematicity in the acquisition of spatial prepositions. In R. Ellis (ed.) *Second Language Acquisition in Context* (pp. 73–82). Englewood Cliffs, NJ: Prentice-Hall.

Schumann, J. (1986) Locative and directional expressions in basilang speech. *Language Learning* 36 (3), 277–294.

Tyler, A. and Evans, V. (2001) Reconsidering prepositional polysemy networks: The case of *over. Language* 77 (4), 724–765.

Tyler, A. and Evans, V. (2003) *The Semantics of English Prepositions: Spatial Scenes, Cognition and the Experiential Basis of Meaning*. New York and Cambridge: Cambridge University Press.

5 L1 Influences in L2 Lexical Inferencing

T. Sima Paribakht and Marjorie Bingham Wesche

Linguistic processing tasks offer rich potential for the study of first language (L1) influences on second language (L2) use and development. In this chapter, we will consider the nature of such influences as revealed through L2 *lexical inferencing,* a complex task involving both declarative and procedural knowledge across multiple linguistic subsystems, as well as the integrative processes of L2 text comprehension. Lexical inferencing, the informed guessing of unfamiliar word meanings in context, seeks word comprehension as part of text or oral discourse[1] comprehension, and also contributes to further lexical development.

While a large body of research exists on lexical transfer,[2] L1 influences on L2 lexical inferencing have received little attention. Most information on this topic comes from introspective L2 learner comments or researchers' observations in contexts where the learners speak different L1s. We will draw on transfer research in L2 reading comprehension as well as in lexical inferencing, focusing on relevant findings from our trilingual research on lexical inferencing from written texts by Persian and French speakers in both L1 and L2 (English) and in L1 by native speakers of English. Persian and French are of interest for their different typological relationships with English. An additional focus was a substudy comparing lexical inferencing processes and outcomes for target L2 words that have readily identifiable word or phrasal 'equivalents' in learners' L1, or are *lexicalized,* with those for words that are not lexicalized.

Background

Lexical inferencing

Lexical inferencing is a complex meaning determination process through which a reader draws on contextual cues and linguistic and world knowledge and combines the information from these sources in the context of his/her cumulative understanding of the text to arrive at a meaning for an unfamiliar word. A correct inference may aid in text comprehension, whereas failure to infer a meaning or to infer an incorrect meaning may impair such comprehension.

Like other complex linguistic tasks, lexical inferencing involves *declarative* knowledge (knowing 'that', or knowledge of or about something, e.g. a rule of grammar) and *procedural* knowledge (knowing how to do something, e.g. using correct grammar consistently without necessarily being able to cite the rule). In lexical inferencing, procedural knowledge is applied in, for example, the search for and the identification of relevant cues in the text or when combining information to arrive at a plausible meaning for the target word. Some studies of lexical inferencing processes have focused on identifying the *knowledge sources* (KSs), or the types of textual cues and reader knowledge used by readers to infer word meanings (e.g. Bengeleil & Paribakht, 2004; de Bot *et al.*, 1997; Haastrup, 1991; Paribakht, 2005; Paribakht & Wesche, 1999; Wesche & Paribakht, 2010). Others have paid more attention to the procedural abilities that learners bring to the task (e.g. Haastrup, 1991, 2008, 2010).

L1 readers often succeed in inferring appropriate meanings of unknown words in written texts, a process that likely contributes substantially to the demonstrated importance of reading in promoting L1 lexical development (e.g. Krashen, 1989). When lexical inferencing is successful, some initial word learning may take place. Consolidation and elaboration of the new knowledge and its long-term retention, however, generally require many subsequent exposures to the new word in diverse contexts. In an L2, lexical inferencing poses many difficulties for readers, so that successful or even partially successful identification of an appropriate word meaning cannot be assumed as an outcome of their encounters with unfamiliar words. As Koda (2005: 63) has pointed out, most L2 readers get much less information from each word in an L2 text than they would in their L1. This is because they know few, if any, of the words as well as they know comparable L1 words. This means that at every level there is more to be understood and learned, which in turn affects success in L2 lexical inferencing.

A large body of research on L2 lexical inferencing over the past several decades has identified factors that influence L2 readers' success in identifying word meanings in context. Their lexical and general L2 proficiency – in relation to text difficulty – play a critical role, as does their relevant world knowledge. Evidence for L1 influence in L2 lexical inferencing success has until recently been mainly anecdotal, but supports the conclusion that readers' L1 background influences both their L2 inferencing behaviors and outcomes.

Lexical knowledge and development

A learner's lexical knowledge, involving among other things both linguistic and conceptual knowledge as well as procedures for integrating them in performance, is essential to language use and underlies further vocabulary acquisition. In an L2, receptive knowledge of written words is relatively easy to measure and it has repeatedly shown strong predictive value for both lexical inferencing success and word learning through extensive reading. Lexical knowledge also involves a 'depth' dimension, reflecting among other things network knowledge – the multiple associations within an individual's lexicon – for which measures have only recently begun to be developed (Albrechtsen *et al.*, 2008; Nassaji, 2004; Read, 1993, 2000; Wesche & Paribakht, 1996). In a recent Danish study of L2 vocabulary and writing, lexical network knowledge was shown to have predictive value for both L1 and L2 lexical inferencing success, providing further insight into the complex role of lexical knowledge in successful inferencing.

Typological distance between L1 and L2

The concept of 'distance' between different languages is long established in linguistics (Lado, 1957; Weinreich, 1953). Recent typological analyses of languages have begun to provide a basis for estimating language distance. The typological profile of a language has been defined as 'a cross-linguistically valid characterization of its structure, highlighting in particular what is universal and what is language specific' (Viberg, 1998a: 119). Such profiles are relevant to the study of transfer in that they offer the possibility of systematic study of L1 influences on L2 knowledge and use. Of interest to the study of transfer in lexical inferencing is the concept of a language's 'lexical profile', providing information such as types and characteristics of word classes from the mapping of semantic fields and subfields as a basis for comparison across languages (Viberg, 1998b). With the development of such profiles for different languages, researchers will be increasingly able to systematically study L1 lexical transfer and its role in L2 lexical processing.

Relative typological distances between given L1s and an L2 are sometimes conceptualized as different starting points for those acquiring that L2, with learners who speak a more distant L1 viewed as facing a longer journey. Successful L2 language processing, including lexical inferencing and related lexical acquisition, is likely to be relatively facilitated for learners whose native language is typologically similar to the L2. This is because cross-linguistic similarities provide greater possibilities for positive transfer, freeing up cognitive resources for other language learning tasks (Odlin, 2003). The result may be more rapid acquisition rates and, over time, cumulative advantages in subsequent comparative proficiency.

Typological proximity between two languages generally reflects historical relationships, which explains the similarities between them across different linguistic subsystems, such as shared orthographic features or narrative structure. The cumulative work of Ringbom and colleagues on English L2 acquisition in Finland has provided important insights regarding the effects of typological distance on L1 transfer from comparisons of

Finnish and Swedish learners of English (Ringbom, 1987, 1992, 2007; Sjöholm, 1993, 1998). Among these is the repeated finding that speakers of Swedish (which, as a Germanic language, is closely related to English) are advantaged in learning English as an L2 compared to culturally very similar speakers of Finnish (which belongs to a quite different language family).

Yu's (1996a, 1996b) study comparing the acquisition of English motion verbs by Chinese and Japanese speakers provides evidence that the relative similarity of a subsystem in L1 and L2 across typologically distant languages can facilitate the learner's acquisition of that subsystem in L2. This appears to be a counterexample to the advantages claimed for proximate languages, but may better be considered an illustration of how transfer likely works. That is, the facilitating effects of typological proximity between L1 and L2 may be based on the cross-linguistic similarities of subclasses of features rather than on more general typological characteristics. While similarities between distant languages may facilitate the learning of some elements, typological proximity between the L1 and the L2 ensures cross-linguistic similarities in many subsystems that can facilitate the learners' task in multiple ways at the same time.

Learners' perceptions of L1/L2 proximity have been found to influence the likelihood of transfer of at least some linguistic features. Kellerman (1977, 1978) found that if learners perceived the L1 and L2 to be closely related, they were more likely to attempt transfer of L1 idiomatic expressions. In studies of L2 inferencing, there is some evidence that readers whose L1 is closely related to the L2 are more likely to report using L1 knowledge, as shown by English L2 learners whose native language was Danish (Haastrup, 1991, 2008) or French (Paribakht & Tréville, 2007) as opposed to those whose L1 was Persian (Paribakht, 2005). In other studies, however, lower proficiency learners of English from both closely related (Danish; Haastrup, 1991) and distant languages (Arabic; Bengeleil & Paribakht, 2004) tended to report using L1 knowledge more often than did more proficient learners.

L1 transfer and other L1 influences

Given the importance of prior knowledge to any kind of learning, it is not surprising that research on L1 transfer in different linguistic subsystems with L2 learners from a variety of L1s has revealed the widespread influence of L1 knowledge and skills on L2 performance. As a learner becomes more proficient in the L2, L1 effects tend to become less obvious, but evidence from highly proficient L2 users suggests that they are long lasting, if increasingly subtle, and are possibly always present in L2 performance (Koda, 2005; Odlin, 2005).

Some L1 transfer effects are readily apparent, for example, those involving formal features in language production such as pronunciation, spelling or grammar. Transfer can also be observed in the interpretation of linguistic features such as sound/symbol relationships, word components or grammatical relationships. Perhaps for this reason, most L1 transfer studies have involved linguistic features. A key lexical area that has been noted in lexical inferencing research, in which L1–L2 proximity helps learners is the availability of cognates (Ard & Holmburg, 1983; Hancin-Bhatt & Nagy, 1994; Tréville, 1996).[3]

Other L1 transfer effects, such as deeply ingrained ways of processing language data, may not be as easily detected. Odlin (2005: 16) suggests that 'language may have an important – but not absolute – influence on cognition'. He cites preliminary research evidence that languages influence their speakers' cognitive capacities in such areas as noticing, categorizing or recalling content. Koda (2005), from a similar position, emphasizes that L1 transfer may affect L2 processing skills as well as linguistic features. Koda (2005: 8–9) further proposes that the effects of transfer on processing skills may be more enduring, as it 'channels subsequent language development and also moulds the cognitive procedures accommodating its structural and functional peculiarities'. In Koda's view, many reading skill components developed in the L1 may be transferred to the L2. Shared orthographic knowledge, for example, likely provides long-term facilitation of visual information sampling ability in the L2.

Recent empirical evidence on lexical processing supports the view that all known meanings of a word are at least briefly activated by its orthographic form, even when the context imposes strong constraints limiting its possible meaning (Koda, 2005: 35). This parallel activation of different meanings for a given word form may, however, occur to different degrees (Singleton, 2006). Such parallel activation implies that readers are involved continuously in meaning selection, even for well-known words, many of which are polysemous or involve determination of which homonym is the intended one. In L2 use, research suggests that each time a familiar L2 word with an L1 lexical equivalent is encountered, its L1 translation is likely to be activated along with any known L2 meanings (Jiang, 2000; Paribakht, 2005). This point supports the notion that bilingual processing is more complex than L1 processing.

A number of cross-lingual studies of L2 lexical processing in the context of L2 reading have addressed the impact of differing orthographies. Some evidence for the transfer of L1 processing skills comes from Ghahremani-Ghajar and Masny (1999), who examined the role played by the different writing systems in Persian and English and their influence on informants' letter recognition strategies. Ghahremani-Ghajar and Masny (1999: 247) conclude that right–left directionality in searching for Persian letters is responsible for the Persian speakers' reading of Roman letters in the same way, i.e. 'Students took a longer time to respond to the left-most position in the Roman letters'. Also, since several vowels are not written in the Persian orthography, Persian readers need to determine appropriate vowels for each word before a combination of consonants becomes meaningful. Therefore, they may spend more time reading individual letters and words. Transfer of this tendency to reading English texts may result in slower reading and text comprehension (Ghahremani-Ghajar & Masny, 1999). A further possible L1 effect stems from the fact that word identification in Persian often involves attention not only to internalized probabilities of letter combinations, but ongoing verification of the potential word in the larger discourse context. In this case, literate Persian speakers may have developed skills in contextual analysis that could advantage their carrying out some language tasks (e.g. confirming the contextual appropriateness of inferred word meanings in lexical inferencing).

Koda (2005) also considers the role of symbol-to-sound relations, noting that in 'transparent' orthographies (such as French), phonological information is assembled mainly through letter-by-letter, symbol-to-sound translation. In less transparent orthographies (such as Persian), phonological information is often obtained only after a word has been identified, based on the reader's knowledge of it. The English orthography lies somewhere between, frequently presenting morphological as well as phonemic descriptions in its graphic representation (Koda, 2005: 84). Thus, phonologically equivalent words may have different spellings (e.g. *there* and *their*; *sight* and *site*). Greater similarity between L1 and L2 sound–symbol relationships should facilitate L2 reading.

Researchers have also found evidence of the effect of syntactic differences between different L1s on L2 lexical inferencing. For example, Nagy *et al.* (1997) reported the ongoing influence of L1 syntax on L2 English inferencing by fluent Spanish–English bilinguals, providing further evidence of the long-lasting and specific nature of some L1 procedures.

Beyond the transfer of specific L1 linguistic knowledge and procedural skills, other kinds of influences may be attributable to learners' L1. For example, a close 'fit' of L1 cultural knowledge to that encoded in the L2 should facilitate lexical inferencing and the retention of new word meanings and provide cumulative advantages over time.

Lexicalization patterns across languages

Each language has a lexical stock that represents the semantic concepts and their combinations used in that language. Words have semantic boundaries, and these boundaries differ from one language to another. For this reason, words in one language generally do not have exact translations in other languages. However, if words or phrases in a learner's L1 share enough semantic components with the L2 words being learned, they can be identified as potential translations of those words. If learners guess or are made aware of these 'equivalents', they have a start toward building appropriate meaning associations for each new word in their lexicon. If both formal and semantic features are close, the initial learning task is even easier.

However, certain semantic 'bundles' (i.e. lexical items) in one language may not have equivalents in another language (i.e. they are not lexicalized). Processing and learning L2 words without L1 equivalents is likely to be challenging. For example, Blum and Levenston's (1979) early study of native speakers of Hebrew versus learners of Hebrew from various linguistic backgrounds found that the latter group tended not to fill in blanks in a cloze test requiring Hebrew words that had no lexical equivalents in their respective L1s. In lexical inferencing, the meaning of a non-lexicalized word may be more difficult to infer, making a text in which it appears more difficult to comprehend.

Paribakht's (2005) lexicalization hypothesis characterizes the lexical inferencing process in terms of *lexemes* (a lexical item's form) and *lemmas* (a lexical item's semantic and syntactic information). She proposes that the process of L2 lexical inferencing may activate an existing lemma in the reader's L1 (or Ln) mental lexicon, leading to more or less appropriate word meaning comprehension. However, if there is no equivalent L1 lemma for the target word in the reader's mental lexicon, initial failure to comprehend the word's meaning is quite likely. The assignment of an appropriate meaning to the lexeme may require the lengthy and complex process of constructing a new lemma from semantic, syntactic and other elements.

Along similar lines, Jiang's (2000) L1 lemma mediation hypothesis postulates that in learning L2 words that have L1 equivalents, learners transfer L1 lemma information to L2 lexemes. That is, while L1 words are learned as both semantic and formal entities, L2 words with L1 lexical equivalents tend to be learned mainly as formal entities or new lexemes, short-circuiting the lemma construction process that characterizes L1 word learning. In his view, the initial adoption of an L1 lemma for an L2 lexeme is likely to have a long-lasting influence on the learner's understanding of that word, in that L1 lemmas for L2 words will continue to be activated in L2 use and may become fossilized at this translation stage.

Trilingual Study

Purpose and research approach

The primary purpose of the trilingual research project was to seek a better understanding of the processes and outcomes of L2 (English) lexical inferencing from written texts, as influenced by readers' native language (L1) knowledge. Our underlying interest has been to understand the conditions that promote successful word comprehension through lexical inferencing by L2 readers, and as part of this process, the conditions that may lead to readers' retention of new word knowledge following inferencing. While the importance of learners' L2 lexical knowledge has been shown to be a major factor in inferencing success and retention, little attention has been paid until recently to the role of learners' L1 lexical knowledge and processing behaviors as they relate to L2 lexical inferencing. In the substudies comprising the trilingual study, we approached the issue of L1 influences on L2 lexical inferencing by comparing the inferencing behaviors and outcomes of two groups of L2 readers who speak dissimilar languages, Persian and French, that have different typological relationships with the L2 (English). A group of native speakers of English provided a further basis of comparison with Persian and French speakers in L1 lexical inferencing, as well as L1 versus L2 inferencing in English.

We examined the use of different KSs by speakers of three languages (English, Persian and French) in their L1, and by the latter two groups in their L2 (English) as they inferred the meanings of unknown words in written texts. This involved instances of both explicit transfer of L1 linguistic KSs (e.g. assuming that an L1 word collocation exists in L2) and the identification of distinctive L1 KS use patterns that held for speakers of Persian or French when inferring word meanings in English. The latter were seen as potentially reflecting L1 transfer of procedural knowledge. Since similarities between L1 and L2 processing may also reflect universal processes or shared characteristics of the L1 and L2, we compared the L1 and L2 KS use patterns of speakers of these two dissimilar languages with each other and with those of English L1 readers. Inferencing behaviors that characterized both the L1 and L2 performance of either Persian or French speakers but distinguished them from the other two groups were further verified through examination of the characteristics of the three languages to determine if they could reasonably be considered instances of L1 transfer. The role of L2 readers' receptive English vocabulary was also studied in relation to their lexical inferencing success and their retention of new word meanings following the inferencing task. Parallel L2 analyses were carried out separately for unknown target words with lexical equivalents in readers' L1 versus those without such equivalents to determine the role of lexicalization in transfer and inferencing outcomes. We interpreted our results in terms of the dissimilarities of Persian and French and their relative typological distances from English.

Choice of Persian, French and English

Persian, French and English, three dissimilar Indo-European languages accessible to the researchers, were chosen for the study. In the absence of precise characterizations of the typological relationships among these three languages, we considered relative L1 and L2 typological distance (Persian being much farther from English than is French), speaker-perceived distance (Persian again being considered by its speakers as more distant) and easily observed differences such as the far larger number of cognates shared by

English and French than by English and Persian. The writing systems also reflect the greater distance of Persian from English, with a different alphabet, a right to left direction of writing and an orthography that does not represent all vowel sounds. In all these respects, French is relatively similar to English. Because of their differing typological distance from English and the considerable distance between these two languages, a cross-lingual study of their speakers performing a lexical inferencing task in English offered the possibility of identifying instances of L1 transfer and other L1 influences.

Research questions

The following research questions guided our study of L1 (Persian and French) influences in L2 (English) lexical inferencing:

(1) What evidence is there of L1 transfer and other L1 influences in English L2 lexical inferencing procedures and outcomes with respect to

    (a) L1-related patterns of KS use?

    (b) Persian L2 versus French L2 readers' success in inferring the meanings of unknown English words?

    (c) Persian L2 versus French L2 readers' retention of new English word knowledge?

    (d) Persian L2 versus French L2 readers' ability to successfully infer meanings for lexicalized versus non-lexicalized target words? Retention of their forms or meanings?

(2) What role, if any, does relative L1–L2 typological distance appear to play in successful L2 lexical inferencing involving these groups? In retention of new word forms or meanings?

Our general expectations were that we would find evidence of L1–L2 similarities in patterns of KS use by the Persian and French speakers that were different from each other and from English L1 patterns, as well as possible differences in L2 inferencing success and retention of new word knowledge, and that these might relate to L1 typological differences from English. In addition, we expected to find common patterns of KS use among all three groups in both L1 and L2 conditions, suggesting shared processing tendencies across these and possibly other Indo-European language users. We anticipated overall L1 versus L2 differences in KS use that would reflect the considerable proficiency gap between L1 and L2 language users. We also looked for similarities between the L1 and L2 English readers' KS use that might indicate progress by L2 learners toward target language norms. Finally, we expected L2 readers to have more difficulty inferring correct meanings for L2 words that had no equivalents in their L1 than for those with equivalents.

Methodology

Participants

Three groups of 20 post-secondary students from English, Persian and French L1 backgrounds, the latter two composed of high intermediate English L2 students in Tehran and Quebec, were selected for the study. All participants scored within a given range on an English reading comprehension test. Their knowledge of receptive English vocabulary was measured using Nation's (1990) Vocabulary Levels Test (VLT). On this test, group differences were not statistically different, although the range of scores for the Persian group was greater, with both higher and lower scores than those of the more homogeneous French-speaking group. The English L1 speakers were undergraduate university students in Ottawa.

Instruments

(1) The English reading comprehension test, developed at the University of Ottawa for English as a second language (ESL) course placement purposes, was used to select the Persian- and French-speaking participants at the high intermediate level of reading proficiency for the study.[4]

(2) The VLT (Nation, 1990) was used to measure the selected Persian- and French-speaking participants' receptive English vocabulary knowledge. The test consists of 90 items from five word frequency levels (2000, 3000, 5000, the University Word List and 10,000 words). It estimates learners' receptive English vocabulary at different word frequency levels, and can be used to help determine if they have enough vocabulary knowledge to read instructional texts that include words from those frequency levels.

(3) The Vocabulary Knowledge Scale (VKS) (Paribakht & Wesche, 1996; Wesche & Paribakht, 1996) was used to measure the Persian- and French-speaking participants' relative knowledge of each target word, before and after the L2 lexical inferencing task, in order to capture their immediate gains in knowledge of these words. (See Appendix A for the VKS elicitation scale and scoring categories.) In this measure, each word is presented individually to the test-taker, who self-evaluates for elicitation Categories 1 and 2, and if possible provides either a synonym/translation or a sentence for Categories 3 through 5. The result is then scored according to the VKS scoring categories. This combination of report and performance data leads to a scale ranging from 1 to 5 for each target word representing a range of knowledge from total unfamiliarity to the ability to use the word with semantic and syntactic accuracy in a sentence.[5]

Target words and texts

Fifty English target words each were selected for the Persian- and French-speaking inferencing tasks.[6] Sets of 25 *lexicalized* target words were first chosen from lists used in previous research. These had a similar frequency range, represented medium to high difficulty for relatively advanced university ESL students and had been screened in previous research to remove French cognates. Examples for the Persian speakers included *to tackle, deteriorating* and *ambivalence*, and for the French speakers, *to pawn, giddy* and *warily*.

Sets of 25 *non-lexicalized* English target words were then assembled for each group for the lexicalization substudy by native speakers of Persian and French who were bilingual in English.[7] First, through a survey of English texts, they identified words they thought had no lexical equivalents in their L1. These words were checked against several bilingual dictionaries and with other native speakers of the given language. Words that were retained represented concepts that could be paraphrased in the L1 but for which single or compound lexical items did not exist in the respective language (e.g. for Persian speakers, *to stalk, proactive* and *prognosis* and for French speakers, *to draft, bungling* and *spree*). Each set of 25 words included 10 nouns, 8 verbs, 4 adjectives and 3 adverbs. The final selection of all the target words was made in consultation with experienced English L2 instructors and verified in a pilot study with L2 readers who had similar reading proficiency to that of the trilingual study participants.

A native English speaker composed brief (200 word) English reading texts on six different themes (e.g. *marriage, genetic engineering*) for each group, embedding seven to nine of the target words in each text so that the target words represented about 3% of the total words in each. The other words were expected to be familiar to the participants.[8] The Persian and French speakers' L1 texts were single, one-page, published, general interest articles aimed at educated adult readers, in which 25 target words had been replaced by pseudowords.[9] These words were constructed to provide similar morphological cues as the original words (e.g. the pseudo equivalent of *devastated, 'beslocked'*, shared its past tense suffix). The English native speakers' L1 inferencing task involved 50 words, since they inferred meanings for the same target words (replaced by pseudowords) and texts as the Persian speakers.

Procedures

Data were gathered in four post-secondary institutions in Canada and Iran. Initial group vocabulary testing was followed by small-group orientation and practice in think-aloud procedures for those selected for participation. Individual sessions with a researcher followed. The VKS (see Appendix A) was used with the Persian and French participants to measure their initial knowledge of the target L2 words, followed by the L2 inferencing task (50 target words) and a second administration of the VKS to gauge readers' retention of new word knowledge. After a break, participants did the L1 inferencing task (25 target words). In L1, English native speakers did the think-aloud training and the same 50-word English inferencing task (with pseudo target words) as the Persian speakers.

The Persian and French speakers read the respective English texts one at a time, first quickly for overall comprehension, and then more slowly, inferring meanings for as many of the unfamiliar target English words (in bold font) as they could. They were asked to orally report what they were thinking and doing as they attempted to infer word meanings, using either their L1 or English. The bilingual researcher prompted participants as necessary to make sure that they kept on task and continued reporting. The researcher also took notes on participants' guesses and anything else that might facilitate later transcription. The L1 inferencing tasks followed similar procedures, but for these two groups involved 25 target words, while the English L1 speakers had 50 target words. All sessions were tape recorded and subsequently transcribed for analysis. The written transcripts plus the researcher's notes taken during each session were the basis of analysis for KS use in lexical inferencing.

Data Analysis

Both qualitative and quantitative analyses were undertaken. Qualitative analysis involved multiple readings of each transcript to

- identify all inferencing attempts for unknown target words;
- identify all KSs that the participant reported using during inferencing;
- determine whether each inferred meaning was both semantically and syntactically appropriate for the context.

The types of KSs used were identified first in the Persian data, using an earlier classification system, and an updated taxonomy was created (Paribakht, 2005). Several new KSs from the other data sets were subsequently added (Paribakht & Tréville, 2007; Paribakht & Wesche, 2006).

Fully successful inferences received 2 points (e.g. 'massacre' for 'genocide'). Partially successful inferences received 1 point. These included a semantically accurate but syntactically inappropriate guess (e.g. an adjective instead of a noun), a superordinate word or an approximate meaning (e.g. 'death' for 'genocide'). A wrong answer or no guess received no points.

The updated trilingual study taxonomy (see Results section) reflects all the KSs identified in the transcripts of student think-aloud comments by L1 readers of English, Persian and French, and the same Persian and French speakers reading in English (L2) while carrying out lexical inferencing tasks based on written texts. The taxonomy, a research outcome as well as the basis for a comparison of KS use in lexical inferencing across groups, provides a comprehensive categorization of the types of KSs used in lexical inferencing applicable to these three Indo-European languages for both L1 and high intermediate English L2 readers.

Quantitative analyses to determine readers' inferencing success and their retention of new word knowledge were based on the number of meanings inferred for previously unknown words by each participant. Numbers of fully and partially successful L1 inferences were calculated for all five conditions and for the lexicalization substudies. The Persian and French speakers' retention of new L2 lexical knowledge was studied by comparing pre and post-inferencing VKS scores for all unknown target words and lexicalized versus non-lexicalized subsets. Relationships linking each group's receptive English vocabulary knowledge with successful inferencing and post-task retention of new word knowledge were further studied through correlation, individual case analysis and statistical tests of group differences and effects of target word lexicalization status.

Results

Most participants made a strong effort to infer target word meanings. In all three L1 conditions, they proposed meanings for almost all the pseudo target words, while in the two L2 conditions, Persian speakers inferred meanings for 79% and French speakers for 87% of the target words unknown to them before the inferencing task. (Persian speakers reported already knowing 9% and French speakers 4%.)

Readers' use of knowledge sources

The trilingual study taxonomy of knowledge source use (Figure 5.1) presents all the KSs identified through qualitative analysis of the think-aloud transcripts from the Persian-, French- and English-speaking participants during their L1 or L2 lexical inferencing tasks. Once finalized, the taxonomy was the instrument for a comparison of KS use patterns across data sets. In the taxonomy, *linguistic* KSs are first categorized as *word, sentence* and *discourse* sources depending on whether the context of the cues is the word itself, the sentence in which the word occurs or the larger discourse context beyond the immediate sentence. Each of these main categories has three or four subcategories that indicate the type of knowledge used. The two *L1 linguistic* subcategories that were reported by

Linguistic sources

Text language-based sources (L1 or L2)

- **Word knowledge**
  - Word association (**wa**): Association of the target word with another familiar word or a network of words.
  - Word collocation (**wc**): Knowledge of words that frequently occur with the target word.
  - Word morphology (**wm**): Morphological analysis of the target word based on knowledge of grammatical inflections, stems and affixes.
  - Word form (**wf**): Knowledge of formal (orthographic or phonetic) similarity between the target word or a part of it, and another word; mistaking the target word for another word resembling it.

- **Sentence knowledge**
  - Sentence meaning (**sm**): The meaning of part or all of the sentence containing the target word.
  - Sentence grammar (**sg**): Knowledge of the syntactic properties of the target word, its speech part and word order constraints.
  - Punctuation (**p**): Knowledge of rules of punctuation and their significance.

- **Discourse knowledge**
  - Discourse meaning (**dm**): The perceived general meaning of the text and sentences surrounding the target word (i.e. beyond the immediate sentence that contains the target word).
  - Formal schemata (**fs**): Knowledge of the macro structure of the text, text types and discourse patterns and organization.
  - Text style and register (**sr**): Knowledge of stylistic and register variations in word choice.

L1-based sources used by L2 readers

- **L1 collocation (*L1wc*)**
  Knowledge of words in L1 that have a collocational relationship with the L1 equivalent of the target word, assuming that the same relationship exists in the target language.

- **L1 word form (L1wf)**
  Knowledge of a formal (orthographic or phonetic) similarity between the target word or a part of it and an L1 word.

Non-linguistic source

- **World knowledge (wk)**
  Non-linguistic knowledge, including knowledge of the topic of the text and other related background knowledge.

Figure 5.1 Trilingual study taxonomy of knowledge source use

L2 English readers are also included. *Non-linguistic* knowledge comprises *world knowledge* (e.g. *topic knowledge, life experience, cultural knowledge*). See Appendix B for examples of the main subcategories.

Table 5.1 presents the percentages of readers' use of KSs from each major category (i.e. *word, sentence, discourse* and *world knowledge*) when inferring word meanings in the five conditions.

Some shared KS use patterns across the five data sets suggest cross-linguistic and L1–L2 commonalities in lexical inferencing. It is also apparent that some KS use patterns differentiate L1 from L2 readers, others characterize readers of English texts in either L1 or L2, and some – of primary interest here – uniquely characterize speakers of either Persian or French reading in both L1 and L2.

As may be seen in Table 5.1, all major categories of KSs were used in lexical inferencing in all five conditions. There was an overwhelming reliance on text language *linguistic* KSs and some use of *non-linguistic* cues (i.e. world knowledge) in all conditions. *Sentence*-level cues were of greatest importance for all groups, accounting for 50–73% of KS use.

Table 5.2 presents a synthesis of readers' use of KS subcategories in each condition. The percentage of each group's average use of each type and overall organization by frequency bands show how KS use patterns compare across language groups and L1–L2 conditions.

An important shared characteristic of KS use across all data sets seen in Table 5.2 was readers' primary dependence on meaning-related KSs (i.e. *sentence meaning* and *discourse meaning*). Likewise, readers tended to use 'local' cues, i.e. those found in the word itself or within the immediate sentence context. With respect to KS subcategories, *sentence meaning* cues, which are both meaning oriented and local, were by far the most

Table 5.1 Readers' use of main KS types: Percentages and relative frequencies

	Linguistic KSs in text language			L1 KS use by L2 readers: L1 word (L1w)	Total linguistic KSs	Total non-linguistic KSs: World knowledge (wk)	Frequency rankings of main KS types
	Word (w)	Sentence (s)	Discourse (d)				
English L1	17%	49%	14%		81%	19%	s>wk>w=d
Persian L1	4%	65%	22%		90%	10%	s>d>wk>w
Persian L2	8%	73%	14%	0.3%	96%	4%	s>d>w>wk>L1w
French L1	29%	50%	10%		89%	11%	s>w>wk>w
French L2	17%	72%	4%	4%	96%	5%	s>w>wk=L1w=d

Note: Percentages are rounded to the nearest integer, or when <1, decimal place.

Table 5.2 Readers' use of KS subcategories: Percentages and rankings within frequency bands

KSs	Very frequent		Frequent	Occasional	Rare
Frequency bands	50–59%	35–49%	10–19%	2–9%	1% or less
English L1 (%)		sm>44	wk>dm> 19 14	wf>wm>sg>wa=sr=wc> 7 6 5 2 2 2	fs>p 0.6 0.1
Persian L1 (%)	sm>53		dm>sg>wk> 14 11 10	fs>sr=wc> 5 3 3	wf>p>wm 1 0.9 0.1
Persian L2 (%)	sm>59		dm=sg> 14 14	wm>wk> 6 4	wf=p=wc>wa<fs>L1wc 1 0.9 0.8 0.5 0.3 0.3
French L1 (%)		sm>36	wm>sg=wk> 13 11 11	wc>wf>dm=fs>wa>p 7 6 5 5 3 2	
French L2 (%)	sm>59		sg>wm> 13 10	wf=wk>L1wf>dm>wa> 5 5 4 3% 2%	p>fs>wc 0.5 0.3 0.1

Note: Percentages are rounded to the nearest digit.

wm: word morphology; sm: sentence meaning; fs: formal schemata; wf: word form; dm: discourse meaning; s/r: style/register; wc: word collocation; sg: sentence grammar; wk: world knowledge; wa: word association; p: punctuation.

important in all conditions, accounting for 36–59% of all KSs used. Other subcategories that were substantially used by all groups included *discourse meaning, sentence grammar* and *word morphology*.

Several overall differences in KS use that distinguish L1 from L2 lexical inferencing can be seen in Tables 5.1 and 5.2. First of all, *world knowledge* is used more in all three L1s than in either L2 condition by Persian and French speakers. This may reflect more thorough, multilevel text comprehension by L1 readers, allowing them to better use their *world knowledge* in generating, and crucially, evaluating lexical inferences in context. Such contextual evaluation accompanying the use of linguistic knowledge is part of the 'advanced processing' that typifies successful inferencing (Haastrup, 2008). A related – also proficiency-related – phenomenon is that both Persian and French readers depend more on *sentence* cues, particularly *sentence meaning*, in L2 than in L1.

Transfer of L1 linguistic knowledge and procedures in L2 lexical inferencing

The most obvious instances of L1 transfer in L2 lexical inferencing were Persian and French readers' reported use of *linguistic* knowledge from their L1. As reflected in Table 5.1, such KSs were used, if infrequently, by both groups, accounting for 0.3% of Persian speakers' and 4% of French speakers' KS use. Participants in each group used only one L1 KS type, in both cases a *word* KS that was important for that group in L1 inferencing. Persian speakers reported using *L1 word collocation* (guessing a target word meaning from an adjacent word whose L1 equivalent tends to co-occur with the L1 word having that meaning), while French speakers reported drawing on *L1 word form* (using as a cue a similarity in form between an L1 word and the L2 target word).

French speakers' greater use than the Persian speakers' of L1 KSs, and specifically, *L1 word form*, may be related to the largely shared alphabet and similar sound–symbol relationships in French and English orthographies and their awareness of frequent cognates.

Of greater importance in our data than the explicit use of L1 lexical knowledge was the considerable evidence of implicit Persian and French L1 influence on procedures governing readers' KS use in L2. This was reflected in unique KS use patterns for each group found in both L1 and L2. The tendency for speakers of a given L1 to emphasize use of certain KSs when inferring word meanings in L1 is presumably efficient for that language, given the consistently high L1 lexical inferencing success found elsewhere and confirmed in this study (below). The tendency to apply the same L1 procedures in L2 lexical inferencing, as in other cases of transfer, involves learners using what they already know in a new but similar situation where it may – or may not – be appropriate.

Overall, the Persian readers were characterized in their L1 lexical inferencing by a heavy reliance on *sentence meaning* (53% of KS use) and frequent use of *discourse meaning* (14%), *sentence grammar* (11%) and *world knowledge* (10%). They occasionally used *word collocation*, but only rarely or never used *word form, punctuation, word association* or *word morphology*. They also occasionally used *discourse*-level *formal schemata* and *style/register*. When inferencing in their L2, English, they depended even more on *sentence meaning* (59%), again followed by *discourse meaning* (14%), *sentence grammar* (14%) and the rare but similar to L1 use of *word form* and *punctuation*. There was some carryover of *word collocation* (0.8%) to L2 inferencing. Persian speakers' use of *world knowledge* and *formal schemata* was reduced in L2 and they never used *style/register* – all KSs like *word collocation* generally relate to high proficiency and L1 inferencing. Unlike in L1 was their use of *word morphology* in L2 inferencing (0.1% in L1, 6% in L2). Overall, they used *discourse* KSs more than any other group in both L1 (22%) and L2 (14%), and *word* KSs least (L1: 4%, L2: 8%). With respect to transfer, likely Persian L1 influence on KS use in English L2 lexical inferencing was most strongly represented in the prominence of *sentence meaning, discourse meaning* and *sentence grammar* cues and the low use of all *word* cues except *word morphology*.

Largely in contrast to the Persian speakers' KS use patterns, the French-speaking readers were most characterized in L1 by their heavy dependence on a variety of *word* cues, which accounted for 29% of their KS use – far more than the other groups. *Sentence meaning*, their most frequent KS, was much less important in L1 than for other groups (36%). *Word morphology* was their second most important KS (13%); they also frequently used *sentence grammar* and *world knowledge* (11% each), with comparatively low dependence on *discourse* KSs (10% overall, representing approximately equal use of *discourse meaning* and *formal schemata*). They also used all the other *word* KSs substantially more than the other groups – i.e. *word collocation* (7%), *word form* (6%) and *word association* (3%). In L2, one sees the same high use of diverse *word* KSs (accounting for 21% including *L1 word form*) and *sentence grammar* (13%) coupled with low use of *discourse* KSs (4% overall). Differences from L1 were the much higher use of *sentence meaning* (59%) and the near disappearance of *word collocation* (tendencies generally related to L1–L2 differences). With respect to transfer, likely French L1 influence on KS use in English L2 lexical inferencing was best reflected in the prominence of diverse *word* KSs and *sentence grammar*, and the relative neglect of *discourse meaning*.

In L2 inferencing, it is apparent that the Persian and French speakers' respective patterns of KS use from *word* and *discourse* sources are not only similar to their L1 patterns but they are also strikingly different from each other as well as from English L1 patterns. Some movement toward English L1 patterns is also seen, for example in the higher use of *word morphology* by Persian speakers in L1 than in L2 and the opposite movement by French speakers (L1: 13%, L2: 10%) toward the English L1 level (6%).

Sentence grammar use is relatively high and similar for Persian and French speakers in both L1 and L2 inferencing (and different from English L1 readers). In both cases, this may represent an L1 effect from these more inflected languages on L2 inferencing. The influence of language instruction may also be important; grammar is heavily emphasized in mother tongue instruction and to some extent in English instruction in both countries.

Discussion of KS use patterns

The KS use patterns noted above that distinguish Persian from French speakers in both L1 and L2 lexical inferencing can, when viewed in light of the characteristics of each language, be reasonably interpreted as representing the transfer of L1 procedural knowledge to L2 lexical inferencing. This knowledge is observed in the processing tendencies of speakers of the two languages in terms of where in the text they tend to look for needed information (e.g. to the *discourse* or *word* level, respectively), and preferred types of linguistic knowledge they seek (e.g. *discourse meaning* for Persian speakers and *word morphology* for French speakers).

The Persian orthography, which limits the value of *word*-level cues as a reliable source of information for lexical inferencing, may largely explain Persian speakers' low use of *word* KSs in both L1 and L2 and their dependence on cues at the *sentence* and *discourse* levels. Since certain vowels are not represented in the Persian orthography, readers are accustomed to drawing on the meaning of the larger (*sentence* and *discourse*) context to identify the exact word they are reading. These L1 Persian processing tendencies appear to be carried over to L2 KS use.

French speakers' relative lack of use of *discourse* KSs in both L1 and L2 and very high use of *word* KSs also distinguishes them. It appears that they are able to get considerable information from *word*- and *sentence*-level cues in English as well as in French, which may help account for their lower use of *discourse* cues.

Persian readers' success in using *word morphology* in English inferencing, a very useful KS for both English and French that they did not use in the L1, is notable. As with *sentence grammar*, English language instructional emphasis in Iran on formal structures almost certainly plays a role, but the fact that Persian, like French, is more inflected probably gives them a conceptual basis for identifying and using morphological cues. French speakers also use *sentence grammar* frequently in L2, but somewhat less than in L1, in the direction of English usage.

These cross-linguistic data support the notion that each L1 provides not so much a different overall starting point for the same journey with respect to acquiring an L2, but a different constellation of starting points relating to given features or subsystem features of a given L2, resulting in different transfer patterns. It may also be conceived in terms of overall difficulty, relating to the broader concept of language distance.

Lexicalization influences

The issue of possible effects of the lexicalization status in L1 of L2 target words was pursued in a substudy that looked separately at KS use by Persian and French L2 readers inferring meanings for lexicalized versus non-lexicalized English words. The findings for both Persian and French speakers indicated that the L1 lexicalization status of the target words had little if any effect on participants' use of given KSs when inferring their

Table 5.3 L1 and L2 lexical inferencing success of English, Persian and French speakers

	Full success			*Partial success*		
	All words	*Lexicalized*	*Non-lexicalized*	*All words*	*Lexicalized*	*Non-lexicalized*
English L1	89%			4%		
Persian L1	79%			4%		
Persian L2	11%	17%	6%	11%	11%	11%
French L1	63%			11%		
French L2	31%	34%	28%	21%	21%	19%

Note: Percentages relate to the number of pre-task unknown words reported by participants. The original percentages have been rounded here to the nearest integer.

meanings. Rather, for each group the pattern of KS use was very similar for both lexicalized and non-lexicalized target words (Paribakht, 2010, 2005; Paribakht & Tréville, 2007). These findings are an indication of the stability of L1 processing tendencies.

Success of L2 readers in inferring unfamiliar word meanings

In addition to the study of L1 influences on KS use in L2 lexical inferencing, we examined how readers' L1 might influence their success in arriving at correct inferences, and their retention of new word knowledge following the inferencing task. Table 5.3 presents information on readers' overall lexical inferencing success, as well as with lexicalized versus non-lexicalized L2 words.

As may be seen in Table 5.3, L1 inferencing for all three language groups was highly successful. Persian speakers were fully successful in 79% of cases while French speakers succeeded in 63%, with English L1 inferencing highest at 89%. The addition of partially successful cases raises these percentages to 83%, 74% and 93%, respectively. However, in L2 inferencing, Persian speakers achieved full success in only 11% of cases and French speakers in 31%. When partially appropriate inferences were added, the percentages were still only 22% for Persian speakers and 52% for French speakers.

Lexicalization status and success in lexical inferencing

The percentages of partially and fully successful L2 inferences are also given in Table 5.3 with respect to the lexicalization status of target words. *T*-tests using weighted scores (i.e. sum of 1 or 2 points, respectively, for partial or full success) indicated a clear lexicalization effect. L2 readers in both language groups were consistently more successful in guessing the meanings of the unfamiliar lexicalized than non-lexicalized target words.[10]

Beyond this shared result was a marked group difference in magnitude; the Persian speakers were far less successful than the French speakers in inferring either lexicalized or non-lexicalized target English words. Their disadvantage was greater when inferring meanings for non-lexicalized words, with full inferencing success almost three times as frequent with lexicalized than with non-lexicalized words (17% vs. 6%), while for French speakers the gap was significant but much smaller (34% vs. 28%). Differences in procedural abilities could not explain this since the two groups had comparable L2 reading proficiency test scores and the Persian speakers were more successful in L1 lexical inferencing.[11]

These results point to the greater challenge posed by non-lexicalized words in immediate word meaning comprehension (see Appendix C for an example from a Persian participant's transcript). Non-lexicalized words may represent a significant challenge for L2 readers in successful comprehension and interpretation of L2 texts, and this effect may be stronger when the L2 is typologically distant from the L1. The relatively dense embedding of non-lexicalized words in our reading texts likely added significantly to the challenge faced by both groups of L2 readers in their text comprehension and lexical inferencing. For learners dealing with a larger number of non-lexicalized words in L2, ongoing failure to successfully infer new word meanings may in this way contribute to a relatively slower overall rate of L2 lexical development.

A further analysis of this issue involved an examination of L2 readers' post-inferencing retention of new lexical knowledge after lexical inferencing to determine its relation to success (below). We then looked at information on group and individual participants' English lexical knowledge and the relationships among success, retention, lexical knowledge and group membership to see if that could help explain the results.

Retention of new word knowledge through lexical inferencing

Both the Persian and French L2 readers showed significant if small gains in new English target word knowledge when administered the VKS following the inferencing task. Average pre-task VKS scores for both groups for the respective L2 target word sets were between VKS Level 1 ('*the word is not familiar at all*') and VKS Level 2 ('*the word is familiar but its meaning is not known*'). Post-task averages were approximately 2 for the Persian speakers and slightly higher for the French speakers. Individual analysis of VKS gains for each participant for each word showed that these gains for most learners and target words represented gains in word form familiarity (i.e. from 1 to 2 on the VKS), which probably explains the similar gain results found for both groups regardless of lexicalization status. However, in 10% of cases for Persian speakers and 16% for French speakers, pre-inferencing VKS responses of 1 to 2 (no meaning knowledge) for L2 target words, moved to post-inferencing VKS responses of at least 3 ('*a correct synonym or translation is given*') and as high as 5 ('*the word is used with semantic appropriateness and grammatical accuracy in a sentence*'). Analysis of individual cases showed that in all cases of post-VKS retention of new meaning knowledge, inferencing had been fully or partially successful. These gains in both word form familiarity and in new meaning knowledge link the lexical inferencing process to early stages of word acquisition, adding to our understanding of the nature of this slow, incremental process.[12]

The results of correlation analyses supported findings from other studies that lexical knowledge is a critical aspect of the L2 proficiency needed as a basis for successful lexical inferencing. Correlations between receptive English L2 vocabulary scores on the VLT and weighted success scores were 0.71 for Persian speakers and 0.79 for French speakers.

Furthermore, participants' receptive vocabulary scores correlated with the number of words on which they had moved from VKS 1–2 to word meaning knowledge (VKS 3–5) at 0.76 for Persian speakers and 0.68 for French speakers.[13] Success scores also correlated with these post-task gains in new meaning knowledge (Persian speakers 0.73; French speakers 0.53).[14]

Further examination of the data indicated a threshold VLT score for receptive English vocabulary knowledge needed to ensure reasonable inferencing success, which held for both Persian and French speakers (Wesche & Paribakht, 2010). Even though Persian speakers had several of the highest VLT scores, the fact that fewer Persian speakers scored above the threshold on the VLT and their lower average scores partially account for the discrepancy in the performance of the two groups. However, examination of individual cases indicated that while the threshold VLT score for inferencing success was the same for both groups in distinguishing multiple word knowledge gains from minimal ones, in almost all cases French speakers at any given vocabulary score level retained knowledge of more new word meanings than did Persian speakers, indicating other factors at work.

Discussion

It seems apparent that Persian–French differences in L2 lexical inferencing success and post-task retention of new word meanings stem from stronger lexical resources brought to the inferencing task by the two groups. The VLT does not fully capture network and other aspects of lexical knowledge that are thought to operate in L2 lexical processing (Albrechtsen *et al.*, 2008). While we cannot know from our data the nature of the French speakers' advantage, several points support the interpretation that it is a complex one related to the different typological relationships between the two L1s and English.

One point is that Persian L2 readers' L1 procedural knowledge related to inferencing, while highly effective in Persian, may have placed them at a disadvantage in English vis-à-vis the French speakers. French L1 KS use patterns appear more similar to English L1 patterns, likely requiring less adaptation to be effective. The Persian speakers were in general not able to take advantage of English *word*-internal cues needed for precise inferences, and while they were accustomed to using *discourse* cues, these distant and dispersed cues, most effective for contextual confirmation of guesses, were often not enough to ensure accurate inferences.

Secondly, the many dissimilarities between Persian and English probably meant that Persian speakers, in spite of their long years of English study, had less declarative lexical knowledge pertinent to English. In contrast, the shared aspects of the linguistic and cultural histories of English and French speakers have created a high proportion of shared word derivations, many cognates and similar overall lexicalization patterns in the two languages that enhance the transferability of declarative lexical knowledge between them. French speakers were in an advantaged position to the extent that they could access that knowledge base when inferring unfamiliar English word meanings. This advantage – which would support better L2 text comprehension, more successful inferencing and better retention – can in our view be largely attributed to the relative typological proximity of French to English, expressed in similarities of linguistic features across the two languages.

Finally, sociocultural factors in the contrasting L2 learning contexts may also have supported greater English lexical development by the French speakers, whose L2 learning occurred in an L2 context that provided diverse opportunities for exposure to the L2 through the media and personal experience. These factors may also have contributed to more rapid L2 vocabulary development for French learners, leading to a cumulative advantage. Furthermore, the divergent performance of the two groups may represent relevant differences in cultural familiarity with text features, such as concepts and points of view presented and schemata underlying the presentation of given topics in English texts. This may also help explain the accentuated disadvantage of Persian speakers in inferring meanings for target English words that lack L1 lexical equivalents.

Conclusions

Lexical processing tasks such as lexical inferencing can provide a rich source of information on lexical transfer, drawing on declarative and procedural linguistic knowledge as well as cultural knowledge, all of which are susceptible to L1-related influences.

Evidence of transfer from the L1 of both specific L1 linguistic knowledge and learned inferencing procedures related to L1 features is found in L2 lexical inferencing in this study. Transfer of procedural knowledge, accessed here through patterns of KS use by readers during lexical inferencing, while less obvious than declarative knowledge, is important and long lasting. The stability of these patterns regardless of the L1 lexicalization status of target L2 words is notable here.

Our research findings reveal the complex nature of L1 influences on L2 lexical inferencing and the related processes of L2 text comprehension and vocabulary learning. They also demonstrate the critical importance of previous L2 vocabulary knowledge in all three processes, and provide insight into how all three processes, through the extent, quality and cumulative nature of learner's L1 vocabulary development, may be influenced by the relative typological distance between learners' L1 and L2.

Finally, our results are in accord with Yu's finding that positive transfer tends to occur at the level of cross-linguistic similarities between subsystems. Overall similarities between a learner's L1 and L2 multiply this effect, so that the incidence of transfer and its cumulative effects may largely correspond to their typological proximity.

Notes

(1) While lexical inferencing is important in the comprehension of oral discourse as well as written texts, most research – including the study reported here – has focused on written language.

(2) We use the term *transfer* here to refer to the influence on language processing and outcomes resulting from similarities and differences between the target language and any other language that has been previously acquired (after Odlin, 1989), based on similarities between learned features across the two languages or a language user's perception of them. L1 transfer in L2 lexical processing thus involves native language influence on some aspect of this process or its outcomes. While one can refer to positive or negative transfer in terms of how its outcomes compare with target language norms, transfer itself appears to be a unitary process (Faerch & Kasper, 1987). Given the varied uses of the term over the past four decades and in different theoretical contexts regarding L2 acquisition, it is not possible to use the word more precisely without a complex definition of many other terms (see Odlin, 1989: 28).

(3) Apparent similarities can sometimes be misleading (e.g. so-called false friends among cognates) (Haastrup, 1991), but between closely related languages this is a small price to pay for the advantages gained.

(4) This test includes three subtests, two of which present extended reading texts followed by comprehension questions, and the third, a multiple-choice cloze test. The participants had 60 minutes to complete the test. The total possible score is 60.

(5) The VKS has been shown to be sensitive enough to pick up incremental gains in the initial stages of learning particular words (Paribakht & Wesche, 1993, 1997; Wesche & Paribakht, 1996). It also allows an analysis of individual or grouped scoring categories for more specific information about what has been learned.

(6) The two word sets had 15 words in common.

(7) Since lexicalization patterns are different for these two languages, separate word lists and texts were needed for each L1 group.

(8) We aimed to have texts with a very high proportion of the words familiar to the readers, based on previous research indicating that a reader needs to know 95–98% of surrounding words to be able to infer meanings for the others (Hazenberg & Hulstijn, 1996; Hirsh & Nation, 1992; Hu & Nation, 2000; Laufer, 1988; Liu & Nation, 1985; Nation, 2006).

(9) Pseudowords with morphological cues relevant to the original target words should essentially require the same inferencing process as unknown lexicalized words.

(10) Since Persian- and French-speaking groups dealt with somewhat different sets of target words in their L2 lexical inferencing tasks, separate analyses were conducted on the 15 shared English target words to ensure that findings were not due to the particular word sets. In these analyses, the Persian speakers were again, notably less successful than the French speakers in inferring the meanings of both lexicalized (18.9% vs. 35.8%, respectively) and non-lexicalized words (7.4% vs. 23.4%, respectively). These success rates were quite similar to those for the complete target word sets, supporting the validity of those findings for the two groups.

(11) In this study, no significant correlations were found between L1 inferencing success and either of the L2 inferencing success variables for either group. Given the procedural abilities involved in reading and inferencing and evidence from elsewhere of the transfer of L1 to L2 procedural skills (Koda, 2005), such a relationship would be expected. It seems likely that the large L1 and L2 proficiency gap and the difficulty of the L2 tasks make it impossible to demonstrate such a relationship here.

(12) We were not able to administer a delayed VKS measure, so we cannot know if these gains were retained. However, without retention at this point any subsequent knowledge development based on the inferencing task would seem unlikely, so these findings are important.

(13) All correlations with the VLT were significant at $p < 0.001$, two-tailed.

(14) $p < 0.001$, $p < 0.05$, respectively.

References

Albrechtsen, D., Haastrup, K. and Henriksen, B. (2008) *Vocabulary and Writing in a First and Second Language – Processes and Development*. Basingstoke: Palgrave MacMillan.

Ard, J. and Holmburg, T. (1983) Verification of language transfer. In S. Gass and L. Selinker (eds) *Language Transfer in Second Language Learning* (pp. 157–176). Rowley, MA: Newbury House.

Bengeleil, N. and Paribakht, T.S. (2004) L2 reading proficiency and lexical inferencing by university EFL learners. *The Canadian Modern Language Review* 61, 225–249.

Blum, S. and Levenston, E. (1979) Lexical simplification in second language acquisition. *Studies in Second Language Acquisition* 2, 85–94.

de Bot, K., Paribakht, T.S. and Wesche, M. (1997) Towards a lexical processing model for the study of second language vocabulary acquisition: Evidence from ESL reading. *Studies in Second Language Acquisition* 19, 309–329.

Faerch, C. and Kasper, G. (1987) From product to process – Introspective methods in second language research. In C. Faerch and G. Kasper (eds) *Introspection in Second Language Research* (pp. 5–23). Clevedon: Multilingual Matters.

Ghahremani-Ghajar, S. and Masny, D. (1999) Making sense in second language orthography. *ITL Review of Applied Linguistics* 125–126, 229–251.

Haastrup, K. (1991) *Lexical Inferencing Procedures or Talking about Words: Receptive Procedures in Foreign Language Learning with Special Reference to English*. Tübingen: Narr.

Haastrup, K. (2008) Lexical inferencing procedures in two languages. In D. Albrechtsen, K. Haastrup and B. Henriksen (2008) *Vocabulary and Writing in a First and Second Language – Processes and Development* (pp. 67–111). Basingstoke: Palgrave MacMillan.

Haastrup, K. (2010) The interaction between types of knowledge in lexical processing: The case of lexical inferencing. Paper presented at the Symposium on Approaches to the Lexicon. Copenhagen: Copenhagen Business School, 8–10 December.

Hancin-Bhatt, B. and Nagy, W. (1994) Lexical transfer and second language morphological development. *Applied Linguistics* 15, 289–310.

Hazenberg, S. and Hulstijn, J. (1996) Defining a minimal receptive second-language vocabulary for non-native university students: An empirical investigation. *Applied Linguistics* 17, 145–163.

Hirsh, D. and Nation, P. (1992) What vocabulary size is needed to read unsimplified texts for pleasure? *Reading in a Foreign Language* 8, 689–696.

Hu, M. and Nation, P. (2000) Unknown vocabulary density and reading comprehension. *Reading in a Foreign Language* 13, 403–430.

Jiang, N. (2000) Lexical representation and development in a second language. *Applied Linguistics* 21, 47–77.

Kellerman, E. (1977) Towards a characterization of the strategy of transfer in second language learning. *Interlanguage Studies Bulletin* 21, 58–145.

Kellerman, E. (1978) Giving learners a break: Native language intuitions about transferability. *Working Papers in Bilingualism* 15, 309–315.

Koda, K. (2005) *Insights into Second Language Reading: A Cross-Linguistic Approach.* New York: Cambridge University Press.

Krashen, S. (1989) We acquire vocabulary and spelling by reading: Additional evidence for the input hypothesis. *Modern Language Journal* 73, 440–463.

Lado, R. (1957) *Linguistics Across Cultures.* Ann Arbor, MI: University of Michigan Press.

Laufer, B. (1988) What percentage of text-lexis is essential for comprehension? In C. Laurén and M. Nordmann (eds) *Special Language: From Humans to Thinking Machines* (pp. 316–323). Clevedon: Multilingual Matters.

Laufer, B. (1997) What's in a word that makes it hard or easy: Some intralexical factors that affect the learning of words. In N. Schmitt and M. McCarthy (eds) *Vocabulary: Description, Acquisition and Pedagogy* (pp. 140–180). Cambridge: Cambridge University Press.

Levelt, W. (1989) *Speaking: From Intention to Articulation.* Cambridge, MA: Bradford Books/MIT Press.

Liu, N. and Nation, I.S.P. (1985) Factors affecting guessing vocabulary in context. *RELC Journal* 16, 33–42.

Nagy, W.E., McClure, E.F. and Mir, M. (1997) Linguistic transfer and the use of context by Spanish-English bilinguals. *Applied Psycholinguistics* 18, 431–452.

Nassaji, H. (2004) The relationship between depth of vocabulary knowledge and L2 learners' lexical inferencing strategy use and success. *The Canadian Modern Language Review* 61, 107–134.

Nation, I.S.P. (1990) *Teaching and Learning Vocabulary.* New York: Newbury House.

Nation, I.S.P. (2006) How large a vocabulary is needed for reading and listening? *The Canadian Modern Language Review* 63, 59–81.

Odlin, T. (1989) *Language Transfer.* Cambridge: Cambridge University Press.

Odlin, T. (2003) Cross-linguistic influence. In C.J. Doughty and M.H. Long (eds) *The Handbook of Second Language Acquisition* (pp. 437–486). Malden, MA: Blackwell.

Odlin, T. (2005) Cross-linguistic influence and conceptual transfer: What are the concepts? *Annual Review of Applied Linguistics,* 25, 3–25.

Paribakht, T.S. (2005) The influence of first language lexicalization on second language lexical inferencing: A study of Persian-speaking learners of English as a foreign language. *Language Learning* 55, 701–748.

Paribakht, T.S. (2010) The effect of lexicalization in the native language on second language lexical inferencing: A cross-linguistic study. In R. Chacón-Beltrán, C. Abello-Contesse and M. del Mar Torreblanca-López (eds) *Insights into Non-Native Vocabulary Teaching and Learning* (pp. 61–82). Clevedon: Multilingual Matters.

Paribakht, T.S. and Wesche, M. (1993) Reading comprehension and second language development in a comprehension-based ESL program. *TESL Canada Journal* 11, 9–29.

Paribakht, S. and Wesche, M. (1997) Vocabulary enhancement activities and reading for meaning in second language vocabulary acquisition. In J. Coady and T. Huckin (eds) *Second Language Vocabulary Acquisition: A Rationale for Pedagogy* (pp. 174–199). New York: Cambridge University Press.

Paribakht, T.S. and Wesche, M. (1999) 'Incidental' vocabulary acquisition through reading: An introspective study. *Studies in Second Language Acquisition,* Special Issue 21, 203–220.

Paribakht, T.S. and Wesche, M. (2006) Lexical inferencing in L1 and L2: Implications for learning and instruction at advanced levels. In H. Byrnes, H. Weger-Guntharp and K.A. Sprang (eds) *Educating for Advanced Foreign Language Capacities: Constructs, Curriculum, Instruction, Assessment* (pp. 118–135). Washington, DC: Georgetown University Press.

Paribakht, T.S. and Tréville, M.C. (2007) L'influence lexicale chez des locuteurs de français et des locuteurs de persan lors de la lecture de textes anglais: effet de la lexicalisation en première langue. *The Canadian Modern Language Review* 63, 399–428.

Read, J. (1993) The development of a new measure of L2 vocabulary knowledge. *Language Testing* 10, 355–371.

Read, J. (2000) *Assessing Vocabulary.* Cambridge: Cambridge University Press.

Ringbom, H. (1987) *The Role of First Language in Foreign Language Learning.* Clevedon: Multilingual Matters.

Ringbom, H. (1992) On L1 transfer in L2 comprehension and production. *Language Learning* 42, 85–112.

Ringbom, H. (2007) *Cross-Linguistic Similarity in Foreign Language Learning.* Clevedon: Multilingual Matters.

Singleton, D. (2006) Lexical transfer: Interlexical or intralexical? In J. Arabski (ed.) *Cross-Linguistic Influences in the Second Language Lexicon* (pp. 130–143). Clevedon: Multilingual Matters.

Sjöholm, K. (1993) Patterns of transferability among fixed expressions in L2 acquisition. In B. Kettemann and W. Wieden (eds) *Current Issues in European Second Language Acquisition Research* (pp. 263–275). Tübingen: Gunter Narr.

Sjöholm, K. (1998) A reappraisal of the role of cross-linguistic and environmental factors in lexical L2 acquisition. In K. Haastrup and A. Viberg (eds) *Perspectives on Lexical Acquisition in a Second Language* (pp. 135–147). Lund: Lund University Press.

Tréville, M.C. (1996) Lexical learning and reading in L2 at the beginner level: The advantage of cognates. *The Canadian Modern Language Review* 53, 173–189.

Viberg, Å. (1998a) Lexical development and the lexical profile of the target language. In D. Albrechtsen, B. Henriksen, I.M. Mees and E. Poulsen (eds) *Perspectives on Foreign and Second Language Pedagogy* (pp. 119–134). Odense: Odense University Press.

Viberg, Å. (1998b) Cross-linguistic perspectives on lexical acquisition: The case of language-specific semantic differentiation. In K. Haastrup and Å. Viberg (eds) *Perspectives on Lexical Acquisition in a Second Language* (pp. 175–208). Lund: Lund University Press.

Weinreich, U. (1953) *Languages in Contact.* The Hague: Mouton.

Wesche, M. and Paribakht, T.S. (1996) Assessing L2 vocabulary knowledge: Depth versus breadth. *The Canadian Modern Language Review* 53 (1), 13–40.

Wesche, M. and Paribakht, T.S. (2010) *Lexical Inferencing in a First and Second Language: Cross-Linguistic Dimensions.* Clevedon: Multilingual Matters.

Yu, L. (1996a) The role of cross-linguistic lexical similarity in the use of motion verbs in English by Chinese and Japanese learners. EdD thesis, University of Toronto.

Yu, L. (1996b) The role of L1 in the acquisition of motion verbs in English by Chinese and Japanese learners. *The Canadian Modern Language Review* 53, 190–218.

Appendices

Appendix A: The Vocabulary Knowledge Scale

Figure 1 VKS Elicitation Scale: Self-Report Categories

Self-report categories	
I	I don't remember having seen this word before.
II	I have seen this word before, but I don't know what it means.
III	I have seen this word before, and I <u>think</u> it means _____ –. (synonym or translation)
IV	I <u>know</u> this word. It means _____. (synonym or translation)
V	I can use this word in a sentence:_____. (Write a sentence.) *(If you do this section, please also do Section IV.)*

Figure 2 VKS Scoring Categories: Meaning of Scores

Self-report categories	Possible scores	Meaning of scores
I	1	The word is not familiar at all.
II	2	The word is familiar but its meaning is not known.
III	3	A correct synonym or translation is given.
IV	4	The word is used with semantic appropriateness in a sentence.
V	5	The word is used with semantic appropriateness and grammatical accuracy in a sentence.

(Paribakht & Wesche, 1996: 178)

Appendix B: Examples of important KSs used in L1 and L2 lexical inferencing

Sentence meaning

'Knowing the Future' (L2 French data); target word: craze

P: I didn't know what [**craze**] meant, but with the rest of the sentence, I think … I'm just going to reread the phrase; … it's (something that one believes deep down).

Sentence grammar

'How to make the New Year more memorable' (L1 Persian data); target word (pseudo): beshkalaanand (to offer)

P: [**beshkalaanand**] It should read *to* (show) *to their grandparents and grandmothers*. I guessed it from the verb.

I: From which one of its verbs?

P: Because there's a verb missing here, it's obvious that it must be a verb.

Discourse meaning

'The Ice Age' (L2 Persian data); target word: bleak

P: [**bleak**] The only guess that I can make, for example, meaning (grim, pale …. desolate)

I: What helped you to make such a guess?

P: The sentence just before it reads *the millions of people who …. the continent were absent*, the words *were absent* …. and *have appeared rather bleak*, it seems as if it must be (desolate).

Word morphology

'Genetic Engineering' (L2 Persian data); target word: genocide

P: [**genocide**] I think it means …. If we parsed it, it'd mean (to kill a generation).

I: How would you parse it?

P: *geno* means gene and generation, and *cide* means to kill. So [**genocide**] should probably mean (to kill a generation).

L1 word collocation

'Preserving our Environment' (L2 Persian data); target word: proactive

P: I think [**proactive**] means (exact); exact measurements. With measurements often such adjectives are used.

I: Why did you make this guess?

P: With the word [measurement] they often use (exact, exact) measurements. I've often heard it this way in Persian, and in English texts, too. ...This is the adjective that can be used.

L1 word form

P: [**untimely**], ça ressemble au mot français 'intimement'.

   ([**untimely**], It looks like the French word 'intimement'.

World knowledge

'L'intuition' (L1 French data); target word (pseudo): dépenaissent (reconnaissent = famous)

P: **dépenaissent** (admit, say, declare) possibly because I know that intuition helps a lot in making discoveries.

Transcription conventions	
P = participant, I = interviewer	[ ] = words spoken in English by Persian or French speakers
Normal font = translation of utterances from Persian or French to English or English L1 utterances	( ) = the inferred meaning(s)
	.... = pause
[**Bold face**] = target words (actual and pseudo)	... = missing text
	Bold face italics: knowledge source
Italics = words/phrases read from the text	

Appendix C: Example of a Persian L2 reader's difficulties with a non-lexicalized word

In the following excerpts, the Persian L2 reader cannot infer the meaning of the non-lexicalized target word 'to clone' and as a result misunderstands the text and has problems guessing the meanings of other unfamiliar target words.

Topic *'Genetic engineering'*; target word: *to clone*

P: I can't guess [**clone**] because [**clone**]… We use [colony] in our language. [colony] means to live in groups but here I believe it wouldn't make sense …. I think the meaning of this [**clone**] must be important because it's been used many times in the text. I think the [point] of the story, that is, the theme, revolves around this word.

I: Why do you think so?

P: Because the example is about sheep and then here in fact the results of this experiment, this [**clone**], it becomes clear where they've got with their research.

*Subsequently, when dealing with the target word [**to trigger**], the participant refers to 'clone' again and tries to make sense of the word.*

Topic *'Genetic engineering'*; target word: to trigger

P: I think it must mean (doing some thing). In other words, it wants to say that in fact, who knows what the new technology might do? Some such meaning ….
[**clones**] here means (groups) but it wouldn't make sense over there. Here I think it says scientists can (raise) some animals, creatures … It has some such meaning. With this meaning for [**to clone**], the sentence there didn't make sense to me.

The participant continues to interpret the meaning of the target word 'to clone' in inferring 'to snoop'.

Topic *'Genetic engineering'*; target word: to trigger

P: It might mean (to investigate) because it says [file]. Files, doctors' files. The criminals might then have access to these files…. As I said [**cloning**] was important in the sentence. That is, if I'd known the meaning of [**to clone**], I might've better understood the text. In fact I know what the text is generally talking about, but I don't exactly understand it because of the word [**clone**].

Wesche and Paribakht (2010: 133)

Part 2

Syntactic Perspectives

The first two chapters in this section consider transfer in the acquisition of certain syntactic patterns in English by first language (L1) speakers of Chinese, whereas the third chapter, by Chang and Zheng, looks at syntactic transfer involving L1 English and second language (L2) Chinese. Despite the differences in native and target languages in the second and third chapters, both studies employ assumptions and formalisms of universal grammar (UG) in their investigations.

In contrast to the chapters employing UG, the study by Li and Yang addresses transfer in a functionalist framework, thus cross-linguistic influence in both grammar and discourse. While some notion of 'discourse topic' seems indispensable for understanding how speakers and writers construct extended texts in Chinese and English (and probably in any other language), the two languages differ considerably in the degree of explicitness required to signal a topical referent. Both languages have nouns and pronouns, but the reliance of English on these explicit lexical markers is much greater; Chinese often does not use such words when the context is clear. The significance of the contrast can be appreciated by considering how frequently English relies on pronouns to maintain topic continuity. Chinese routinely dispenses with forms such as those underlined in the English sentence ***That car*** *is too expensive, and **its** color is not good.* **I** *don't like* **it** *and don't want to buy* **it**, because the implied referent is easily identifiable in the context. Using a back-translation task, Li and Yang show that learners at an earlier stage of acquisition tend to omit the elements required in the English target much more often than do more advanced learners. Their results thus suggest a strong influence of what they and other analysts of Chinese call the 'topic chain'. Overcoming the difficulty of learning to supply an element obligatory in the target but not in the native language poses serious challenges for acquisition. Li and Yang raise the possibility that zero elements resulting from the L1 topic chain are a domain where fossilization may be routine, since even advanced learners in their study showed a persistence of the problem, albeit at lower rates than those seen in the less advanced groups.

Chapter 7 by Yusong Gao considers problems of transfer involving argument structures in grammatical patterns (e.g. what kinds of subjects and objects can occur with particular types of verbs). Adopting UG as his theoretical framework, his analysis focuses on anticausative and middle constructions (MCs), which are common in the languages of the world but which vary considerably in their formal properties from one language to the next. Thus, for instance, the English sentence *The window broke* has a fairly close translation equivalent in Spanish, *La ventana se rompió* (The window RFLX broke), but the difference between the languages appears to have interesting consequences for second language acquisition (SLA) in the light of research by Silvina Montrul discussed by Gao. The Spanish reflexive pronoun *se* is normal in so-called anticausative sentences such as the one just given, with *se* in effect signaling to listeners or readers to interpret *la ventana* (the window) as the subject of the verb, not as the direct object. Montrul's research indicated that Spanish speakers are inclined toward more favorable judgments of the so-called *get*-passive pattern in *The window got broken* than of *The window broke*. Spanish speakers thus seem to have engaged in a matching process where a kind of interlingual identification was made between the L1 reflexive *se* and the English *get*-passive, even though there are major differences in the formal properties of the Spanish pronoun and the English verb phrase. In other words, L1 morphosyntactic patterns apparently influenced judgments of grammaticality of an L2 structure. The results in Gao's study are nevertheless quite different from those of Montrul. Examining the intuitions of L1 Chinese and L1 Korean speakers about English MCs (e.g. *This book reads easily*), Gao found relatively little evidence of a matching process, even though both Chinese and Korean have special morphemes often required in anticausative constructions and MCs. Despite such results, Gao points to the fact that Korean learners' judgments tended to be more skeptical about the grammaticality of English MCs in comparison with the judgments of Chinese speakers. The relatively lenient judgments of the latter group reflect, Gao surmises, the rather wide range of possible MCs in Chinese so that the aberrant sentence *The Eiffel Tower sees easily from this window* has an acceptable Chinese translation even while the pattern is ungrammatical in English. Korean, in contrast, has stronger constraints than either Chinese or English as to what can be a sentence subject. Thus, the case for transfer in Gao's analysis has less to do with a matching process of morphosyntactic patterns and more to do with an abstract influence based on fundamental typological properties that vary across languages.

Like Gao's study, Chapter 8 by Hui Chang and Lina Zheng focuses on the transfer of syntactic argument structures within a UG framework. However, in the Chang and Zheng study, English is the L1 and Chinese the L2, as noted above. Chinese arguably has a wider array of causative patterns than English, and this variety seems to pose a serious acquisition challenge for English speakers. Learners do show an ability to capitalize on cross-linguistic similarities in periphrastic constructions such as *This story makes me sad,* where the causative *make* has a close counterpart in the Chinese verb *shi*. Translations with *shi* proved frequent in a test designed by Chang and Zheng to determine how many types of Chinese causative patterns beginning and intermediate learners could use. While students' choices of periphrastic constructions with *shi* and other causative verbs often led to accurate translations, their answers showed an overreliance on such constructions since, in several cases, Chinese causative structures using either affixes or compound verb patterns were required for accurate translations. The similarity of English and Chinese thus proved to be a mixed blessing: although the transfer of periphrastic patterns was often positive, in many other cases it was negative.

6 An Investigation of Topic-Prominence in Interlanguage of Chinese EFL Learners: A Discourse Perspective

Shaopeng Li and Lianrui Yang

Introduction

In many respects, English and Chinese are typologically different. Chinese is a topic-prominent (TP) language in which the category of topic plays an important role in the formation of a sentence, whereas English is a subject-prominent (SP) language in which the category of subject is an indispensable syntactic element (Li & Thompson, 1976). SP languages typically rely on certain coding devices such as subject/object case marking, number agreement between subjects and predicates and (in somewhat fewer SP languages) dummy subjects as seen in the *it* in the sentence *It is not clear that Jill can come*. In contrast, such coding devices are typically absent in TP languages. Given this typological difference between Chinese and English, the likelihood of transfer in the interlanguage of Chinese English as a foreign language (EFL) learners seems rather high.

The distinction between SP and TP languages has indeed provided a useful point of departure for second language acquisition (SLA) research (e.g. Cai, 1998a, 1998b; Jung, 2004; Sasaki, 1990; Yang, 2008; Yip & Matthews, 1995). Nevertheless, some details of the TP/SP distinction warrant close scrutiny in order to understand better the task that Chinese learners face when constructing extended discourse in a typologically different language such as English. Accordingly, we focus on the notion of *topic chain*, which Chu (1998: 324) defines as 'a set of clauses linked by a topic in the form of zero anaphora'. Later in this chapter, examples of topic chains will be given, followed by an empirical investigation showing the usefulness of the notion for understanding second language (L2) writing. First, however, a closer look will be taken of the relation between topics and subjects.

Topics and Topic Chains

Li and Thompson (1976) rely on additional categories to make the SP/TP distinction. The former type refers to those languages in which 'the structure of sentences favors a description in which the grammatical relation of subject-predicate plays a major role' (Li & Thompson, 1976: 459). By contrast, TP languages are those in which 'the basic structure of sentences favors a description in which the grammatical relation of topic-comment plays a major role' (Li & Thompson, 1976: 459). While topics are thus linked to comments and subjects to predicates, the notion of topic is often seen to be applicable to the study of both SP and TP languages. To the extent that topics involve referents, what Givón (1983) calls 'topic continuity' is a necessary condition for listeners or readers to be able to keep track of the same referent in extended discourse. Speakers and writers therefore need to construct phrases, clauses and sentences that make topics continuously accessible for their audience. As Givón (1984: 138, emphasis in the original) puts it, 'the main behavioral manifestation of important topics in discourse is **continuity**'. With regard to languages that give overt grammatical signals of a subject (as in the case of the English subject pronouns *he* and *she*), Givón (1984: 138) asserts that 'the subject case tends to code the most important, current, and continuous topic'.

Whether in a TP or an SP language, introducing a topic explicitly establishes a point of reference for the ensuing discourse which often constitutes new information, that is, information that is not recoverable from the preceding text. In Chinese, the topic chain serves as a key device for signaling the continuity of an established topic. This unit does not always correspond to the traditional notion of a sentence. A clause can be part of a topic chain, but, at the same time, it can serve as a component of a different sentence. In addition, the domain or scope of a topic chain can stretch across not only sentence boundaries but also across paragraph boundaries. This suggests that a topic chain can be a unit larger than a sentence or even a paragraph.

Topic chains result from the fact that referring expressions which can be inferred contextually by the reader are frequently omitted in Chinese discourse (Yeh & Chen, 2003). When the referent is established through a clear referring expression, it may continue to be highly accessible even with minimal devices expressing topic continuity. In other words, even minimal patterns of cohesion may serve to help readers or listeners track referents effectively and thus to consider the particular stretch of discourse coherent. Underpinning the whole system is the overt established topic which defines any particular topic chain.

Tsao (1979: vii), who is believed to have been the first researcher to use the term *topic chain*, stated that it is a stretch of actual discourse composed of one or more clauses, headed by a topic which serves as a common link among all the clauses. As such, it functions as a discourse unit in Chinese (Tsao, 1979: vii; cf. Tsao, 1990: 63). Chu (1998) presented a more restricted view, contending that because the topic is mainly a discourse notion, it can be identified only on the level of discourse when it serves as an inter-clausal link. Consequently, Chu (1998: 324) defined a topic chain as 'a set of clauses linked by a topic in the form of zero anaphora'. To him, there is no point in talking about a topic within a single-clause sentence.

According to Li (2005), a topic chain is a concatenation of clauses sharing an identical topic that occurs overtly one time. All the other clauses are linked to the chain by zero noun phrases (NPs) that are coreferential (whether anaphorically or cataphorically) with the topic. The underlined words in the following translations correspond to what would be zero NPs in the Mandarin original. The second example comes, with some modifications, from Chen (1987).

(1)

Na	*liang*	*che*	*jiaqian*		*tai*	*gui*	*yanse*	*ye*
that	CLF	car	price		too	expensive	color	either
bu	*hao*			*bu*	*xihuan*		*bu*	*xiang*
not	good			not	like		not	want
mai	*zuotian*	*qu*	*kan le yixia*					
buy	yesterday	go	look					
hai	*kai le*	*yi*	*huier*		*haishi*	*bu*	*xihuan*	
also	drive	a	while		still	not	like	

=**That car** is too expensive, and **its** color is not good. **I** don't like **it** and don't want to buy **it**. I went to see **it** yesterday and I drove **it** for a short time, but **I** still dislike **it**.

(2)

Tang Mingde	*jinghuang de*	*wangwai*	*pao,*	*zhuang*	*dao*
Tang Mingde	in panic	out	ran	bumped	onto
yige	*dahande*	*shenshang*			
a	big guy's	body			
Ta	*kan*	*qing le*	*narende*	*meiyan*	
he	saw	clearly	that guy's	eyes	
renchu	*na*	*ren*	*shi*	*shui*	
recognized	that	guy	was	who	

=**Tang Mingde** ran out in panic and **he** bumped onto **a big guy**. **He** saw **that guy's** eyes clearly and **he** recognized who the guy was.

In the first example, six zero NPs occur, as the underlined units in the English translation indicate, each NP being (both in the original and in the translation) coreferential with the overt NP referring to the car. In the second example, there are two human referents in the discourse, but the topic chain stays clear. The first reference (to Tang Mingde) establishes the chain, which remains transparent partly because other words (e.g. *na* and *ren*) establish a clear referential contrast and because the context thus established forestalls any real ambiguities.

As the preceding examples show, Chinese discourse relies heavily on zero anaphora (ZA), which involves elements that, if not deleted, would most typically be NPs that somewhat redundantly specify the context. As the examples also show, ZA occurs much more frequently in Chinese than in English. Li and Thompson (1981: 657) have summed up the tendency thus: 'a salient feature of Mandarin grammar is the fact that NPs that are understood from context do not need to be specified' (cf. Liang, 1993). ZA may occur in almost any syntactic position in a Chinese sentence including positions where the use of nouns or pronouns would be more likely in English.

Second Language Research on Discourse

Typological transfer and discourse transfer

Research has shown two contradictory claims on the role of topic/ subject prominence typology in SLA. One claim is that irrespective of learners' first language (L1), there is no L1 influence (e.g. Fuller & Gundel, 1987). The opposing view is that the L1 of learners does play a major role in their L2 learning (e.g. Jin, 1994).

Discourse transfer refers to the use of some of the discourse patterns of the learner's L2 in the same way in which they are employed in the learner's L1 (Kasper & Schmidt, 1996; Kellerman, 1995; Wu, 2001). Such transfer is operationally defined in the present study as the kind that happens when the language learner transfers L1-based discourse patterns to the L2 context. The notion of discourse transfer has long been recognized as a cognitive activity, as in the assertion of Bartelt (1992: 113) that 'discourse transfer is a rule-governed cognitive process', in which the known rules of the native language are used as hypotheses in mastering the L2. Since the ZA so common in Chinese shows a highly context-dependent use of language, the overt signals such as nouns and pronouns often required in English become a challenge in that new cognitive routines have to be acquired in order to employ signals expected in the target (cf. Wang *et al.*, 1998).

With regard to possible L1 Chinese influence, some research (e.g. Huang, 1984, 1989; Shi, 1989; Tsao, 1977) posits a rule of *Topic NP Deletion*, which operates across discourse to delete the topic of a sentence under identity with a topic in a preceding sentence. The typological difference between Chinese and English thus implies a competition between L1 rules involving the omission of syntactic and semantic information and L2 rules to make explicit such information. Our study will accordingly focus on the discourse patterns of the learners' L2 to explore whether Chinese EFL learners use L1 rules.

Previous studies on topic prominence in interlanguage

The introduction of the notion of topic prominence by Schachter and Rutherford (1979) and Rutherford (1983) into SLA research has encouraged detailed investigations of a wide range of languages. Naturally, certain complications arise from this linguistic diversity. While Chinese is a prototypical example of a TP language, others such as Japanese and Korean have both TP and SP characteristics, and Li and Thompson sometimes consider Korean and Japanese as a separate type yet sometimes as akin to Chinese and other TP languages. Fuller and Gundel (1987) grouped speakers of Chinese, Japanese and Korean together in a typological contrast with languages that are unambiguously SP (Spanish, Arabic and Persian). Their comparison focused on typological variables such as ZA, pseudo passives, double-subject constructions, periphrastic constructions and subject-verb concord. To measure the degree of topic prominence of learners' L2 narratives, a three-point implicational scale was employed. No difference was found in topic-prominence between the speakers of more TP and less TP languages in their L2 English narratives, results that called into question the position of Rutherford (1983) that subtle language-specific differences would affect interlanguage production.

There are reasons to be skeptical about the conclusions of Fuller and Gundel, however. For one thing, the numbers of individuals representing the different L1 groups were small (for example, there were only two Chinese speakers). Moreover, it seems quite possible that the students recruited in their study were so advanced that any L1 effects would wash out. In contrast, our cross-sectional study can be viewed as counterevidence to the conclusions of Fuller and Gundel, since the relatively large sample of low-proficiency students in our investigation does show what one would expect if transfer is at work.

Another reason to suppose that discourse transfer is related to topic-prominence comes from a longitudinal study by Huebner (1983) of an adult learner of English whose L1 is Hmong, a TP language. Huebner found that the learner continued to treat all the copulas as topic boundary markers in the earlier stages of SLA. In these stages, the learner also consistently interpreted the subject NP in English as definite, which is consistent with the role of initial NPs in TP languages. The learner's interlanguage showed a progression from the TP to the SP stage, with evidence of the progress coming from growing complexity in his morphosyntactic patterns.

Still another reason to consider typological properties as transferable is seen in the findings of Jin (1994), who looked at the production patterns of 46 adult native speakers of English learning Chinese as an L2. Two important results emerged from his study. First, L2 learners with very limited proficiency in Chinese tended to rely on structures that are similar . to English. Second, as soon as some TP features in learners' interlanguage increased significantly, other clustered TP structures such as double-subject constructions began to occur. Jin viewed his findings as counterevidence to the conclusions of Fuller and Gundel (1987). Native language influence also appears to be especially strong among L1 Chinese speakers in their earlier years of using English (Yang, 2008), with TP patterns especially common. With increasing proficiency, however, SP patterns grow in frequency and TP patterns decline.

In view of the controversies, our chapter can shed some light in that it considers how likely or unlikely transfer might be in an EFL setting (in contrast to the English as a second language [ESL] environments in the studies of Rutherford and of Fuller and Gundel) and in that the possibility of transfer is explicitly examined in relation to widely varying degrees of L2 proficiency among learners who all perform a task relevant to the issue of constructing L2 discourse: namely, a translation task.

Research Questions and Hypotheses

The study reported here explores whether the TP features in Chinese discourse exist in the interlanguage of Chinese learners of English. The following research questions guide our research:

(1) Do learners use fewer TP structures and more SP structures at higher proficiency levels?
(2) Is ZA transferable in connected discourse?

From those questions come the following hypotheses:

(1) The characteristics of Chinese topic chains will be transferred to the interlanguage of Chinese EFL learners, thus resulting in the overuse of ZA.
(2) The interlanguage discourse of Chinese EFL learners shows effects of discourse transfer but with more transfer evident among less-proficient learners.

Method

Participants

The participants in this study were 90 native speakers of Mandarin Chinese studying English in China. Group 1 consisted of 30 first-year high school students (who were 15–16 years old and who had studied English for about 4 years), while Group 2 consisted of 30 first-year university students majoring in English (who were 19–20 years old and who had studied English for about 7 years) and Group 3 consisted of 30 first-year postgraduate students majoring in English at the same university (who were 24–26 years old and who had studied English for more than 10 years). Proficiency levels among the groups varied as follows (albeit with some individual exceptions), using as our norm the Common European Framework of Reference for Languages: A2 (Group 1), B1 (Group 2) and B2 (Group 3).

Instrument and procedure

The task was designed to compare written English productions of Chinese university students involving two passages which the researchers had translated from English into Chinese (the passages coming from EFL textbooks). The task given to students was to translate the two Chinese passages into English, each of which consisted of two paragraphs that were characterized by typical Chinese TP features, namely, topic chains and ZA. These passages were translated from passages originally written in English for the primary school textbooks *Go for It* (Book 3) (People's Education Press, 2002) and *Essential English for Foreign Students* (Book 1) (Eckersley, 1955). This task, in effect an exercise in back translation, was designed to elicit the learners' production of anaphora. There were six topic chains in which 26 anaphora (including zero, pronominal and nominal anaphora) were identified in the two Chinese passages, one of which is Example (1) given earlier.

Glosses of the more difficult English words were provided to the participants in order to ensure that these words would not prevent them from completing the task successfully. After reading the instructions and making sure they understood them, the participants proceeded with the task, which had a time limit of 20 minutes. Although some students may have used the books as course texts, the results suggest that they would not likely have remembered many details. The translation exercise took place in the participants' regular classes.

Data analysis

An example of how three learners performed on the task appears in Table 6.1.

Results

Distributions of different types of anaphora in the test among the three groups

Table 6.1 shows the typical performances of individuals with differing proficiency. The distribution of types of anaphora used by the three

Table 6.1 Sample translation performances

Proficiency level	Translation by participants	Zero anaphora	Overt anaphora
Beginning	**That car** is too expensive, the color is not good. **I** don't like∅ and don't want to buy∅. I went to see∅ yesterday and drove∅ a little time, but still dislike∅.	N5	N0
Intermediate	**That car** is too expensive, the color is not good. **I** don't like∅ and don't want to buy∅. I went to see **it** yesterday and I drove **it** a little time, but I still dislike **it**.	N2	N3
Advanced	**That car** is too expensive, the color is not good. **I** don't like **it** and don't want to buy **it**. I went to see **it** yesterday and I drove **it** a little time, but I still dislike **it**.	N0	N5

participant groups can be seen in Table 6.2 and Figure 6.1, which show that the beginning and intermediate groups used the ZA more extensively than the advanced group, who in turn used nominal and pronominal anaphora more frequently.

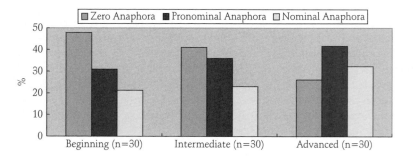

Figure 6.1 Percentage of different types of anaphora in the test

Table 6.2 Number of different types of anaphora in the test

Proficiency groups	No. of different types of anaphora		
	ZA	Pronominal anaphora	Nominal anaphora
Beginning (*n* = 30)	373	241	166
Intermediate (*n* = 30)	320	280	180
Advanced (*n* = 30)	206	325	249

Specific distributions of ZA in the test among the three groups

Table 6.3 displays the proportion of the number and the percentage of ZA in all the test items.

Table 6.3 Number and percentage of ZA in the test

	No.	Percentage
Beginning (n = 30)	373	47.82%
Intermediate (n = 30)	320	41.03%
Advanced (n = 30)	206	26.15%

The percentages in Table 6.3 reflect occurrences of ZA in relation to possible cases. For example, 373 cases of ZA were identified in the writing of the 30 beginning learners and the percentage is thus 373/780 = 47.8% (with the denominator representing 30 students × 26 test items). The table thus indicates that less-proficient students tend to show more instances of ZA. The tendency is clearly weaker among the more proficient groups, especially in the most advanced one. Raw figures such as 373 in Table 6.3 are inversely proportional to those in Table 6.2, showing as they do that there is a decrease in ZA along with an increase of explicit nominal and pronominal anaphora.

Multiple comparisons between proficiency levels

A one-way analysis of variance (ANOVA) was conducted on the rates of ZA in the proficiency groups. As seen in Table 6.4, a significant difference occurs in the frequency of ZA across the three groups ($F = 57.466$, $p = 0.000$).

A *post hoc* analysis was also undertaken, with the results of multiple comparisons between proficiency levels shown in Table 6.5; in all cases, inter-group differences are statistically significant.

Table 6.4 Result of one-way ANOVA

ANOVA

ZA

	Sum of squares	df	Mean square	F	Sig.
Between groups	485.489	2	242.744	57.466	0.000
Within groups	367.500	87	4.224		
Total	852.989	89			

Table 6.5 Results of multiple comparisons between proficiency levels

Multiple Comparisons: Comparisons between different proficiency levels
ZA: Zero Anaphora
LSD: Least-significant difference

(I) level	(J) level	Mean difference (I–J)	Std. error	Sig.	95% confidence interval Lower bound	Upper bound
Beginning		1.767*	0.531	0.001	0.71	2.82
		5.567*	0.531	0.000	4.51	6.62
Intermediate		−1.767*	0.531	0.001	−2.82	−0.71
		3.800*	0.531	0.000	2.75	4.85
Advanced	Beginning	−5.567*	0.531	0.000	−6.62	−4.51
	Intermediate	−3.800*	0.531	0.000	−4.85	−2.75

*Mean difference significant at the 0.05 level.

Discussion

The results of our study indicate that at each proficiency level the patterns of overt anaphora and ZA are consistent with the hypotheses stated above. Most significantly, the high incidence of ZA suggests the influence of the Chinese topic chain, especially among less-proficient learners. Whereas the translations of the beginners showed the highest incidence of ZA, those of the most advanced group showed the lowest, thus the least reliance on a TP discourse pattern. The inverse pattern for SP features is just as strong: that is, the beginners showed the least use of nominal and pronominal anaphora, while the most advanced group showed the greatest use. Although our results are cross-sectional, not longitudinal, they are consistent with a generalization that in the normal course of acquisition, SP features become relatively common and TP features become relatively rare for Chinese learners of English.

As the results suggest, even advanced learners are still susceptible to the influence of the topic chain, which indicates that L1 transfer persists over a relatively long period of time, thus suggesting possible fossilization (Selinker, 1972). Put another way, it may be that a 'discourse accent' persists. Overcoming such an accent may, however, be even more difficult than overcoming negative phonetic transfer. In discussing discourse transfer, Odlin (1989) considered both structural and non-structural factors. Given that there is clearly a difference between the degree of structurally explicit signals to process discourse in Chinese and in English, it follows that the degree of inferencing required in the two languages will also be different across a wide range of contexts. If, as suggested here, fossilization is a hazard, the barrier may arise largely from the difficulty of learning a wide range of new contextual conventions involving what can be implicit and what must be explicit in the target language discourse.

Conclusion

The present study suggests that negative transfer will result from a lack of discourse awareness. In other words, mismatches may arise between learners' grammatical knowledge and the demands of extended discourse contexts. It therefore seems pedagogically sound to explore with students some of the many contexts that communicating in a new language will involve (with time and syllabus priorities being obvious constraints on what can be taught). How effective such instruction might be in Chinese school settings remains an intriguing question to ponder. Han (2010) has offered longitudinal analyses of fossilization involving plurals and articles, and similar longitudinal studies might prove insightful with regard to developmental sequences of SP features in L2 English among speakers of TP languages. To investigate transfer in more detail, it could also help to look at how speakers of an SP language do on a back-translation task like the one used in our study. Comparing L2 learners from both TP and SP L1 backgrounds can surely lead to a better understanding of typological factors in discourse transfer.

References

Bartelt, H.G. (1992) Transfer and variability of rhetorical redundancy in Apachean English interlanguage. In S.M. Gass and L. Selinker (eds) *Language Transfer in Language Learning* (pp. 101–118). Amsterdam: Benjamins.

Cai, J.T. (1998a) The influence of Chinese topic-prominent features on Chinese EFL learners' compositions. *Foreign Language Teaching and Research* 4, 17–21.

Cai, J.T. (1998b) L1 transfer and topic-prominence structure. *Journal of Jiefangjun University of Foreign Languages* 6, 15–19.

Chen, P. (1987) Discourse analysis of Chinese zero anaphora. *Chinese* 5, 16–19.

Chu, C.C. (1998) *A Discourse Grammar of Mandarin Chinese*. New York: Peter Lang.

Eckersley, C.E. (1955) *Essential English for Foreign Students*. London: Longmans.

Fuller, J.W. and Gundel, J.K. (1987) Topic-prominence in interlanguage. *Language Learning* 37 (2), 1–18.

Givón, T. (1983) Topic continuity in discourse: An introduction. In T. Givón (ed.) *Topic Continuity in Discourse: A Quantitative Cross-Language Study* (pp. 1–41). Amsterdam: Benjamins.

Givón, T. (1984) *Syntax: A Functional–Typological Introduction, Volume I*. Amsterdam: Benjamins.

Han, Z. (2010) Grammatical inadequacy as a function of linguistic relativity: A longitudinal case study. In Z. Han and T. Cadierno (eds) *Linguistic Relativity in Second Language Acquisition: Evidence of First Language Thinking for Speaking* (pp. 154–182). Bristol: Multilingual Matters.

Huang, J. (1984) On the typology of zero anaphora. *Language Research* 20, 85–105.

Huang, J. (1989) Pro-drop in Chinese: A generalized control theory. In O. Jaeggli and K. Safir (eds) *The Null Subject Parameter* (pp. 185–214). Dordrecht: Kluwer Academic.

Huebner, T. (1983) *A Longitudinal Analysis of the Acquisition of English*. Ann Arbor, MI: Kornonma Press.

Institute of Curriculum Research (2002) *Go for It (Book 3)*. Beijing: People's Education Press.

Jin, H.G. (1994) Topic-prominence and subject-prominence in L2 acquisition: Evidence of English to Chinese typological transfer. *Language Learning* 44, 101–122.

Jung, E.H. (2004) Topic and subject prominence in interlanguage development. *Language Learning* 54 (4), 713–738.

Kasper, G. and Schmidt, R. (1996) Developmental issues in interlanguage pragmatics. *Studies in Second Language Acquisition* 18, 149–169.

Kellerman, E. (1995) Crosslinguistic influence: Transfer to nowhere? *Annual Review of Applied Linguistics* 15, 125–150.

Li, C. and Thompson, S.A. (1976) Subject and topic: A new typology. In C. Li (ed.) *Subject and Topic* (pp. 457–489). New York: Academic Press.

Li, C. and Thompson, S.A. (1981) *Mandarin Chinese: A Functional Reference Grammar.* Los Angeles, CA: University of California Press.

Li, W.D. (2005) *Topic Chains in Chinese: A Discourse Analysis and Applications in Language Teaching.* Munich: Lincom Europa.

Liang, T. (1993) Zero anaphora in Chinese: Cognitive strategies in discourse processing. PhD thesis, University of Colorado.

Odlin, T. (1989) *Language Transfer: Cross-Linguistic Influence in Language Learning.* Cambridge: Cambridge University Press.

Rutherford, W. (1983) Language typology and language transfer. In S.M. Gass and L. Selinker (eds) *Language Transfer in Language Learning* (pp. 358–470). Rowley, MA: Newbury House.

Sasaki, M. (1990) Topic prominence in Japanese EFL students' existential constructions. *Language Learning* 40 (4), 337–368.

Schachter, J. and Rutherford, W. (1979) Discourse function and language transfer. *Working Papers in Bilingualism* 19, 1–12.

Selinker, L. (1972) Interlanguage. *International Review of Applied Linguistics* 10, 209–231.

Shi, D.X. (1989) Topic chain as a syntactic category in Chinese. *Journal of Chinese Linguistics* 17, 223–261.

Tsao, F. (1977) Subject and topic in Chinese. In R. Cheng, L. Ying-Che and T. Ting-Chi (eds) *Proceedings of Symposium on Chinese Linguists* (pp. 167–195). Linguistic Institute of the Linguistic Society of America. Taipei: Student Book Company.

Tsao, F. (1979) A functional study of topics in Chinese: The first step towards discourse analysis. PhD thesis, Cornell University.

Tsao, F. (1990) *Sentence and Clause Structure in Chinese: A Functional Perspective.* Taipei: Student Book.

Wang, Y.K., Chen, Y.S. and Hsu, W.L. (1998) Empirical study of Mandarin Chinese discourse analysis: An event-based approach. In *Proceedings of Tenth IEEE International Conference on Tools with Artificial Intelligence* (pp. 466–473). New York: IEEE.

Wu, S.H. (2001) Discourse transfer phenomena as manifested in interlanguage performance of four Chinese ESL university-level students: An analytic/interpretive investigation of what Chinese learners bring to NS-NNS interaction. See http://sunzi1.lib.hku.hk/ER/detail/hkul/2684742 (accessed 15 March 2008).

Yang, L.R. (2008) Topic prominence in typological interlanguage development of Chinese students' English. PhD thesis, Shanghai Foreign Studies University.

Yeh, C.L. and Chen, Y.C. (2003) Zero anaphora resolution in Chinese with partial parsing based on centering theory. In *Proceedings of International Conference on Natural Language Processing and Knowledge Engineering* (pp. 683–688). Beijing, China.

Yip, V. and Matthews, S. (1995) Interlanguage and typology: The case of topic-prominence. In L. Eubank, L. Selinker and M.S. Smith (eds) *The Current State of Interlanguage* (pp. 17–30). Amsterdam: Benjamins.

Appendix

Test

Translation Task:

1. ①**我**最大的问题是太忙了。年轻时有很多时间，但最近起得很早，整天呆在学校，然后直接(directly)回家吃晚饭。上高中以前花很多时间跟朋友们一起玩儿，但现在不再有时间了。②我过去晚上常看电视或者跟奶奶聊天(chat)，但现在必须学习。③我喜欢音乐，爸爸以前常带我去音乐会。④最近，我几乎没有时间去，写作业，然后睡觉，真的很想念以前的日子。

2. ⑤**那辆车**价钱太贵，颜色也不好，⑥**我**不喜欢，不想买。昨天去看了一下，还开了一会儿。还是不喜欢。

7 Investigating the Impact of L1 Morphology and Semantics on L2 Acquisition of English Detransitivized Constructions by Chinese and Korean Learners

Yusong Gao

Introduction

Argument expression in relation to verb types has long been an important area of inquiry for both first (L1) and second language (L2) researchers and has led to varying claims about structure and about acquisition. Much of the controversy reflects the complex interface between semantics and syntax, where sentence construction is semantically determined but morphosyntactically expressed (Hale & Keyser, 1993; Haspelmath, 1993; Levin & Rappaport, 1995, 2005). Moreover, successful acquisition requires coming to terms with the properties of both forms and meanings in distinct constructions.

Previous studies have suggested that the outcomes of the acquisition of L2 argument structure are due to influences from the learner's L1. However, there remains a significant challenge to understand the details of such influence, that is, exactly what and how learners transfer from their L1 to an L2 (Inagaki, 2001; Juffs, 1996; Kim, 2005; Kondo, 2005; Montrul, 1997, 2000; Oh, 2010; White, 1991). The present chapter examines the impact of L1 semantics and morphology on the acquisition of argument structure by investigating Chinese and Korean learners' acquisition of two English detransitivized constructions, i.e. middle constructions (MCs; e.g. *The book reads well*) and anticausative constructions (e.g. *The window broke*). It is shown that English, Chinese and Korean differ grammatically in this domain in ways that can indicate whether L1 influence exists in detransitivized constructions.

The chapter is organized as follows: the next section presents a brief overview of the debate over the role that L1 semantics and morphology play in the acquisition of argument structure. The focus then narrows to a comparative analysis of the formation of MCs and anticausative constructions in English, Chinese and Korean, followed by an account of an experimental investigation of transfer and then by a general discussion in the last section.

L1 Influence on L2 Acquisition of Argument Structure

In recent years, a number of studies have considered the role of L1 morphology (e.g. Montrul, 1997, 2000, 2001a, 2001b; Kim, 2005; Kondo, 2005; Oh, 2009, 2010; Oh & Zubizarreta, 2006; Whong-Barr & Schwartz, 2002). These studies have provided interesting yet conflicting analyses of the role of the native language in the acquisition of L2 argument structure. There exists a consensus that the L1 is at play, but what and how L2 learners transfer from their L1 to an L2 remains controversial.

Especially relevant to the present study are two by Montrul (2000, 2001a), who investigated the acquisition of causative constructions. Studying grammaticality judgments of learners of L2 Turkish, L2 Spanish and L2 English, she found that incomplete knowledge of the meaning of causative forms could explain many patterns in the data (an explanation often termed the *default event template hypothesis*). Even so, language-specific differences suggesting transfer were also evident. For example, Spanish-speaking learners of English often rejected zero-derived forms implying causation (e.g. *The window broke*) yet accepted alternating verbs with the *get*-passive (e.g. *The window got broken*) significantly more than did a comparable Turkish-speaking group. While incomplete knowledge of the grammatical properties of English words helps explain the judgments of Spanish speakers, they also seem to have been influenced by a belief that L2 forms and meanings should somehow correspond to those in the L1. In Spanish, it is not enough to say *La ventana rompió* (The window broke); rather, a reflexive form *se* is required in order to construct a sentence semantically equivalent to *The window broke*: *La ventana se rompió*. The need for a *se* form in the L1 apparently influenced Spanish speakers' often favorable judgments of the *get*-passive (*The window got broken*). Moreover, Spanish-speaking learners of Turkish were less accurate in their judgments of zero-derived intransitive forms (e.g. *Gemi bat-mış*, Ship sink-PERFECT, 'The ship (apparently) sank') but more accurate with the overt morphology of intransitive forms (*e.g. Pencere kır-ıl-dı*, Window break-PASS-Past, 'The window broke') than were English-speaking learners of Turkish. Once again, the intuitions of Spanish speakers were apparently affected by a matching process whereby a kind of interlingual identification was made between the L1 reflexive *se* and the Turkish passive form *-il*. It appears that in these L2 English and L2 Turkish cases, the judgments of Spanish speakers support what is often called the modular transfer hypothesis, which has considered in depth how, for example, passives and causative constructions pattern in the morphology and syntax of causative constructions and how such patterns affect the challenges that learners encounter with a new language (cf. Kondo, 2005).

L1 influence was also evident in the acquisition of double object (DO) constructions by Korean speakers of English (Whong-Barr & Schwartz, 2002). Such constructions can have either an indirect + direct object (as in *John gave Mary a book*) or a direct + prepositional object (as in *John gave a book to Mary*). There are two main varieties of DO constructions, goal and benefactive, which in English are typically coded distinctly with the propositions *to* and *for*. Oh (2010) offers the following examples:

(1)   a.   John gave Mary a book/a book *to* Mary. (Goal construction)
      b.   John baked Mary a cake/a cake *for* Mary. (Benefactive construction)
           (Oh 2010: 410)

Morphologically speaking, Korean and English goal DOs are the same in the sense that neither requires any special morphology on the verb. However, unlike their English counterparts, Korean benefactive constructions require the morpheme *cwu-*:

(2)   John-i   Mary-eykey   kheyikhu-lul   kwuwe-*cwu*-ess-ta.
      John-Nom   Mary-Dat   cake-Acc   bake Ben-Past-Dec
      John baked Mary a cake. (Oh, 2010: 415)

(Nom = nominative, Acc = accusative, Ben = benefactive, Dec = declarative, Dat = dative)

Given this morphological difference, Whong-Barr and Schwartz (2002) predicted that Korean-speaking children would demonstrate an asymmetry between goal and benefactive DOs in their acquisition of English DOs: If a matching process (like the one evident in Montrul's research) took place, learners should accept goal DOs but not benefactive DOs because the latter are morphologically different from their English counterparts. Using an oral grammaticality judgment task (GJT), Whong-Barr and Schwartz compared Korean-speaking learners' performances between the two types of DOs and found that they correctly rejected illicit benefactive DOs and not illicit goal DOs. This asymmetry was argued to be the evidence for morphological transfer.

Such findings on morphological transfer have not gone unchallenged, however, as seen in various studies (e.g. Kim, 2005; Oh, 2010; Oh & Zubizarreta, 2006). Kim, for example, tested how sensitive the judgments of learners were in cases where Korean morphologically distinguishes verb subtypes of transitives and intransitives that are not marked with bound morphemes in English (e.g. *melt, sink, open* and *close*). Kim's results indicate that Korean morphology did not make a notable impact on Korean English as a second language (ESL) learners' performance.

As to L2 acquisition of English DOs, Oh (2010) argues that Korean speakers' rejection of benefactive DOs originates from the transfer of the syntactic and associated semantic properties of Korean benefactive verbs, rather than from the morphological difference between English and Korean. More specifically, unlike English, Korean has no ditransitive benefactive verbs (but the form *cwu* can be added to virtually any verb to signal a benefactive meaning). Oh also argues that the acquisition of the semantics of goal DOs is a precondition for the acquisition of the benefactive DOs.

To summarize, researchers generally agree that the L1 plays a significant role in the acquisition of L2 argument structure. However, they differ on what and how L2 learners transfer from their L1 to an L2. The controversy comes as no surprise, given the fact that L1 transfer encompasses a wide range of phenomena (e.g. retention, avoidance, hypercorrection and simplification), and the fact that the term *morphological transfer* can refer to diverse phenomena such as either the comprehension or production of bound morphemes or the use of derivational or inflectional morphemes – or of both (Jarvis & Odlin, 2000). Therefore, further research that examines L1 influence in the domain of argument structure is necessary. This chapter accordingly focuses on the acquisition of English MCs and anticausative constructions by Chinese and Korean learners.

Grammatical Properties of Anticausative and Middle Constructions

Causative alternations in English, Korean and Chinese

The term *anticausative* refers to the intransitive use of a transitive verb where the original object (or, more technically, the patient argument) occurs as a subject (e.g. *The window broke*). Semantically, the transitive has a causative meaning (e.g. *I broke the window*) whereas the intransitive describes an inchoative situation which is conceived of as occurring without an agent, perhaps spontaneously (e.g. *The window broke*). Cross-linguistically, inchoative constructions are semantically similar, evoking a situation as occurring without an agent (Haspelmath, 1993). Morphologically speaking, however, different languages employ different grammatical devices to mark such meanings. In English, transitive and intransitive forms are often the same (as with the verb *broke* in the above examples), requiring no extra morphemes. Korean, in contrast, frequently employs affixes to mark such meanings (Cho, 1995; Kim, 2006; Son, 2006; Yeon, 2001). More specifically, there is a causative/inchoative alternation involving bound morphology, as seen in Table 7.1. In the causative type, the basic intransitive form (as in [3a]) contrasts with a transitive one derived by suffixing an *i* after the verb stem (as seen with the *i* after *nok* in [3b]). In the anticausative type, a basic transitive form (4a) contrasts with an intransitive one (having

Table 7.1 Differences between causative and anticausative types in the Korean causative alternation

Causative type	Anticausative type
(3) a. (inchoative)	(4) a. (causative)
Elum-i nok-ass-ta.	Inho-ka mwun-ul yel-ess-ta.
ice-Nom melt-Past-Dec	Inho-Nom door-Acc open-Past-Dec
The ice melted.	Inho opened the door.
b. (causative)	b. (inchoative)
Chelswu-ka elum-ul nok-**i**-ess-ta.	Mwun-i yel-**li**-ess-ta.
Chelswu-Nom ice-Acc melt-**Cau**-Past-Dec	door-Nom open-**Incho**-Past-Dec
Chelswu melted the ice.	The door opened.
(Son, 2006: 29)	(Son, 2006: 104)

dec: declarative; cau: causative; incho: inchoative.

an inchoative meaning) derived by suffixing, in the case of (4b), the form *li*. (The forms *i* and *li* and also *hi* are often analyzed as allomorphs of a morpheme represented as *hi*, but there are semantic differences associated with the varying forms.)

There is also the neutral type whose transitive and intransitive variants share the same form:

(5)   a. (causative)
      John-i   tol-ul   wumciki-ess-ta.
      John-Nom stone-Acc move-Past-Declarative
      John moved the stone.

    b. (inchoative)
      tol-i   wumciki-ess-ta
      stone-Nom move-Past-Dec
      The stone moved. (Yeon, 2001: 383)

In contrast to this class of verbs allowing transitive/intransitive alternations, there is a class of unaccusative verbs, which have non-volitional subjects, as in *nathana 'appear'*. Such unaccusatives do not take suffixes such as *i* and *li* in (3b) and (4b). Kim (2005: 37) offers the following examples:

(6)   a. thokki-ka   nathana-ss-ta
      rabbit-Nom   appear-Past-Dec
      The rabbit appeared.

    b. *thokki-ka   nathana-i-ss-ta
      rabbit-Nom   appear-Incho-Past-Dec
      *The rabbit was appeared.

In Chinese, causative alternation consists of two types. The first involves no morphological change from an alternation:

(7) a. shuishoumen   **chen**-le   chuan.
         Sailor(s)   sink--asp   boat.
         The sailors sank the boat.

     b. chuan   **chen**-le.
         boat   sink-asp.
         The boat sank.

Chinese does not mark verbs for tense, although the -*le* in the examples indicates a marker of perfective aspect (and *not* any causative meaning).

In the second type of causative construction, the intransitive verb is the base form, whereas its causative use requires the support of another causative verb, as in the compound verb *dapo* in (8b) and the periphrastic construction *shi...shiqu* in (8c). In neither type does the intransitive use require any bound morphology (He & Wang, 2002; Yang, 1999).

(8) a. beizi   **po**-le.
         cup   break-asp
         The cup broke.

     b. ta   **dapo**-le   beizi.
         he   hit-break-asp   cup.
         He broke the cup.

     c. zhongzu   dongluan   **shi**   zheli de   renmin   **shiqu**-le jiayuan.
         race   riot   made   here   people   lose-asp   family.
         The race riot made the people here lose their families.

Middle constructions in English, Chinese and Korean

Several analysts have offered typical examples of what is often termed the *middle construction*:

(9) a. This book reads easily. (Goldberg & Ackerman, 2001: 799)
     b. The pen writes fluently. (Adapted from Hoekstra & Roberts, 1993: 218)
     c. Jane discourages easily. (Yoshimura & Taylor, 2004: 311)
     d. This kind of glass breaks often. (Rapoport, 1999: 150)
     e. No Latin text translates easily for Bill. (Stroik, 1992: 131)

These examples suggest that the English MC has at least the following properties:

- The MC usually appears in the simple present tense and denotes generic events. That is, it either has a property/capacity reading (e.g. [9a]) or a habitual reading (e.g. [9d]).
- The MC takes the active form, but in the subject position is a non-agent argument (e.g. patient [9a], instrument [9b] and experiencer [9c]).
- An MC formed with an agentive verb usually involves an arbitrary agent that is semantically implicit but syntactically suppressed; however, some sentences can contain a *for somebody* prepositional phrase as in (9e), which introduces the agent of the event concerned.
- An MC generally requires the modification of certain adverbs like *easily* and *well* or other types of adjunct.

Although analyses of the semantics of the English MC do not agree on all points, two constraints are, arguably, necessary conditions. The first is a constraint involving lexical aspect. Following Vendler's (1967) classification of verbs, a considerable number of researchers propose that verbs of activity and accomplishment undergo middle formation, whereas stative and achievement verbs do not (Fagan, 1988, 1992; Klingvall, 2003; Zwart, 1997). This explains why the sentences in (9) are acceptable, but those in (10) are ill-formed.

(10)   a.   *The answer knows easily. (Hoekstra & Roberts, 1993: 194)
       b.   *Anniversaries forget easily. (Hoekstra & Roberts, 1993: 201)

Another identified constraint concerns the nominal argument which a verb takes. The standard view on the nominal subject of an MC is that it is the internal argument which is moved out of the underlying object position into the subject position for case reasons (Stroik, 1992). Thus, the nominal subject remains a patient, like the nominal subject of a passive. However, several researchers (Fagan, 1992; Gao, 2008; Oosten, 1977; van Voorst, 1988; Yushimura & Taylor, 2004) contend that the patient argument in the MC appears to play an agent-like role in the sense that the inherent properties of the nominal argument have to be construed as responsible for the occurrence of the event involved. This explains the asymmetrical behavior of *buy* and *sell*. *Sell* forms a legitimate middle, but *buy* does not, as shown in (11).

(11)   a.   The book sells well.
       b.   *The book buys well. (Yoshimura & Taylor, 2004: 298)

By this analysis, the inherent properties of a book include a capacity for it to be sold yet not to be bought. Closer scrutiny of the linguistic data nevertheless provides clear evidence that the two identified constraints are necessary, but not sufficient conditions, as shown in the sentence

English acquires easily. The verb *acquire* is an accomplishment verb, and the properties of English (e.g. phonology, lexis and syntax) may facilitate the process of acquisition. The ill-formedness of the above sentence does suggest that there may be other constraints on MC formation. In any case, the aim of the present study is to examine L1 influence, leaving the exploration of other constraints for further research.

In Chinese, sentences such as (12a) and (12b) are often regarded as MCs (Cao, 2005; Gao, 2008; Gu, 1992; Sung, 1994, 1997). (The CL indicates a noun classifier.)

(12)   a.   Zhe   ben   shu   du   *qilai*   hen   rongyi.

     This   CL   book   read   verb-particle very   easily.

     The book reads easily.

   b.   Zhe   shan   chuanghu guan   *qilai*   hen   rongyi.

     This   CL   window   close   v-particle   very   easily.

     This window closes easily.

Thus, the Chinese MC, unlike its English counterpart, is usually formed by adding a verb particle *qilai* to the main verb (Cao, 2005; Sung, 1994, 1997). This particle consists of two morphemes, the literal meanings of which are 'up' (*qi*) and 'come' (*lai*), respectively. As a verb particle, its basic meaning is *upward* (He, 2004; Sung, 1994, 1997). In addition, *qilai* is used to denote the initiation and/or the continuation of an action (He, 2004; Smith, 1991; Sung, 1994; Yang, 1995). The function of *qilai* as a marker of MCs was proposed by Sung (1994: 62), who claimed that the particle has become an overt middle morpheme that 'gives the verb a non-eventive generic reading usually reflected in other languages by the middle construction'.

As to the semantic constraints, the Chinese MC is also sensitive to aspectual restrictions: thus, stative verbs and achievement verbs do not occur in Chinese MCs, as seen in the ungrammaticality of (13).

(13)   a.   *Haolaiwu   dapian   xihua *qilai*   hen   rongyi.

     Hollywood   blockbuster   like v-particle   very   easily.

     *Hollywood blockbusters like easily.

   b.   *Shanding   dao   *qilai*   hen   rongyi.

     Mountaintop   reach   v-particle   very   easily.

     *The mountaintop reaches very easily.

Another significant area of contrast between English and Chinese involves psych verbs, which often do not have identical semantic properties in the two languages. The state of being frightened can be expressed in an

MC in English but not in Chinese. In a generative analysis from the 1990s, Chinese and English are said to encode different event structures in such cases. Juffs (1996), expanding on an analysis of Pinker (1989), proposed that psych verbs in Chinese, unlike their English counterparts, do not allow a lexical conceptual structure [ACT (+effect) [GO [STATE]]] to be realized in a verb root. In Juffs' analysis, psych verbs in Chinese are intransitive verbs denoting only a state or result. In other words, Chinese psych verbs are stative or achievement verbs; consequently, verbs such as *jingxia* cannot undergo MC formation, as seen here:

(14) *Zhe   ge   xiao   hai   jingxia *qilai*   hen   rongyi.
      This   CL   little   child   scare v-particle   very   easily.

      This little child scares very easily.

A different cross-linguistic contrast involving psychological predicates is evident in the base forms of some Chinese perception verbs (verbs denoting sight, sound, touch, taste and smell), which Lin (2004) considers as activity verbs whose English counterparts are achievement verbs; examples include *kan* 'see' and *ting* 'hear'. Consequently, these verbs can function as MCs in Chinese, but not in English:

(15) Eiffel ta   cong zhe   ge   chuanghu   kan *qilai*   hen   qingxi.
      Eiffel Tower   from this   CL   window   perceive v-particle   very   clear.

      *The Eiffel Tower sees clearly from this window.

Still another difference between English and Chinese is that responsibility shifts do not impose any restriction on a Chinese MC, as in (14); a clear view of the Eiffel Tower cannot be attributed to the properties of the tower itself, but to the position the viewer takes. The above examples suggest that the Chinese MC does not necessarily predicate properties over the nominal subject. In turn, the nominal subject need not be responsible for the occurrence of the event concerned.

Unlike English and Chinese, Korean has no real MC, and the MC-like structures in Korean are actually passives (Cho, 1995; Kim, 2006). The closest approximations to real MCs can be classified, according to Cho (1995), into two types: K1 and K2. K1 refers to a construction formed with verbs undergoing causative alternation between a neutral default and a causative reading. When these verbs semantically correspond to the genuine MCs of other languages, no bound morphology is required. On the other hand, the K2-type represents the pseudo-MC (PMC) formed with verbs of an anticausative/inchoative bound morpheme such as *li* (as seen in [4b]). Sentence (15a) represents the K1 construction and (15b) the K2.

K1 type:

(16)   a.   cha-ka   cal   wumciki-n-ta
            car-Nom   well   move-Pres-Dec
            The car moves well. (Cho, 1995: 58)

K2 type (PMC)

       b.   chayk-i   cal   phal-*li*-n-ta
            book-Nom   well   sell-PMC-Pres-Dec
            The book sells well. (Cho, 1995: 59)

Due to an animacy constraint on the sentence subject in Korean, inanimate entities cannot easily occur in the subject position (Kim, 2006). Certain constructions do, however, resemble English MCs as when an instrument is the subject. The following example shows that such a pattern requires two morphological changes: the instrument is marked with the topic marker *nun*, and the main verb takes a PMC/passive form marker *li*.

(17)   a.   I   ppaltay-*nun*   cal   ppal-*li*-n-ta
            this   straw-TOP   well   suck-PMC-Pres-Dec
            This straw sucks well. = This drinking straw works well. (Cho, 1995: 55)

It is clear that Korean PMCs demonstrate different morphological patterns. The K1 pattern involves no change, whereas the K2 requires overt marking. In the K2, the subject still takes the nominative case, but a PMC/passive morpheme is suffixed to the verb. In the final pattern discussed, PMCs with an instrument as the subject, two morphological alterations from the default pattern are required: the subject takes the topic marker *nun*, and the PMC/passive morpheme is suffixed to the verb.

The Present Study

Research hypotheses

As seen in the preceding section, neither Chinese nor Korean closely resembles English with regard to anticausative constructions and MCs. From the perspective of L1 transfer, the challenges for Chinese learners are diverse. On the one hand, they have to realize that in English, unlike in Chinese, the MC requires no morphological marking of MCs. If learners use L1 morphological marking as their reference point for understanding the L2, they might judge English MCs to be aberrant and so not use them. On the other hand, they need to learn that English psych verbs can be used in MCs whereas perception verbs cannot. With regard to the anticausative construction, a different problem involving morphology arises, in this case, one involving contrasts between Korean and English. Chinese learners appear to have no trouble in this domain since neither Chinese nor English anticausatives require morphological marking. Korean learners, on the other hand, may experience difficulty with English anticausatives because Korean verbs of this type require a PMC marker such as *li*. This analysis of contrastive challenges thus leads to the following hypotheses:

> *Hypothesis 1 (H1): Chinese learners will judge legitimate English MCs of different types as equally ungrammatical. Korean learners, by contrast, will be more inclined to accept English MCs whose Korean counterparts correspond to the K1 type. English MCs that correspond to the K2 type are likely to be judged as ungrammatical, especially when they have an instrumental meaning coded in the syntactic subject.*
>
> *Hypothesis 2 (H2): Chinese learners are more likely to reject English MCs formed with psych verbs than other types. However, Chinese learners are less likely to reject MCs formed with perception verbs than other types. By contrast, Korean learners' judgments of all types of illicit MCs will be similar.*
>
> *Hypothesis 3 (H3): Chinese learners will not passivize anticausative verbs. Korean learners, by contrast, will tend to passivize those whose Korean counterparts are formed with anticausative verbs.*

Participants

The participants in this study were 30 Chinese learners of English, 16 Korean learners of English and 24 native speakers of English. The Chinese were freshmen majoring in English in a university in northwestern China. The Koreans were new arrivals in an ESL program in British Columbia, Canada, where they were preparing to enter a local university. These learners had studied English in high school in South Korea before coming to Canada. Of the 24 native speakers of English recruited as controls, 19 were either students or staff members at a university in British Columbia, and the rest (four from the United States and one from Britain) were teachers of English in a college in northwestern China.

Instruments

A GJT and a forced-choice task (FCT) were developed to elicit L2 learners' data. In the GJT, the participants were asked to judge the acceptability of a total of 106 sentences. Their responses were measured on a 5-point Likert scale ranging from –2 (totally unacceptable) to +2 (completely acceptable), with –1 (mostly unacceptable), 0 (sounds odd but acceptable) and 1 (mostly acceptable) in between. The order of sentence presentation was randomized so that sentences of a similar type would not appear sequentially.

Of the 106 sentences, 64 were the target items (i.e. MCs and other structures referred to in H1–H3). The rest were fillers consisting of a variety of English structures such as expletive, compound and adjectival patterns, as well as complex sentence structures. They were included to increase the structural diversity of the test items, which, in turn, would help to disguise the target sentences. Each target item belonged to one of the types or subtypes exemplified in Table 7.2. To test L2 learners' judgments of illicit MCs formed with stative verbs and achievement verbs, 16 MC-like sentences were created. These sentences were further divided into four categories: STA, PSYSUB, ACH and PER. The first two groups are illicit MCs formed with stative verbs whereas the last two groups represent MCs formed with achievement verbs. STA stands for MCs formed with three cognition verbs (verbs involving mental or cognitive processes, e.g. *know*) and one possession verb (i.e. *own*). PSYSUB refers to MCs formed with psych verbs with a subject experiencer (e.g. *like*). PER refers to MCs formed with perception verbs (e.g. *hear*) whose Chinese counterparts undergo MC formation. ACH stands for achievement verbs (e.g. *reach*).

Table 7.2 shows subcategories of the types just described, which are represented by 16 sentences. Four MCs formed with agentive verbs are put in the category of AGENT, another four MCs formed with psych verbs of object experiencer are in the category of PSYOBJ; still another four are MCs whose nominal subject refers to an instrument (INSTR). The remaining four are MCs formed with verbs undergoing causative alternation. They are further divided into K1CAU and K2CAU, where the former represents MCs formed with verbs whose Korean counterparts are K1 causative verbs; and the latter represents MCs formed with verbs whose Korean counterparts are K2 anticausative verbs.

The FCT was adapted from Ju (2000) and Kondo (2005) to investigate the effect of context, argument type and L1 morphology on L2 passivization of English inchoative sentences. In the FCT, each test item consisted of two sentences. The participants were asked to indicate which form in the second sentence was more grammatical, the active or the passive. The first sentence set a context for the event that the second sentence described, as

Table 7.2 Types and tokens of MCs in the GJT

Type	Token
AGENT	The book reads well.
PSYOBJ	John frightens easily.
INSTR	The knife cuts well.
K1CAU	Chocolate ice-cream melts quickly.
K2CAU	The window opens easily.
STA	*The answer knows easily.
ACH	*The top of the mountain reaches with difficulty
PSYSUB	*Hollywood blockbusters like easily.
PER	*The Eiffel Tower sees clearly from the window.

seen in Example (17a); Example (17b) varies slightly in that the adverbial clause at the beginning (*As I walked through the automatic door*) establishes the context for the main clause that follows. In both cases, the context was provided to indicate that the event occurs without involvement of a volitional agent, which would facilitate the participants' selection of the active form. The FCT consisted of 68 test items, of which 30 were target items and the rest were fillers. The target sentences relevant to the present study were categorized into three groups: INTR, CAU and ANTICAU. INTR represents five sentences formed with intransitive unaccusative verbs which cannot undergo transitive alternation (e.g. *disappear*). The remaining five were formed with verbs capable of undergoing transitive alternation, which were further divided into two types. The first (henceforth CAU) consisted of English verb tokens whose Korean counterparts are causative (e.g. *freeze* 'el-ta'), while the second (henceforth ANTICAU) consisted of English verb tokens whose Korean counterparts are anticausative (e.g. *open* 'yul-**li**-ta').

(18) a. A car slid off the road and into the lake. Shortly after, the car (disappeared/ was disappeared).

   b. As I walked through the automatic door, the door (closed/was closed) immediately.

Results

This section will first consider the results from the GJT to evaluate the first two hypotheses, and then the focus will shift to the results from the FCT to evaluate H3. Table 7.3 presents the means and standard deviations of the participants on their judgment of English MCs. It can be seen that Chinese learners' ratings of the five types of legitimate

Table 7.3 Means and standard deviations of the GJT performance

	Chinese (n = 30) means/SD	Korean (n = 16) means/SD	English (n = 24) means/SD
AGENT	0.2583/1.0494	−0.6562/1.1434	1.1563/0.6115
PSYOBJ	0.491/0.492	0.2344/1.0144	0.990/0.898
INSTR	0.8167/0.8904	0.3594/1.0205	1.4792/0.3721
K1CAU	0.833/0.864	1.625/0.466	1.875/0.304
K2CAU	0.583/0.777	0.281/1.140	1.771/0.329
STA	0.0583/0.6813	−1.000/0.7853	−1.656/0.3745
ACH	0.1333/0.5443	−0.6563/0.6447	−1.313/0.4848
PSYSUB	−0.0417/0.7908	−0.6563/0.6447	−1.6354/0.4543
PER	−0.0667/0.8855	−0.9063/0.8004	−1.500/0.5265

MC are not uniform. They did rate AGENT items much the same as they did PSYOBJ and K2CAU items, judging all three types marginally acceptable (mean = 0.2583, 0.491, 0.583 for AGENT, PSYOBJ and K2CAU, respectively). However, they rated K1CAU much the same as they rated INSTR, judging both almost acceptable (mean = 0.833, 0.8167 for K1CAU and INSTR, respectively). In contrast, the Korean learners judged AGENT unacceptable (mean = −0.6562), whereas they rated PSYOBJ, INSTR and K2CAU almost the same, judging them marginally acceptable (mean = 0.2344, 3594, 0.281 for PSYOBJ, INSTR and K2CAU, respectively). They rated K1CAU the highest, judging it acceptable (mean = 1.625). In contrast to both English as a foreign language (EFL) learner groups, the native speakers of English usually accepted all types of legitimate MCs, rating K1CAU and K2CAU the highest, PSYSUB the lowest and AGENT and INSTR in between.

The results of one-way ANOVAs (in a repeated measures design) revealed that the difference in performance between the five MC types was significant for all participant groups ($F = 2.893$, $p = 0.025$ for the Chinese; $F = 15.701$, $p = 0.000$ for the Korean; and $F = 11.307$, $p = 0.000$ for the English participants). Follow-up pairwise comparisons (Table 7.4) showed that Chinese learners rated INSTR and K1CAU significantly higher than AGENT, which cannot be attributed to any effect of L1 morphology. In addition, although their performance between PSYOBJ, AGENT and K2CAU was not significantly different, the fact that they rated PSYOBJ numerically higher than AGENT suggests that they did *not* transfer L1 semantics into L2.

Korean learners' performance, on the other hand, presents a mixed picture about L1 influence. The pairwise comparisons showed that they rated K1CAU significantly higher than the other types, indicating that they

Table 7.4 Mean differences of the participants' performance on legitimate MCs

	Chinese	Korean	English
AGENT vs. PSYOBJ	−0.233	−0.891**	0.167
AGENT vs. INSTR	−0.558**	−1.016***	−0.323*
AGENT vs. K1CAU	−0.575*	−2.281***	−0.615***
AGENT vs. K2CAU	−0.325	−0.938*	−0.719***
PSYOBJ vs. INSTR	−0.325	−0.125	−0.490*
PSYOBJ vs. K1CAU	−0.342	−1.391***	−0.781***
PSYOBJ vs. K2CAU	−0.0917	−0.0469	−0.885***
INSTR vs. K1CAU	−0.0167	−1.266***	−0.292*
INSTR vs. K2CAU	0.233	−0.0781	−0.396**
K1CAU vs. K2CAU	0.250	1.344***	0.104

*** $p < 0.001$, ** $p < 0.01$, * $p < 0.05$.

were most accurate with this type, a finding which supports H1. However, contrary to the same hypothesis, INSTR was rated significantly higher than AGENT. As for the English-speaking participants, they showed themselves more disposed to favorable ratings of K1CAU and K2CAU than of INSTR, but more so for INSTR than for AGENT and PSYOBJ. Nevertheless, their ratings of K1CAU and K2CAU did not differ significantly, nor did their ratings of AGENT and PSYOBJ.

With regard to the illicit MCs, no significant difference was found between the four types in the judgments of the Chinese and Korean participants (F (3, 29) = 0.737, p = 0.533 for the Chinese; and F (3, 15) = 1.976, p = 0.131 for the Korean participants). As the bottom four rows of Table 7.3 indicate, all participant groups were reluctant to accept the illicit MCs. More specifically, the Chinese group's mean scores for PSYSUB, PER, STA and ACH are around zero, showing that they were not certain about their grammaticality. In addition, their similar performance with the four types suggests that PER, whose Chinese counterparts are grammatical, did not create extra difficulties for the Chinese learners (i.e. the spurious correspondence between an ungrammatical English pattern and a grammatical Chinese pattern did not lead to many false positive judgments). Therefore, the prediction in H2 that Chinese participants would transfer L1 semantics to L2 was not borne out, and the similar prediction of H2 about Korean learners is not fully supported either since one significant difference emerged between the rating of stative and achievement verbs (Table 7.5). However, unlike the two learner groups, the native speaker participants rated the four types of MCs very differently. One-way ANOVAs (repeated measures) revealed that they tend to judge more favorably, for example, the MCs formed with achievement verbs than those with stative verbs (Table 7.5).

To summarize, the findings from the GJT do not provide strong support for the first two hypotheses, except in the case of Korean learners' higher ratings of K1CAU than of other types.

Table 7.5 Mean differences of the participants' performance on illicit MCs

	Chinese	Korean	English
STA vs. PSYSUB	0.100	−0.344	−0.0208
STA vs. ACH	−0.0750	−0.344*	−0.344***
STA vs. PER	0.125	−0.0938	−0.156*
PSYSUB vs. ACH	−0.175	0.000	−0.323***
PSYSUB vs. PER	0.0250	0.250	−0.135*
ACH vs. PER	0.200	0.250	0.188

*** $p < 0.001$, ** $p < 0.01$, * $p < 0.05$.

Table 7.6 Means and standard deviation obtained by the participants in FCT

	Chinese mean (%)/SD	Korean mean (%)/SD	English mean (%)/SD
INTR	0.1714/0.2028	0.2000/0.2733	0.0000/0.000
CAU	0.0714/0.1793	0.6875/0.2500	0.0416/0.1412
ANTICAU	0.4871/0.2474	0.6249/0.3415	0.1513/0.1941

Table 7.6 presents the results from the FCT. As described above, participants were required to choose between a passive and an active form in this task. If they selected the passive option, a score of one point was assigned, whereas no point was assigned if they selected the active form. The raw scores were transformed into percentages to show the extent of their passivization. Table 7.6 shows that both learner groups differed considerably from the native speaker group in passivizing non-alternating verbs such as *appear*. Clearly, this does not support H3, which predicts that both Chinese and Korean learners would correctly use non-alternating unaccusative verbs.

Discussion

Taken together, the findings offer no strong support for any of the assertions in the three hypotheses with regard to language transfer. Although Korean learners most accurately judged GJT items of the K1CAU type (thus supporting H1), their performance on other items suggests that various factors besides the L1 influenced their judgments. Moreover, the FCT results did not demonstrate significant differences in Korean speakers' performance on verbs corresponding to the causative or anticausative categories in their native language (H3). While the Chinese participants did not reject English MCs as emphatically as the Koreans did, their judgments are not consistent with the transfer predictions in H2, including in cases with sentences corresponding to the putative middle marker *qilai*. Furthermore, even though psych verbs are not allowed to undergo MC formation in Chinese, the Chinese participants marginally accepted examples of the PSYOBJ subtype, rating items in this category even higher than those in AGENT. In addition, their uniform performance on four types of illicit MCs suggests that the PER category does not pose an extra challenge for Chinese learners, despite the fact that perception verbs can appear in MCs in Chinese.

Despite the evidence raising doubts about transfer, there were some intriguing differences between the Chinese and Korean participants. First of all, Chinese learners were more inclined than Korean learners to overgeneralize in the GJT. As noted above, they judged illicit MCs either marginally acceptable or only a little unacceptable, whereas Korean learners rejected them with greater certainty. Secondly, Chinese learners were more accurate than Korean learners in their judgment of AGENT and INSTR items. They tended to rate INSTR and AGENT sentences as marginally acceptable. By contrast, Korean learners judged INSTR marginally acceptable but strongly rejected AGENT items. These dissimilarities in group performances suggest that some sort of L1 knowledge influences their judgments of L2 items, but the forms and meanings of the L1 do not play the straightforward role that could be inferred if H1–H3 had been fully supported. The discussion will now examine more closely these systematic differences and explore what role L1 knowledge may have played, especially in relation to two questions:

(1) why Chinese learners were more inclined than Korean learners to overgeneralize on the GJT;
(2) why Korean learners performed better on PSYOBJ and INSTR than on AGENT items.

With regard to the first question, an observation by Gass (1996: 321) seems relevant: 'L1 influences occur not only as direct linguistic reflexes, but they also indirectly reflect underlying organizational principles of language'. In the case of the English MC, a typological explanation seems plausible. It is widely acknowledged that restrictions on the sentence subject category vary a great deal across languages. In Chinese, the relationship between the subject and the predicate is not the actor-versus-action relationship, but a topic–comment relationship (Chao, 1968; Li & Thompson, 1981, Li & Yang, Chapter 6 in this volume). Accordingly, Chinese is less restricted than English and Korean in subject selection. It does not require the subject to take responsibility for the occurrence of the action concerned (as in Example 14, *Eiffel ta cong zhe ge chuanghu kan qilai hen qingxi.* *'The Eiffel Tower sees clear from this window'). Indeed, patient-as-subject structures (e.g. *This book reads easily*) are much more common in Chinese than in English. In English, the subject need not be animate, but it has to be somewhat responsible for the event occurring, and so responsibility figures more prominently than animacy (Lakoff, 1977; van Voorst, 1988). Compared with Chinese or English, Korean is much more restrictive, since it is animacy rather than responsibility that figures importantly in determining whether an argument can be the sentence subject (Kim, 2006). When encoding the situation in which an inanimate object takes responsibility for the occurrence of an event, there is a hierarchy of causal factors, as in the following examples where the material – and inanimate – causes of the events (the liquor in [18a] and the hammer in [18b]) are *not* coded as subjects.

(19) a. Sul-ttaemue   ku-ka   cu-ess-ta
          Liquor-because   he-Nom   die-Past-Dec
          Due to liquor, he died.

      b. (nukunka-ka)   mangchi-lo   youlichang-ul   kka-ess-ta
          (Someone-Nom)   hammer-with   window-Acc   break-Past-Dec
          Someone broke the window with the hammer.

(Adapted from Kim, 2006: 120–121)

The different degrees of conservatism demonstrated in the Chinese and Korean groups' performance on the GJT can therefore be attributed to the different restrictions on the subject position in their L1.

With regard to the second question, why Korean learners performed better on PSYOBJ and INSTR than on AGENT items, there is something of a paradox. It might seem plausible to expect that there would be more negative judgments of INSTR items if learners consistently searched for morphemes in the L2 sentences that corresponded in one way or another to L1 morphemes (as Montrul found, for example, in the way that Spanish speakers rated English MCs as discussed earlier). Nevertheless, the Koreans showed more accurate judgments of INSTR than of AGENT items. This performance may be explained in terms of responsibility since instruments can 'do' things (as in the example *The knife cuts well*) and can thus be seen as responsible for the occurrence of an event. It might be this conceptualization of an instrument as the material cause that led the Koreans to rate INSTR marginally acceptable. In the case of their better performance on PSYOBJ than on AGENT, it is plausible that Korean learners transferred an animacy constraint on subjects to their L2. In other words, the animate nature of the subject in MCs formed with PSYOBJ (e.g. *John frightens easily*) may make MCs of this type more acceptable. By contrast, the nominal subject in MCs formed with agentive verbs does not show the property of animacy (e.g. *The bread cuts easily*), nor can it be conceptualized as a doer of an action.

The complex pattern of results in this study probably owes something to the fact that two different tests were used, i.e. the GJT and the FCT. It should be noted that the FCT was a productive task in which the participants' attention was likely drawn to the functions of the structures because of the contextual frame provided. Therefore, choosing between active and passive forms may have prompted more reflection on discourse as well as semantics, with cross-linguistic differences in formal patterning less of a concern. The GJT, on the other hand, tested the participants' grammatical knowledge in a decontextualized situation in which they were more likely to pay greater attention to the formal aspects of a sentence.

To conclude, the overall findings suggest that transfer may sometimes reflect the underlying organizational principles of specific languages. The performance of Korean learners suggests an influence of an animacy constraint on subjects in their L1, whereas the performance of Chinese learners may reflect more lenient restrictions on subjecthood in Chinese. In general, the Korean learners were more conservative than the Chinese learners in their judgments of English MCs and in their selection of active verb forms in the FCT. The present study indicates that L1 morphology interacts with other considerations, and its effect on L2 learners is restricted by a number of factors which transcend patterns of formal similarity and dissimilarity between the L1 and the L2.

Note

(1) Funding for the present study was provided in part by a grant to the author from the Ministry of Education of the People's Republic of China for social sciences and humanities (09XJC740009) and a grant for Research Enhancement Projects for Young Researchers by Northwest Normal University (SKQNGG11026).

References

Cao, H. (2005) On the semantic characteristics of middle constructions in Mandarin Chinese language. *Studies of the Chinese Language* 2005, 205–213.

Chao, Y. (1968) *A Grammar of Spoken Chinese.* Berkeley, CA: University of California Press.

Cho, S.D. (1995) On verbal intransitivity in Korean: With special reference to middle construction. Unpublished doctoral dissertation, University of Hawaii.

Fagan, S. (1988) The English middle. *Linguistic Inquiry* 19, 181–203.

Fagan, S. (1992) *The Syntax and Semantics of Middle Constructions: A Study With Special Reference to German.* Cambridge: Cambridge University Press.

Gao, Y.S. (2008) L2 acquisition of English MC and its related structures by Chinese and Korean learners: Towards an event structure-based account. Unpublished PhD dissertation, Guangdong University of Foreign Studies.

Gass, S.M. (1996) Second language acquisition and linguistic theory: The role of language transfer. In W.C. Ritchie and T.K. Bhatia (eds) *Handbook of Second Language Acquisition* (pp. 317–345). San Diego, CA: Academic Press.

Goldberg, A.E. and Ackerman, F. (2001) The pragmatics of obligatory adjunct. *Language* 77, 798–814.

Gu, Y. (1992) The syntax of resultative and causative compounds in Chinese. Unpublished doctoral dissertation, Cornell University.

Hale, K. and Keyser, S.J. (1993) On argument structure and the lexical expression of syntactic relations. In K. Hale and S.J. Keyser (eds) *The View from Building 20: Essays in Linguistics in Honor of Sylvain Bromberger* (pp. 53–109). Cambridge, MA: MIT Press.

Haspelmath, M. (1993) More on the typology of inchoative/causative verb alternations. In B. Comrie and M. Polinsky (eds) *Causatives and Transitivity* (pp. 87–120). Amsterdam: John Benjamins.

He, Y. (2004) Semantic types of verb-direction construction 'V+qilai' and their syntactic features. *Studies in Linguistics* 24, 23–31.

He, Y.J. and Wang, L.L. (2002) The syntax of causatives in Chinese. *Chinese Language Learning* 2002 (04), 1–9.

Hoekstra, T. and Roberts, I. (1993) Middle constructions in Dutch and English. In E. Reuland and W. Abraham (eds) *Knowledge and Language. Vol. 2. Lexical and Conceptual Structure* (pp. 183–220). Dordrecht: Kluwer.

Inagaki, S. (2001) Motion verbs with goal PPs in the L2 acquisition of English and Japanese. *Studies in Second Language Acquisition* 23, 153–170.

Jarvis, S. and Odlin, T. (2000) Morphological type, spatial reference, and language transfer. *Studies in Second Language Acquisition* 22, 535–556.

Ju, M.K. (2000) Overpassivization errors by second language learners: The effect of conceptualizable agents in discourse. *Studies in Second Language Acquisition* 22, 85–111.

Juffs, A. (1996) *Learnability and the Lexicon: Theories and Second Language Acquisition Research*. Amsterdam: John Benjamins.

Juffs, A. (1998) Some effects of first language argument structure and morphosyntax on second language sentence processing. *Second Language Research* 14, 406–424.

Kim, J.Y. (2005) L2 acquisition of transitivity alternations and of the entailment relations for causatives by Korean speakers of English and English speakers of Korean. Unpublished doctoral dissertation, University of Hawaii.

Kim, K. (2006) Transitivity in English and Korean: A contrastive analysis with pedagogical implications. Unpublished doctoral dissertation, Ball State University.

Klingvall, E. (2003) Aspectual properties of the English middle construction. *The Department of English in Lund: Working Papers in Linguistics* 3.

Kondo, T. (2005) Overpassivization in second language acquisition. *International Review of Applied Linguistics in Language Teaching* 43, 129–161.

Lakoff, G. (1977) Linguistic gestalts. In W.A. Beach and S.E. Fox (eds) *Papers from the 13th Regional Meeting of the Chicago Linguistic Society* (pp. 236–286). Chicago: Chicago Linguistic Society.

Levin, B. and Rappaport, M. (1995) *Unaccusativity: At the Syntax–Lexical Semantics Interface*. Cambridge, MA: MIT Press.

Levin, B. and Rappaport, M. (2005) *Argument Realization*. Cambridge: Cambridge University Press.

Li, C. and Thompson, S. (1981) *Mandarin Chinese: A Functional Reference Grammar.* Berkeley and Los Angeles, CA: University of California Press.

Lin, J. (2004) Event structure and the encoding of arguments: The syntax of the Mandarin and English verb phrases. Unpublished doctoral dissertation, MIT.

Montrul, S. (1997) Transitivity alternation in second language acquisition: A crosslinguistic study of English, Spanish and Turkish. Unpublished doctoral dissertation, McGill University.

Montrul, S. (2000) Transitivity alternations in L2 acquisition: Toward a modular view of transfer. *Studies in Second Language Acquisition* 22, 229–273.

Montrul, S. (2001a) Causatives and transitivity in L2 English. *Language Learning* 51, 51–106.

Montrul, S. (2001b) First-language constrained variability in the second language acquisition of argument-structure-changing morphology with causative verbs. *Second Language Research* 17, 144–194.

Oh, E. (2009) Transfer of morphology revisited. *Language and Linguistics* 44, 127–160.

Oh, E. (2010) Recovery from first-language transfer: The second language acquisition of English double objects by Korean speakers. *Second Language Research* 26, 407–439.

Oh, E. and Zubizarreta, M.L. (2006) Against morphological transfer. In K.U. Deen, J. Nomura, B. Schulz and B.D. Schwartz (eds) *Proceedings of the Inaugural Conference on Generative Approaches to Language Acquisition: North America. University of Connecticut Occasional Papers in Linguistics 4* (pp. 261–272). Cambridge, MA: MITWPL.

Oosten, J. (1977) Subject and agenthood in English. In W.A. Beach, S.E. Fox, S. Philosoph (eds) *Papers from the 13th Regional Meeting of the Chicago Linguistic Society* (pp. 459–471) Chicago: Chicago Linguistic Society.

Pinker, S. (1989) *Learnability and Cognition: The Acquisition of Argument Structure.* Cambridge, MA: MIT Press.

Rapoport, T.R. (1999) The middle, agents, and for-phrases. *Linguistic Inquiry* 30, 147–155.

Smith, C.S. (1991) *The Parameter of Aspect.* Dordrecht: Kluwer.

Son, M. (2006) Causation and syntactic decomposition of events. Unpublished doctoral dissertation, University of Delaware.

Stroik, T. (1992) Middles and movement. *Linguistic Inquiry* 23, 127–137.

Sung, K. (1994) Case assignment under incorporation. Unpublished doctoral dissertation, University of California.

Sung, K. (1997) *An Introduction to Syntax.* Beijing: Social Science Press.

van Voorst, J.V. (1988) *Event Structure.* Amsterdam: John Benjamins.

Vendler, Z. (1967) *Linguistics and Philosophy.* Ithaca, NY: Cornell University Press.

White, L. (1991) Argument structure in second language acquisition. *French Language Studies* 1, 189–207.

Whong-Barr, M. and Schwartz, B.D. (2002) Morphological and syntactic transfer in child L2 acquisition of the English dative alternation. *Studies in Second Language Acquisition* 24, 579–616.

Yang, S. (1995) The aspectual system of Chinese. Unpublished doctoral dissertation, University of Victoria.

Yang, S. (1999) The unaccusative phenomenon—A study on the relationship between syntax and semantics. *Contemporary Linguistics* 1, 30–43.

Yeon, J. (2001) Transitivity alternation and neutral-verbs in Korean. *Bulletin of the School of Oriental and African Studies, University of London* 64, 381–391.

Yoshimura, K. and Taylor, J.R. (2004) What makes a good middle? The role of qualia in the interpretation and acceptability of middle expressions in English. *English Language and Linguistics* 8, 293–321.

Zwart, J.W. (1997) On the relevance of aspect for middle formation. Unpublished manuscript, University of Groningen.

8 The Role of L1 in the Acquisition of Chinese Causative Constructions by English-Speaking Learners

Hui Chang and Lina Zheng

Introduction[1]

In recent years, the acquisition of argument structure has generated much interest in second language (L2) acquisition (see also Chapter 7), especially problems involving the relation between syntax and semantics in interlanguage. One area of special concern is the acquisition of causative constructions, which are the linguistic representations of causality, as in *The story makes me very sad*. Causative constructions denote events in which the causer (e.g. the story) performs or at least initiates something, and the caused events in which the causee (e.g. me) carries out an action or undergoes a change of condition or state (e.g. sad) as a result of the causer's action (Comrie, 1989: 165–166). Thus, the causing events serve as the external factors of the change, while the caused events are the outcomes. The causative constructions can be formalized as [*x* ACT] CAUSE [*y* BECOME <STATE>].

Causative constructions in Chinese are normally formed syntactically with the help of causative light verbs, or lexically with compound causative verbs (examples of which will be given in the next section).[2] In contrast, English causative constructions are normally formed either with bound morphemes which function as causative affixes (e.g. the –*fy* in *simplify*) or with causative light verbs (e.g. *They make somebody do something*). In general, Chinese has a wide variety of constructions to express the corresponding English causative constructions. With this cross-linguistic contrast in mind, our chapter investigates the role of transfer in English-speaking learners' acquisition of Chinese causative constructions.

The chapter is organized as follows: the next section provides a cross-linguistic analysis of Chinese and English causative constructions within the theoretical framework of the minimalist program (Chomsky, 1995), after which there is a review of studies on the L2 acquisition of causative constructions. The focus then turns to an empirical study on the acquisition of Chinese causative constructions by English-speaking learners, and the results are considered with special attention to the evidence for first language (L1) English influence.

A Cross-Linguistic Analysis of Causative Constructions

Causative verbs can be classified into four categories according to their morphological features: causative light verbs, affixed causative verbs, converted causative verbs and compound causative verbs. Causative light verbs, such as *make*, *let* and *cause* in English, and *shi* (make), *rang* (let), *ling* (make) and *jiao* (make) in Chinese, are free morphemes having a special syntactic status that will be discussed shortly.[3] Affixed causative verbs, the second category, include words having bound morphemes as in *enlarge*, *modernize* and *purify* in English and *jinghua* (purify) and *meihua* (beautify) in Chinese; such verbs express causation with prefixes or suffixes. Converted causative verbs, the third category, are free morphemes converted (or zero-derived) from nouns or adjectives, as with *surprise* and *empty* in English and *fengfu* (rich) and *chongshi* (full) in Chinese. The fourth category, compound causative verbs, is a quite common pattern in Chinese, but not in English. Compound causatives consist of two parts, the first being the verb initiating actions, which appears earlier in the clause and denotes the cause, and the second part expressing the change of state. The focus in compound causative verbs is on the second part. For example, in the verb *dasui* (break), the first morpheme *da* (hit or beat) is a verb initiating an action, and the second morpheme *sui* (broken) is the result of the action *da*. In this compound causative, it is *sui* (the resulting broken state) rather than *da* (the causing action) that is emphasized.

As noted above, causative light verbs have a special syntactic status in that they form an integral part of periphrastic causative constructions as in (1) and (2).

(1)   *Laoshi*   *rang*   *ta*   *dasao*   *jiaoshi*.
      teacher   let   him   clean   classroom
      The teacher lets him clean the classroom.

(2)   *Zhe-ge*   *gushi*   *shi*   *wo*   *hen*   *nanguo*.
      this-CL   story   make   me   very   sad
      This story makes me very sad. (CL = noun classifier)

In periphrastic causative constructions, the determiner phrase (DP) before the light verb is the causer (e.g. *Zhe-ge gushi*), while the part after denotes the causee and the action that the causee does or the state that the causee is in. Even if the DP before a light verb denotes a person or persons, it functions only as the causer, not necessarily as the agent. Thus, this pattern has the syntactic form [DP v_{cause} DP VP (AdjP)]. English and Chinese correspond closely in this regard, as seen in the close cross-linguistic parallels in (1) and (2) The structural specifics of a minimalist analysis are evident in the tree diagram of (1) in Example (3). Here, TP refers to the tense phrase, vP is the phrase headed by light verbs and VP refers to the verbal phrase.

(3)

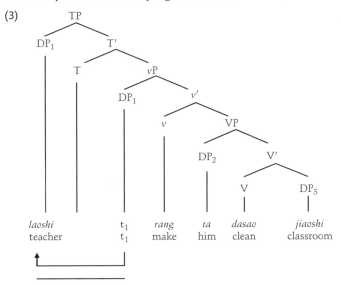

In the syntactic derivation of periphrastic constructions, DP_1 is base-generated in the specifier of vP and raises to the specifier of TP as the subject of the sentence in the course of the syntactic derivation of the periphrastic construction. The overt causative verb is base-generated and remains in the head position of vP because of the weak verbal feature of Chinese and English T. Since the causative light verb is phonologically overt, it cannot trigger the raising of VP, and as a result, VP remains in situ.

Affixed causative verbs typically pattern as in (4).

(4) *Gongren*   *jinghua*   *shui.*
     worker   purify   water
     The worker purifies water.

While English has a rather large repertory of affixed causative verbs, Chinese is morphologically impoverished, having few affixed causative verbs. Although there is a causative suffix *hua* in Chinese, which is similar to English causative affixes *en-, -en, -ize* and *-fy*, its application is restricted to a handful of adjectives and nouns. Furthermore, in contrast to English pairs such as *sad/sadden*, Chinese *-hua* cannot be added to psyche adjectives; for instance, the adjectives *gaoxing* (glad or happy) and *beishang* (sad) cannot be combined with *hua* into *gaoxinghua* or *beishanghua*.

Although the examples given so far might suggest that the syntactic and morphological correspondences between Chinese and English are usually straightforward, this is not always the case. Another common pattern in Chinese shows the *-hua* suffix in a *ba*-construction[4] as in (5), where the object of the causative *jinghua* is placed in the preverbal position along with the free morpheme *ba*.

(5) *Gongren*   *ba*   *shui*   *jinghua*.
     worker   ba   water   purify
     The worker purifies water.

When English affixed verbs such as *frighten* do not have morphologically close counterparts in Chinese, the corresponding Chinese can be a periphrastic construction (6a), a *ba*-construction (6b) or a lexical causative (6c), all three patterns being possible as translations of *The dog frightens me*:

(6) a.   *Na-tiao*   *gou*   *shi/rang*   *wo*   *haipa*.
         that-CL   dog   make   me   fear

     b.   *Na-tiao*   *gou*   *ba*   *wo*   *xiazhe*   *le*.
         that-CL   dog   ba   me   frighten   le[5]

     c.   *Na-tiao*   *gou*   *jingxia-le*   *wo*.
         that-CL   dog   frighten-le   me

In cases where there is indeed a morphologically close match, as between English *purify* and Chinese *jing-hua*, a generative analysis that involves raising is appropriate. The syntactic derivation of morphological causative constructions is shown in (7), which is based on (4).

(7)

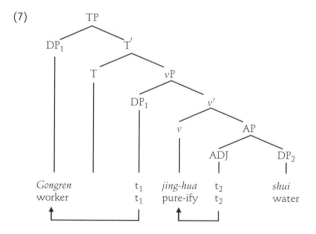

In such cases, DP₁ is base-generated in the specifier of *v*P and raises to the specifier of TP as the subject of the sentence. The overt causative affix is base-generated in the head position of *v*P. The head of AP raises to the head of vP and merges with the overt causative affix into a morphological causative verb, for the head of vP is an affix which cannot exist independently. The merged morphological causative verb stays in the head of vP because of the weak verbal feature of Chinese and English T.

English lexical causative constructions are composed of converted causative verbs or middle verbs[6] or the *put*-type verbs plus the DP and the prepositional phrase (PP). Chinese, however, has a somewhat different set of options, as seen in (8), (9) and (10):

(8) *Xuesheng*   *jinu*   *laoshi.*
     student   anger   teacher
     The student angers the teacher.

(9) *Xiaohai*   *dasui-le*   *huaping.*
     child   break-le   vase
     The child broke the vase.

(10) *Tamen*   *ba*   *shu*   *fang*   *zai*   *zhuozi*   *shang.*
     they   ba   book   put   at   table   on
     They put books on the table.

As noted earlier, the Chinese compound causative verb *dasui* (break) consists of two morphemes, the first, *da* (hit or beat), being a verb that initiates an action, and the second, *sui* (broken), being the result of the action *da*. Example (9) thus contrasts with Example (8), which is *not* a compound and which behaves more like the stative verb in (6c). The verb in Example (9) could also appear in a *ba*-construction. As for (10), the *ba*-construction corresponds somewhat to the English lexical causative constructions composed of the *put*-type verbs plus DP and PP, but the free morpheme *ba* in Chinese does not have an English counterpart.

The syntactic derivation of one lexical causative construction is shown in (11), which is based on (8).

(11)

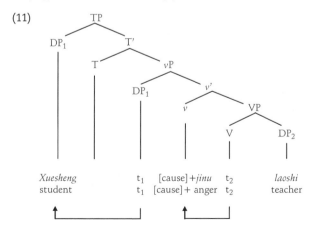

Table 8.1 English causative constructions and the corresponding Chinese constructions

English	Chinese
Periphrastic with *make*-type verbs	Periphrastic with *shi*-type verbs
Morphological with affixed causatives	Morphological with causatives with *-hua* when correspondences exist
	Periphrastic with *shi*-type verbs, *ba*-constructions or lexical with compound causative verbs when correspondences do not exist
Lexical with converted causatives	Periphrastic with *shi*-type verbs, *ba*-constructions or lexical with compound verbs
Lexical with middle verbs	*Ba*-constructions or lexical compound causative verbs
Lexical with *put*-type verbs	*Ba*-constructions

The DP_1 is base-generated in the specifier of vP and raises to the specifier of TP as the subject of the sentence in the course of the syntactic derivation of the lexical causative constructions. There is a null or covert causative verb in the head of vP and it cannot stand independently because it is affixal in nature. Thus, the head of VP raises to the head of vP and the two structures merge into a lexical causative verb. The merged lexical causative verb stays in the head of vP because of the weak verbal feature of English and Chinese T. In this way, a lexical causative construction is generated.

Table 8.1 lists the different options commonly used in both languages. It should be noted that only the first two categories are closely comparable, especially periphrastic constructions, where *make* and other light verbs in English clearly correspond to *shi* and other light verbs in Chinese and where the overall periphrastic construction in each language is similar.

Previous Studies on the Acquisition of Causative Constructions

Most previous studies on the acquisition of causative constructions are concerned with overgeneralization errors of causatives with intransitive verbs and the role of the L1. For example, Moore (1993), Hirakawa (1995), Yip (1995), Juffs (1996), Montrul (1999, 2001) as well as Cabrera and Zubizarreta (2003, 2005) all found that L2 users tend to accept causative constructions with intransitive verbs, especially the unaccusative verbs – even those without causative/inchoative alternation.[7] As for the role of the L1, Montrul (1999, 2001) claimed that cases of overgeneralized causatives with the unaccusative verbs of manner-of-motion are motivated by L1 transfer, while those with non-alternating unaccusatives and unergatives are motivated by universal grammar. However, Cabrera and Zubizarreta (2003) claimed that overgeneralized causatives in the L2 are motivated by the transfer of different L1 properties at different stages of acquisition. Less-advanced L2 learners tend to focus on the L1 constructional properties of causatives, while advanced learners tend to focus on L1-specific lexical properties of verb classes. Cabrera and Zubizarreta (2005) modified their claim in Cabrera and Zubizarreta (2003) and argued that beginners and intermediates transfer only L1 constructional properties of causatives, but not L1-specific lexical properties of verb classes, while advanced learners transfer both types of properties.

Helms-Park (2001) also investigated the role of L1 in the acquisition of English causatives by speakers of Vietnamese and Hindi-Urdu. While Vietnamese primarily uses suppletion or serial verbs (and other periphrastic structures), Hindi-Urdu relies heavily on bound morphology. The results of production, comprehension and grammaticality judgment tests indicated significant differences between the two L1 groups both in periphrastic constructions (with the Vietnamese speakers using more of them) and in choices of causatives related to L1-specific semantic factors. Helms-Park (2003) found that some L1 Vietnamese participants often produced causative serial verb constructions, while Hindi-Urdu speakers did not. Since Vietnamese relies heavily on serial verbs and Hindi-Urdu does not, Helms-Park attributed the verb serialization in English causatives to the transfer of such constructions from Vietnamese.

Wong (1983) was one of the earliest researchers to study L1 Chinese learners' acquisition of L2 English causative constructions. Examining production data, she found that Chinese learners' uses of L2 constructions containing the light verb *make* occurred over twice as often as the uses by those with other L1 backgrounds. She saw *shi*-constructions as the cause, along with less reliance in Chinese on bound morphology. Juffs (1996) also examined the acquisition of English causative constructions by Chinese learners. Elicited production data and grammaticality judgments showed that learners tended to accept and use more English periphrastic causatives than did English native speakers. However, their performance on the causative constructions containing psyche causative verbs (e.g. *frighten* and *interest*) and unaccusative verbs with causative/inchoative alternation was closer to that of English native speakers as learner proficiency increased. As with the Helms-Park studies, such results suggest that syntactic and semantic knowledge can be transferred.

In contrast to Wong (1983), Cai (1999) found that Chinese learners were more sensitive to English than to Chinese causative patterns. By attending to target language details, learners proved able to overcome L1 effects in acquiring English causative verbs. More recently, Zhang (2005a) has formulated a semantic salience hierarchy model to account for the acquisition sequence of L2 causative constructions. According to his model, periphrastic constructions should be acquired first by L1 Chinese speakers because they exist extensively in both languages, and morphological causative constructions should be acquired later, even though both languages have overt causative affixes. English lexical constructions with converted causative verbs should be acquired last since they do not have overt morphological causative markers. Using sentence judgment tasks, Zhang's (2005a, 2005b) studies of psyche causative verbs and color causative verbs indicated that periphrastic causative constructions are acquired first, followed by affixed causative verbs, and the converted causative verbs are acquired last, thus lending support to his model.

To the best of our knowledge, no studies have been conducted to examine the acquisition of L2 Chinese causative constructions by English speakers, much less studies that take into account syntactic, morphological and lexical characteristics. Thus, very little is known about the role of the L1 in the acquisition of the different classes of Chinese causative constructions. The present study aims to help fill the gap and achieve some understanding of how English-speaking learners acquire causative constructions.

The Present Study

Our study investigates whether the similarities and differences between causative patterns in Chinese and English affect the acquisition of Chinese causative constructions by English-speaking learners of Chinese. As the comparisons in the preceding section suggest, there is reason to believe that both positive and negative transfer can occur.

Participants

A total of 45 adult native speakers of English took part in the study, all of them students majoring in Chinese at Shanghai Jiao Tong University. All came from the United States and most were Asian-Americans. Before coming to Shanghai, the majority had studied Chinese as a foreign language in the United States. From the results of a placement test, 20 were assigned to the beginning class and 25 to the intermediate class. In the beginning class, instructors spoke some English to facilitate understanding, while in the intermediate class, instructors mainly spoke Chinese. All the participants lived on campus and often communicated with native speakers of Chinese.

Test design

In order to examine the acquisition of all three types of Chinese causative constructions and the role of the L1, a translation task of 12 sentences from English to Chinese was designed (see the Appendix). Two of the sentences were periphrastic constructions containing *make* and *let*, respectively, whose Chinese counterparts are also periphrastic constructions. Four morphological causative constructions were also included. Two of them contained the affixed causative verbs *purify* and *beautify*, which have Chinese morphological counterparts, and two others contained the affixed psyche causative verbs *frighten* and *horrify*, which do not have Chinese counterparts. In addition, six lexical causative constructions were included. Two of them contained the converted causative verbs *anger* and *surprise*, another two the middle verbs *break* and *melt*, and two the verbs *put* and *roll* plus DPs and PPs, with PPs functioning as object complements. These six sentences would further show what kind of Chinese causative constructions L1 English speakers acquired earlier and better. In order to control for the possible influence of tense, the verbs in all 12 sentences were in the past tense. All test items were presented in a randomized order.

Procedure

Taking the translation test during class time, the participants were required to finish the task independently within 20 minutes. No discussion or consulting reference books or dictionaries was permitted.

In the scoring procedures, no answer was counted if the translation into Chinese did not have a causative construction. If a particular sentence was partly translated but did have a causative construction, it was counted. If the participants used *pinyin* instead of Chinese characters for some particular English words, the response was also counted.

Results

The results of the translation task are presented in the sequence of periphrastic, morphological and lexical constructions in the source sentences.

Periphrastic causative constructions

The constructions that the participants supplied in their translations of the two English periphrastic causatives containing *make* and *let* (Sentences 1 and 8 in the Appendix) are presented in Table 8.2.

As Table 8.2 shows, 19 out of the 20 beginners provided valid information for the English periphrastic causative containing *make*, all students using Chinese periphrastic constructions, among which 14 contained the causative light verb *rang* and 4 contained the causative light verb *shi*. A sample target-like response is illustrated in (12).

(12) *Xiaoxi   rang/shi wo   hen   nanguo.*
     news   make   me   very   sad
    The news makes me very sad.

Table 8.2 Patterns used to translate English periphrastic causative constructions

Participants	Target constructions	Make	Let	Total
Beginners (n = 20)	Valid number	19	16	35
	Periphrastic causative constructions	19 (100%)	16 (100%)	35(100%)
	Other constructions	0 (0%)	0 (0%)	0 (0%)
Intermediates (n = 25)	Valid number	25	21	46
	Periphrastic causative constructions	24 (96%)	20 (95%)	44 (96%)
	Other constructions	1 (4%)	1 (5%)	2 (4%)

There were also translations using *ba*-constructions as in one case shown in (13), where *ba* is not target-like and should be replaced by a causative light verb.

(13) *Xiaoxi   *ba*   *wo*   *hen*   *xiang*   *ku.*
      news   ba   me   very   want   cry

All 25 intermediate learners provided countable responses for the English construction containing *make,* and 24 used Chinese constructions with *rang* (16 cases), *shi* (7) or *ling* (1). The only inaccurate use was a *bei*-construction[8] as shown in (14).

(14) *Zhege   *xiaoxi*   *bei*   *wo*   *hen*   *nanguo.*
      this-CL   news   bei   me   very   sad

The *make*-construction is the most typical periphrastic causative in English and its Chinese counterpart is supposed to be periphrastic, and it turned out that nearly all the participants did supply periphrastic constructions in their translations. As for the source construction having *let,* 16 out of the 20 beginners provided valid information and all of them used Chinese constructions containing *rang.* Among the 25 intermediate learners, 21 provided valid information. Twenty supplied periphrastic causative constructions, with 19 *rang*'s and 1 *jiao,* as in (15).

(15) *Laoshi*   *rang/jiao*   *wo*   *du*   *ci.*
      teacher   let   me   read   word
      The teacher lets me read words.

As with *make* constructions, nearly all translations of *let* constructions used periphrastic constructions.

Accordingly, almost all the learners in this study seemed to recognize that the Chinese counterparts of English periphrastic constructions were also periphrastics. As expected, the participants used the Chinese light verb *rang* more often in their answers, even when the target construction might have *shi*. The especially high frequency of *rang* in the target language thus appears to affect what learners use (see also Note 3).

Morphological causative constructions

The patterns evident in the translations of the two English morphological causative constructions, which have Chinese counterparts (Sentences 7 and 11 in the Appendix), are presented in Table 8.3.

The responses differ somewhat from those in Table 8.2 in that fewer learners provided valid answers: 29 out of a possible 40 among the beginners and 45 out of 50 among the intermediates. Among the beginners, periphrastic constructions accounted for over half of the responses (15), whereas only one learner provided a causative with a bound morpheme (in translating a construction with *purify*). Among the eight choices of periphrastic constructions translating the *purify* pattern, four used *shi*-constructions, three *rang*-constructions and one a *ba*-construction, which are not acceptable in Chinese, as shown in (16).

(16) *Tamen   shi/rang/ba   shui   ganjing le.
     they   make   water   clean   le
     They made the water clean.

The patterns in (16) contrast with those of (4) and (5). Periphrastic constructions containing *shi* and *rang* are non-target-like, and the

Table 8.3 Patterns used to translate English morphological causative constructions which have Chinese counterparts

Participants	Target constructions	Purify	Beautify	Total
Beginners (*n* = 20)	Valid number	17	12	29
	Periphrastic causative constructions	8 (47%)	7 (58%)	15 (52%)
	Morphological causative constructions	1 (6%)	0	1 (3.5%)
	Other constructions	8 (47%)	5(42%)	13 (44.5%)
Intermediates (*n* = 25)	Valid number	23	22	45
	Periphrastic causative constructions	11 (48%)	16 (73%)	27 (60%)
	Morphological causative constructions	3 (13%)	2(9%)	5 (11%)
	Other constructions	9 (39%)	4 (18%)	13 (29%)

ba-construction is likewise non-target-like, because *gangjing* is an adjective, not an affixed causative verb with *hua*. Only one of the beginners used a Chinese morphological construction containing *jinghua*, which is the counterpart of *purify*, as seen in (17).

(17) *Tamen*   *jinghua-le*   *shui.*
     they   purify le   water
     They purified the water.

The other eight periphrastic constructions of the beginners all contained non-causative compound adjectives like *ganjing* (clean), *chunjie* (pure) and *mingliang* (bright), all of which are totally unacceptable in Chinese. An example is given in (18).

(18) **Tamen*   *chunjie-le*   *shui.*
     they   pure-le   water.

Among the intermediate learners, periphrastic constructions were also the predominant response pattern, but more learners did use constructions with the bound morpheme *-hua*. Three used constructions containing *jinghua* (purify) as in Example (17), and two supplied constructions containing *meihua* (beautify). Other responses were about as varied as among the beginners. Nine intermediates translated *purify* constructions with non-causative compound adjectives like *ganjing* and *chunjing*, and four translated *beautify* constructions with the non-causative compound adjective *piaoliang* or the non-causative compound verb *meirong* (beautify one's face). Once again, there was considerable variation in the intermediates' choice of periphrastic constructions, with *rang-*, *shi-* and *ba-*constructions, as seen already with the beginners.

The results in Table 8.3 thus indicate that the participants did not have a strong awareness of Chinese morphological causative constructions, although the intermediate learners tended to have a better command of affixed causative verbs. Despite the morphological similarity between forms such as *meihua* and *beautify*, few learners seemed able to profit from the resemblance. More often than not, learners in both groups resorted to non-target-like Chinese periphrastic causatives or the constructions with non-causative compound adjectives or verbs.

Table 8.4 summarizes the patterns in the participants' translations of the two English morphological causative constructions which do not have Chinese counterparts (Sentences 3 and 9 in the Appendix).

Once again, fewer beginners than intermediates supplied answers that could be counted. They also differed in using far fewer periphrastic

Table 8.4 Patterns used to translate English morphological causative constructions which do not have Chinese counterparts

Participants	Target constructions	Horrify	Frighten	Total
Beginners (n = 20)	Valid number	14	15	29
	Periphrastic causative constructions	4 (29%)	4 (27%)	8 (28%)
	Other constructions	10 (71%)	11 (73%)	21 (72%)
Intermediates (n = 25)	Valid number	20	18	38
	Periphrastic causative constructions	12 (60%)	7 (39%)	19 (50%)
	Lexical causative constructions	2 (10%)	4 (22%)	6 (16%)
	Other constructions	6 (30%)	7 (39%)	13 (34%)

constructions, especially in the translations of *horrify* sentences. One example of such a response is as follows.

(19) *Laohu*   *rang/shi*   *women*   *haipa.*
     tiger   make   us   fear
     The tiger makes us fear.

As expected, neither group of participants used morphological causative constructions, but both often opted for other kinds. For example, eight beginners' translations contained non-causative compound psyche verbs like *haipa* (fear) or adjectives like *kepa* (horrible) as shown in (20a), and two of them even contained the monosyllabic psyche verb *pa* (fear) as shown in (20b).

(20) a.   **Laohu*   *haipa/kepa*   *women*   *le.*
          tiger   fear   us   le

     b.   **Laohu*   *pa-le*   *women.*
          tiger   fear-le   us

As already seen in (6), when the English morphological causatives do not have Chinese counterparts, the corresponding Chinese can be periphrastic causatives, *ba*-constructions or lexical causatives with compound verbs. As a result, the 4 periphrastic constructions that the beginners supplied were target-like, but none of the other 10 constructions were target-like when compound state psyche verbs or adjectives were used instead of compound causative psyche verbs. In Chinese, compound state psyche verbs or adjectives cannot be directly followed by experiencers. The 10 anomalous constructions of the beginners reflect word-for-word translations.

The translations of the intermediates were often similar to those of the beginners. In addition, however, some students employed lexical causative constructions to translate either the *horrify* (two individuals) or the *frighten* (four individuals) sentences, including a response with the causative compound psyche verb *xiadao* (horrify) seen in (21).

(21) *Laohu*   *xia-dao-le*   *women.*
      tiger   horrify-le   us

The fact that the intermediate learners began to use target-like lexical causative constructions with compound causative verbs, which do not have close structural parallels in English, indicates that these more advanced learners sometimes eschew word-for-word translations and opt for constructions unique to the target language. Moreover, the fact that no one in either group attempted to use a bound form in his/her interlanguage Chinese suggests that the bound morphology of English words with *–fy* and *–en* (at least the words *terrified* and *frightened*) did not seem transferable.

Lexical causative constructions

Table 8.5 reports results involving the participants' translations of the two English lexical causative constructions having the converted (aka zero-derived) causative verbs *anger* and *surprise* (Sentences 4 and 6 in the Appendix).

While nearly all of the participants in the intermediate group supplied valid answers, the number of beginners doing so was somewhat smaller. None of the participants in either group used bound morphology in their responses. Another commonality between the two groups was the frequent use of periphrastic causatives, which account for over half of the total valid

Table 8.5 Patterns used to translate English lexical causative constructions consisting of *anger* and *surprise*

Participants	Target constructions	Anger	Surprise	Total
Beginners (*n* = 20)	Valid number	17	16	33
	Periphrastic causative constructions	9 (53%)	8 (50%)	17 (52%)
	Other constructions	8 (47%)	8 (50%)	16 (48%)
Intermediates (*n* = 25)	Valid number	23	24	47
	Periphrastic causative constructions	14 (61%)	15 (63%)	29 (62%)
	Lexical causative constructions	2 (9%)	0 (0%)	2 (4%)
	Other constructions	7 (30%)	9 (37%)	16 (34%)

responses. Other constructions were also frequent, such as word-for-word translations of the non-causative compound psyche verb *shengqi* (anger) and the experiencer *fuqin* (father), which were non-target-like. No beginners supplied the Chinese lexical causative constructions with the compound causative verb *ji-nu* (arouse-anger), and only two in the intermediate group did. An example of an intermediate answer appears in (22):

(22) *Ta*   *ji-nu-le*   *tade*   *fuqin.*
     he   arouse-angry-le   his   father
     He angered his father.

The intermediate Chinese learners supplied, overall, more target-like periphrastic constructions; furthermore, the lexical causative constructions and the compound verbs they used were more diverse.

Table 8.6 details the patterns in the participants' translations of the two English lexical causative constructions containing the middle verbs *break* and *melt* (Sentences 5 and 12 in the Appendix).

In this case, far fewer beginners supplied valid answers (with either target-like *ba*-constructions or target-like lexical causative constructions composed of compound causative verbs); one reason that so few translations of the *melt* sentence could be counted was that the Chinese character for *ronghua* (melt) was difficult for some beginners to write. Although a far larger number of the intermediates did supply valid answers, the number is still smaller than what was seen in most of the preceding tables. In both groups, many participants used periphrastic constructions, while none used bound morphology, as also seen in most of the tables considered so far. In the beginning group, there was one target-like lexical causative construction formed by the causative

Table 8.6 Patterns used to translate lexical causative constructions containing break and melt

Participants	Target constructions	Break	Melt	Total
Beginners (*n* = 20)	Valid number	10	6	16
	Periphrastic causative constructions	3 (30%)	3 (50%)	6 (37%)
	Lexical causative constructions	1 (10%)	2 (33%)	3 (19%)
	Other constructions	6 (60%)	1 (17%)	7 (44%)
Intermediates (*n* = 25)	Valid number	24	17	41
	Periphrastic causative constructions	12 (50%)	10 (57%)	22 (54%)
	Lexical causative constructions	5 (21%)	5 (29%)	10 (24%)
	Other constructions	7 (29%)	2 (14%)	9 (22%)

compound verb *dapo* (break), and there were also six non-target-like constructions formed by the Chinese monosyllabic adjectives *po* (broken) or *huai* (broken) followed by an object, as illustrated in (23), along with one case of a *bei*-construction, where *bei* should be replaced by *ba*, as shown in (24).

(23) **Zuotian*   *jieke*   *po/huai-le*   *nage*   *ping.*
      yesterday   Jack   broken-le   that-CL   bottle.

(24) **Jieke*   *bei*   *pingzi*   *po-sui-le.*
      Jack   bei   bottle   break-le
      Jack was broken by the bottle.

As already noted, the *melt* sentence proved especially difficult for the beginners, but the intermediates also encountered problems (and for both groups this was the last item on the test, which suggests that time constraints were also involved). Along with periphrastic translations having *shi-* or *ba-*constructions, there were some with the compound causative verb *ronghua* and also a *bei*-construction. Examples of some choices, all of which are target-like, appear in (25).

(25) a.   *Taiyang*   *ba*   *xue*   *hua-le.*
         sun   ba   snow   melt-le
         The sun melted the snow.

     b.   *Taiyang*   *rong-hua-le*   *xue.*
         sun   melt-le   snow
         The sun melted the snow.

     c.   *Xue*   *bei*   *taiyang*   *rong-hua-le.*
         snow   bei   sun   melt-le
         The snow was melted by the sun.

The translations of the two English lexical causative constructions containing middle verbs suggest that, on the one hand, participants could acquire the target-like *ba*-constructions or lexical causative constructions composed of compound causative verbs, but, on the other hand, there was also a strong tendency to overuse *shi*-constructions.

Finally, Table 8.7 presents the constructions that the participants used when translating the lexical causative constructions consisting of *put/roll* + DP + PP (Sentences 2 and 10 in the Appendix). The latter sentence proved much harder – especially for the beginners – to translate, which suggests a vocabulary problem for many, with *gun*, the normal Chinese translation equivalent of *roll*, apparently not in the active vocabulary of several learners. Once again, periphrastic constructions constituted the most frequent response type, and once again, no participant in either group attempted to use a morphological causative. Among the periphrastic

Table 8.7 Patterns used to translate lexical causative constructions consisting of put/roll + DP + PP

Participants	Target constructions	Put + DP + PP	Roll + DP + PP	Total
Beginners (n = 20)	Valid number	19	5	24
	Periphrastic causative constructions	10 (53%)	3 (60%)	13 (54%)
	Lexical causative constructions	0	1 (20%)	1 (4%)
	Other constructions	9 (47%)	1 (20%)	10 (42%)
Intermediates (n = 25)	Valid number	25	18	43
	Periphrastic causative constructions	17 (68%)	13 (72%)	30 (70%)
	Lexical causative constructions	0	2 (11%)	2 (5%)
	Other constructions	8 (32%)	3 (17%)	11 (25%)

translations of the *put* sentences of the beginners, two response types predominated: 10 target-like *ba*-constructions, as exemplified in (26a), and 9 word-for-word translations, as shown in (26b), which are not congruent with Chinese word order. Among the intermediates, the pattern was similar, but with 17 *ba*-constructions and 8 others, 7 of which were word-for-word translations.

(26) a. *Jian   ba   tade   liwu   fang   zai   zhuozi   shang.*
        Jane   ba   her   gift   put   at   table   on
        Jane put her gift on the table.

    b. **Jian   fang   tade   liwu   zai   zhuozi   shang.*
        Jane   put   her   gift   at   table   on
        Jane put her gift on the table.

As for the *roll* sentence, the periphrastic pattern was predominant in the intermediates' answers and also among the few beginners able to provide a valid answer, with the intermediates using 13 target-like *ba*-constructions and the beginners a total of 3. Besides the *ba*-construction, as exemplified in (27a), another pattern used was a lexical causative construction with the compound causative verb *gundong* (roll and move), as seen in (27b). A variant of the latter type omits *dong*, hence the parentheses. The *gun* and *gundong* constructions are acceptable in Chinese, but their meaning is different from the source sentence. More accurately translated, *down the mountain* would be rendered as the complement of *yikuai shitou*, not the adverbial of the verb *gun*.

(27) a. *Maike   ba   yikuai   shitou   gunxia   shan.*
        Michael   ba   one-CL   stone   roll-down   mountain
        Michael rolled a rock down the mountain.

   b. *Maike   yanzhe   shan   gun(dong)   yikuai   shitou.*
        Michael   along   mountain   roll-down   one-CL   stone
        Michael rolled a rock along the mountain.

The translations of the two English lexical causative constructions containing V + DP + PP show that many participants realized that the Chinese counterparts were *ba*-constructions, but some still used non-target-like literal translations whose word order was different from their Chinese counterparts.

Discussion

The results of the translation task indicate that participants could use Chinese periphrastic causative constructions quite well, but most showed no signs of using morphological and lexical causative constructions. As expected, the intermediate learners' performance on causative constructions was better than the beginners' performance. While these conclusions follow straightforwardly from the results, the role of L1 transfer is complex and requires considering other factors as well.

The L1 English speakers often successfully used Chinese periphrastic constructions, but they also over-relied on them. Positive transfer may well explain the successes, given the great similarity of some periphrastic constructions in the two languages, but the non-target-like translations suggest that the participants resorted to such constructions when they did not know the normal Chinese pattern (as in Example 16). The syntactic transparency of periphrastic constructions offers an easy, if inaccurate, alternative when the bound morphology or other lexical resources required for target-like uses are not known. Since morphological and lexical causative constructions involve the interface between syntax, semantics and lexicon, our results are consistent with the interface hypothesis (Sorace, 2011; Sorace & Filiaci, 2006), which asserts that a syntactic system is easier to acquire than the interface of syntax and semantics, syntax and morphology or syntax and lexicon.

The rather weak performance of the participants with regard to morphological and lexical causative constructions is evident in three ways: the infrequent use of bound morphology, the use of non-causative instead of causative verbs and inaccurate word-for-word translations, which often resulted in non-target-like word orders where experiencers were directly followed by state psyche verbs.

Most learners demonstrated little or no ability to use affixed or compound causative verbs well. It cannot be determined whether most of the lexical items (which course instructors affirmed had indeed been taught) were completely unfamiliar or were, instead, a part of the passive but not active vocabulary knowledge of learners. Either way, it proved difficult or even impossible for most participants to write these words, and they frequently resorted to simpler periphrastic constructions, sometimes even in Chinese pinyin. More often than not, the participants used Chinese monosyllabic verbs, thus suggesting little familiarity with the highly productive pattern of compounding in the target language.

Learners encountered serious problems in distinguishing meaning differences among Chinese causative light verbs, a finding consistent with the morpholexical approach model of constructionism developed by Herschensohn (2000: 203), which holds that L2 morpholexical variation, the locus of cross-linguistic variation, is more difficult to grasp than syntactic differences. Herschensohn proposes that pure syntactic knowledge is easiest to acquire as it stems from universal grammar, whereas one of the main challenges is to distinguish word and affix meanings in the target lexicon. Such meanings need to be learned on an individual basis, which thus poses serious challenges for language learners.

Although the success of English speakers in using target-like periphrastic constructions suggests positive transfer, skeptics might object by saying that learners had simply become attuned to a syntactically transparent pattern in the target with no actual help from similarity between English and Chinese. However, such an objection seems implausible in view of a study discussed earlier, the investigation by Helms-Park (2001) of the acquisition of English causative constructions by two groups of immigrants in Canada. One group consisted of speakers of Vietnamese, and the other consisted of speakers of Hindi-Urdu. Vietnamese, but not Hindi-Urdu, shows clear cross-linguistic similarities with English in periphrastic constructions where there is, for instance, a construction in Vietnamese quite similar to the causative *make* pattern of English. If skeptics were correct, Vietnamese speakers in the Helms-Park study should not have done any better than Hindi-Urdu speakers in producing periphrastic patterns. This was not the case, however. Vietnamese speakers tended to use far more periphrastic constructions. Even though the target language in our own study differs, the logic of the Helms-Park study strongly argues for positive transfer in our results as well.

The overall pattern in our evidence suggests a strong role for transfer. When causative constructions were congruent in Chinese and English, the interlanguage patterns proved target-like, especially in cases involving periphrastic constructions. When the constructions were not congruent, the participants still transferred their English constructions, leading to non-target-like constructions as in the case of *put*-type verbs plus DP and PP. Although the outcomes are different, the pattern of transfer evident in translating word for word is the same, a pattern consistent with the full transfer position of Schwartz and Sprouse (1996), namely, that the L1 is the initial state of the L2 and that the syntactic features of the L1 will transfer to the L2. Our findings also support Harley (1989), who emphasizes the heavy reliance on the L1 by L2 learners.

Conclusion

This chapter has investigated the acquisition of Chinese causative constructions by English-speaking learners with a focus on the role of the L1. The results suggest that the participants have acquired Chinese periphrastic causative constructions quite well, but morphological and lexical causative constructions are still difficult for them, as are certain lexical patterns involving compounding. The mixed outcomes seem consistent with constructionism and with the interface hypothesis. The interlanguage constructions of the participants, target-like or not, suggest that language transfer resulted from translating word for word. To further examine the acquisition of Chinese causative constructions and the role of the L1, other production and judgment data are needed, including data coming from L2 Chinese learners with different L1 backgrounds.

Notes

(1) The present study is supported by the Chinese National Social Science Fund (No. 11CYY028) and the 2013 Shanghai Municipality Funded Training Project of Young Academics in Colleges and Universities. We are grateful to the editors of the book for their constructive suggestions for revision and those students of Shanghai Jiao Tong University who participated in our study. Any possible errors are ours.

(2) According to Pinker (1989: 85–86), a causative verb is a verb that takes as its direct object an entity directly acted on by an agent and affected by the action in a physical or metaphorical way.

(3) Syntactically and semantically, these four Chinese causative light verbs are quite similar. However, *rang* (literally *let*) is the most frequent one in modern Chinese, spoken or written. *Shi* (literally *make*) is also frequent in written Chinese. *Ling* is very seldom used today, especially in spoken Chinese, and is mainly seen in idioms. *Jiao* is quite colloquial and is only used in some dialects today.

(4) *Ba*-constructions are semantically resultative. According to Huang *et al.* (2004: 26), *ba* functions as a causative verb comparable to the causative use of *make* in English. In *ba*-constructions, the objects of the verbs are introduced in the preverbal position by *ba* and the objects are 'disposed' in the event denoted by the verbs. Although *ba*-constructions are thus periphrastic, they are not identical to periphrastic causative constructions with *shi*-type verbs since only a [DP v_{cause} DP AdjP] structure can be expressed by a *ba*-construction, and an extra verb is needed.

(5) There are two *le*'s in Chinese. The *le* here is a particle used at the end of sentences. The other *le* is the perfect aspectual marker and is a bound morpheme and used after transitive verbs, as shown in (5c).

(6) Middle verbs refer to those verbs like *break* and *melt*, which can be used either as a causative verb (thus transitive as in *I broke the window*) followed by a causee or as an unaccusative verb (thus intransitive as in *The window broke*). Therefore, middle

verbs are characterized by causative/inchoative alternation. (See also Chapter 7 in this volume.)

(7) According to the unaccusative hypothesis (Perlmutter, 1978), there are two subclasses of intransitive verbs: unergative verbs and unaccusative verbs. They have an identical surface structure of 'subject + verb', but a different deep structure. Unaccusative verbs have underlying objects but no underlying subjects, and these underlying objects move to subject positions and serve as surface subjects. For example, in the sentence *An accident happened,* the subject *An accident* is actually an underlying object of the verb *happened* in the deep structure. Unaccusative verbs with causative/inchoative alternation refer to those that alter between transitives and unaccusatives, such as *break* and *melt* (also refer to Note 6). Unergative verbs have underlying subjects, but no underlying objects. The subjects of unergative verbs are base-generated and there is no movement. For example, in the sentence *He works in a company,* the subject *He* is also the underlying subject of the unergative verb *works* in the deep structure.

(8) *Bei*-constructions are similar to the English sentences marked for passive voice in that *bei* literally means *by.* Unlike in English, however, no auxiliary is needed in *bei*-constructions, and the agent occurring with *bei* precedes the verb, as seen here:

Xin	bei	wo	shao-	le.
letter	bei	me	burn	le

The letter was burned by me.

References

Cabrera, M. and Zubizarreta, M.L. (2003) On the acquisition of Spanish causative structures by L1 speakers of English. In J.M. Liceras, H. Zobl and H. Goodluck (eds) *Proceedings of the 6th Generative Approaches to Second Language Acquisition Conference (GASLA 2002)* (pp. 24–33). Somerville, MA: Cascadilla Press.

Cabrera, M. and Zubizarreta, M.L. (2005) Overgeneralization of causatives and transfer in L2 Spanish and L2 English. In D. Eddington (ed.) *Selected Proceedings of the 6th Conference on the Acquisition of Spanish and Portuguese as First and Second Languages* (pp. 15–30). Somerville, MA: Cascadilla Proceedings Project.

Cai, Y. (2000) Prominence of causativization and its influence on L2 acquisition. *Modern Foreign Languages* 23 (2), 174–182.

Chomsky, N. (1995) *The Minimalist Program.* Cambridge, MA: MIT Press.

Comrie, B. (1989) *Language Universals and Linguistic Typology: Syntax and Morphology.* Oxford: Oxford Basil Blackwell.

Harley, B. (1989) Transfer in the written compositions of French immersion students. In H. Dechert and M. Raupach (eds) *Transfer in Language Production* (pp. 3–19). Norwood, NJ: Ablex.

Helms-Park, R. (2001) Evidence of lexical transfer in learner syntax: The acquisition of English causatives by speakers of Hindi-Urdu and Vietnamese. *Studies in Second Language Acquisition* 23 (1), 71–102.

Herschensohn, J. (2000) *The Second Time Round: Minimalism and L2 Acquisition.* Amsterdam: John Benjamins.

Hirakawa, M. (1995) L2 acquisition of English unaccusative constructions. In D. MacLaughlin and S. McEwen (eds) *Proceedings of Boston University Conference on Language Development 19, Vol. 1* (pp. 291–302). Somerville, MA: Cascadilla Press.

Huang, C.-T.J., Li, Y.-H.A. and Li, Y.-F. (2004) *The Syntax of Chinese.* Cambridge: Cambridge University Press.

Juffs, A. (1996) *Learnability and The Lexicon.* Amsterdam: John Benjamins.

Montrul, S. (1999) Causative errors with unaccusative verbs in L2 Spanish. *Second Language Research* 15 (2), 191–219.
Montrul, S. (2001) Causatives and transitivity in L2 English. *Language Learning* 51 (1), 51–106.
Moore, M. (1993) Second language acquisition of lexically constrained transitivity alternations: Acquisition of the causative alternation by second language learners of English. Unpublished PhD thesis, University of South Carolina.
Perlmutter, D.M. (1978) Impersonal passives and the unaccusative hypothesis. In J. Jaeger et al. (eds) *Proceedings of the 4th Annual Meeting of the Berkeley Linguistics Society* (pp. 157–189). Berkeley, CA: Berkeley Linguistics Society.
Pinker, S. (1989) *Learnability and Cognition: The Acquisition of Argument Structure*. Cambridge, MA: MIT Press.
Schwartz, B. and Sprouse, R. (1996) L2 cognitive states and the Full Transfer/Full Access model. *Second Language Research* 12 (1), 40–72.
Sorace, A. (2011) Pinning down the concept of 'interface' in bilingualism. *Linguistic Approaches to Bilingualism* 1 (1), 1–33.
Sorace, A and Filiaci, F. (2006) Anaphora resolution in near-native speakers of Italian. *Second Language Research* 22 (3), 339–368.
Wong, S-L.C. (1983) Overproduction, underlexicalization, and unidiomatic usage in the 'make' causatives of Chinese speakers: A case for flexibility in interlanguage analysis. *Language Learning and Communication* 2 (2), 151–163.
Yip, V. (1995) *Interlanguage and Learnability*. Philadelphia, PA: John Benjamins.
Zhang, J.-Y. (2005a) *The Semantic Salience Hierarchy Model*. Victoria, BC: Trafford Publishing.
Zhang, J.-Y. (2005b) The acquisition of English causative color verbs by Chinese university students. *Foreign Language Teaching and Research* 37 (6), 446–452.

Appendix: The Translation Task

Directions: Please translate the following English sentences into Chinese.

1. The news made me very sad.
2. Jane put her gift on the table.
3. The tiger horrified us.
4. His decision surprised us.
5. Jack broke that vase yesterday.
6. He angered his father.
7. They purified the water.
8. The teacher let me read words.
9. The cat frightened me.
10. Michael rolled a rock down the mountain.
11. They beautified their city.
12. The sun melted the snow.

Part 3

Phonological Perspectives

While both of the chapters in this section offer empirical examples of phonological transfer, they differ in a number of ways, with Chapter 9 focusing on an important property of the English suprasegmental system, stress, and with Chapter 10 focusing on a different target language, Spanish, and on a segmental feature *not* found in that language, retroflexion (which is, however, found in the source languages). In Chapters 9 and 10, the first language (L1) source languages also differ, with Chinese in the suprasegmental study and retroflexing languages of India in the segmental investigation. The study of retroflexion has, moreover, the goal of using evidence of transfer today to make inferences about transfer in a contact situation that took place long ago.

The chapter by Hong Li, Lei Zhang and Ling Zhou addresses the challenge that word-level stress in English poses for speakers of Chinese. Along with their interest in transfer, the authors look closely at how much the differences in the age of learners may or may not affect the acquisition of word-stress patterns in the target language. Drawing on theories and methods of the late Susan Guion and others, Li, Zhang and Zhou conducted experiments to determine which of the following factors might affect acquisition among L1 Chinese speakers: syllable structure, lexical class and knowledge of stress in vocabulary already acquired. Whereas the findings of Guion and colleagues often indicated important effects due to age differences, the findings of Li, Zhang and Zhou show no such differences, a result they see as related to the learning environment: that is, the Chinese participants were acquiring English in a formal setting in which English as a foreign language (EFL) rather than English as a second language (ESL) would be the best descriptor. Although the investigators had only a single L1 group in contrast to, for example, Gao's study which compares L1 Korean and L1 Chinese speakers (Chapter 7), Li, Zhang and Zhou are able to demonstrate a strong likelihood of transfer effects partly from their contrastive analysis and partly from the similarity of their methods to those in Guion's studies. They explain the rather even prominence of each syllable in a Chinese word as due to the frequent need for speakers of Chinese to mark the syllable with a distinct tone (and for listeners to identify the tone). The influence of such a system seems likely since the factors of syllable structure and lexical class did not figure in the results in the same ways that they did in the investigations of Guion and others who looked at other L1 groups.

Chapter 10 by David Mitchell also deals with transfer in sound patterns, but the author focuses on segmental phonology, and he uses instrumental phonetics to study the feature in question: retroflexion. Speakers of Hindi, Tamil and other languages of India which have retroflex consonants were asked to repeat Spanish words uttered in a recording by a native speaker of Spanish. Unlike Hindi and other native languages of the participants, Spanish does not have retroflex consonants, yet the participants fairly often used such consonants when attempting to reproduce the consonants in the target Spanish word – even in some cases where a straightforward interlingual identification of a non-retroflex consonant in the native language with one in the target language would have been possible (e.g. between a dental /t/ in Spanish and a dental /t/ in Hindi in a Spanish word such as *borbotón* ['bubbling']). Mitchell offers this evidence of present-day transfer as support for what he and others have seen as an analogous case of language contact in the Indian subcontinent about 3000 years ago. Historical linguists have long believed that speakers of Indo-Aryan (IA; an ancient Indo-European language which is the source of modern languages such as Hindi and Bengali as well as the early sacred language Sanskrit) entered the Indian subcontinent from West or Central Asia and came into contact with speakers of Proto-Dravidian (the source of other modern Indian languages such as Tamil and Telugu). Like other ancient Indo-European languages such as Greek and Latin, the earliest varieties of IA apparently did not have many words showing retroflex consonants even though modern IA languages do. A number of Indo-Europeanists who are skeptical about a contact explanation have argued that retroflexion could have developed independently of contact with speakers of Proto-Dravidian, a language which seems to have many retroflex consonants; skeptics typically argue that retroflexion might have taken place in IA with little or no transfer being involved (apart, perhaps, from using Dravidian loanwords with retroflex consonants). However, some characteristics of retroflexion in modern IA languages do not logically follow from patterns of sound change invoked by the skeptics. These exceptions to (arguably) language-internal sound changes are, however, consistent with Mitchell's findings about transfer, which thus suggests that much retroflexion in modern IA languages probably did arise from attempts of ancient Dravidian speakers to pronounce IA words (or, as the author puts it, to 'impose' retroflexion on dental consonants). Mitchell's study thus parallels that of Helms-Park (discussed in Chapter 1) in the sense that the second language acquisition (SLA) research of today can sometimes offer a window on past language contact situations.

9 L1 Influence on the Learning of English Lexical Stress Patterns: Evidence from Chinese Early and Late EFL Learners

Hong Li, Lei Zhang and Ling Zhou

Introduction

Second language (L2) research on pronunciation has traditionally focused more on learner problems involving segmental (vowels and consonants) as opposed to suprasegmental phenomena (including stress, tone and intonation). Even so, suprasegmentals do matter for any learner seeking to become a proficient speaker. Among the various suprasegmental phenomena, stress plays a crucial role, since listeners often rely on stress placement to identify words (Cutler, 1984). Research interest in suprasegmentals has continued side by side with segmental work, as seen in recent studies (e.g. Trofimovich & Baker, 2006) indicating that inaccurate production of L2 prosodic features contributes in complex ways to a foreign accent, and as seen in several studies of the late Susan Guion and colleagues which have also shed valuable light on the implications of the contrasts in prosodic systems across languages (e.g. Guion *et al.*, 2006).

In languages where stress placement plays a major systemic role, the acquisition of stress patterns begins early. Houston *et al.* (2000) found evidence that knowledge of language-specific stress patterns influences the speech processing routines of infants as well as adults. Infants of approximately eight months of age display a bias toward the dominant stress patterns in their first language (L1) for segmentation of two-syllable words from continuous speech and cannot reliably segment words in a language with a prosodic system different from their L1.

Word stress differs across languages, and while some resemble each other in stress patterns, they often differ dramatically. For example, more similarities in lexical stress patterns can be found between Spanish and English than between French and English. Cross-linguistic studies of perceptions of adults have found that listeners from a language with contrastive stress (like Spanish) are better at distinguishing non-words that differ only in stress placement than are listeners from a language without contrastive stress (Depoux et al., 1997, 2001). In greater contrast still, Sino-Tibetan languages employ lexical tone much more than word stress, and the tone patterns are associated with an accentual phrase.

The evidence from studies we have cited thus suggests that structural differences in suprasegmentals have consequences for how L2 learners perceive and use the prosodic patterns of a new language. Other evidence also points in the same direction, as in a recent study (Guion, 2005) that examined how native language prosody and age of acquisition influence the learning of L2 English stress patterns among early and late Korean–English bilinguals. Guion found that prosodic differences between English and Korean could help explain how Korean speakers acquire English stress patterns. Korean–English bilinguals demonstrated non-native-like knowledge of the distributional stress patterns across the lexical classes of noun and verb, particularly among late bilinguals. Guion suggested that the differing results between older and younger bilinguals might result from Koreans' low sensitivity to word-level stress distributions as a result of early exposure to the phrase-level prosodic system of their L1.

The age of L2 acquisition has often been viewed as the most important predictor of a foreign accent. Long (1990), for example, proposed that a native-like accent would be impossible unless first exposure was quite early, and learners older than 12 would not be able to acquire native-like phonological knowledge in an L2 (cf. Flege et al., 1999). Beyond the age of 12, the degree of accentedness will rely on L2 exposure and use (Long, 2013). Recent studies (Guion, 2005; Guion et al., 2004) have indicated that the age of L2 exposure affects the ability to learn a new prosodic system, but they did not fully support Long's conclusion that learners older than 12 cannot acquire L2 phonological knowledge; instead, the evidence indicated that late learners also demonstrated native-like knowledge of some aspects of English stress placement. The importance of age differences remains less clear in cases of L2 instruction in school settings. Thus, the aim of this chapter is to investigate how such differences may or may not be a factor in the acquisition of English stress patterns among Chinese learners of English as a foreign language (EFL) whose L1 prosodic system is quite different from the English system. Working on the assumption that Chinese suprasegmental patterns will influence the learning of English word stress patterns by Chinese EFL learners, we tested the knowledge of English stress patterns of early and late Chinese learners of English who have learned English in a formal setting.

Background: Chinese and English Stress Patterns

As our goal is to investigate the effects of Chinese prosodic patterns on the learning of English stress patterns by early and late Chinese EFL learners, an analysis of the Chinese prosodic system should be presented. We focus our analysis of stress patterns on disyllabic words as they comprise 73.6% of the modern Chinese lexicon (Wu & Zhu, 2001). Our analysis begins with a comparison of Chinese and English suprasegmental features before we proceed to analyze the similarities and differences of the word stress patterns in Chinese and English.

Traditionally, Chinese is classified as a tone language and English as a stress language (Chan, 2005). Tones, i.e. the pitches carried by the vocalic part of syllables, are used to differentiate lexical items. Tone is a key element in Chinese syllables and a distinctive feature in the Chinese prosodic system. Mandarin Chinese has four tones: high level (Tone 1), high rising (Tone 2), low dipping (Tone 3) and high falling (Tone 4). For example, a single syllable [tu] serves as the syllabic template for four different words: distinguished in speech by four distinct tones and in writing by four different characters: 秃 (tū), 涂 (tú), 土 (tǔ), 兔 (tù) (meaning 'bald', 'daub', 'soil' and 'rabbit', respectively). In English, stress can sometimes signal different meanings, as with *condúct* and *cónduct*. Although such pairs represent just one subclass of patterns in the complicated English stress system, they do offer an interesting site for a contrastive analysis of Chinese and English patterns of suprasegmentals.

The two languages also contrast greatly in syllable structure. In each Chinese syllable there are from one to four phonemes. The syllabic structure of words can be expressed as (C) V (C), where the vowel is the nucleus with one consonant before and/or after it. The syllabic structure of English is far more complex, with varying numbers of consonants possibly appearing both before and after the vowel. Stress patterns in the syllables in the two languages are also quite different. In Chinese, the distinction between stressed and unstressed syllables is not transparent. Native Chinese speakers tend to pronounce each and every syllable in a word distinctively except for the untoned syllables (Zhang & Li, 2011). There is a certain difference between stressed and unstressed syllables, but it is not easy to recognize in oral communication. As tones can signal meaning differences in Chinese words, speakers make their tones quite distinct; if not, the words would sound untoned and an unintended meaning might be construed by the listener. As a result, nearly all syllables in a word are apt to be stressed more or less by Chinese speakers. In English, the distinction between stressed and unstressed syllables is clear, with the stressed much stronger than the unstressed syllable. Word stress patterns are more complicated in multisyllable English words in which the stress has degrees. Syllables with different degrees of stress thus form a continuum,

Table 9.1 Main characteristics of Chinese and English disyllable word stress patterns

	Status and function of WS	WS rules	Relationship between WS and LC	Relationship between WS and SS
English[1]	Stress can signal different word meanings.	Rules are complex and the place of stress is not fixed.	Stress sometimes indicates the LC of a word.	(1) Long vowels or diphthongs are often stressed; (2) coda consonant clusters are often stressed.
Chinese	Stress does not distinguish word meanings.	Stress may be audible on the second syllable for ordinary words, and on the first syllable for untoned words.	Stress placement does not indicate LC.	(1) No distinction between long and short vowels exists; (2) no consonant clusters exist.

WS: word stress; LC: lexical class; SS: syllabic structures; SC: syllabic clusters.

from the most strongly stressed to the weakest, unstressed syllable. In the word *introduction,* for example, the third syllable, which has the main stress, is stronger than any other syllable in the word. The first syllable, which receives secondary stress, is stronger than the second, and the fourth is the weakest of all. Underlying the complexity of stress patterns in English multisyllable words are complex word stress rules such as the main stress rule and the alternating stress rule (Chomsky & Halle, 1968: 59–83).

The main features of Chinese and English disyllable word stress patterns are summarized in Table 9.1. Some of the characteristics cited in the table will be discussed in more detail in the next section. In general, it seems clear that there exist more differences than similarities between Chinese and English stress placement. Accordingly, Chinese learners of English have to acquire a prosodic system which is quite different from that in their native language.

Literature Review

Most previous studies on the acquisition of English stress patterns by L2 learners have involved exclusively either early or late learners. Of the few studies that have examined the age factor, some (e.g. Guion, 2005, 2006; Guion *et al.*, 2004) have identified an age effect. These studies have mainly investigated three aspects of knowledge likely to influence the acquisition of English stress patterns by L2 learners: knowledge of syllabic structure, distributional stress patterns of nouns and verbs and analogical extension of stress patterns from phonologically similar known words. In English, long vowels (e.g. [iː] in *beet*) tend to be stressed more often than short vowels (e.g. [i] in *bit*), and syllables with more coda consonants are more likely to receive stress than syllables with fewer or no coda consonants. Furthermore, bisyllabic nouns are more likely to have initial stress while bisyllabic verbs are more likely to have final stress. Experiments with non-words have shown that native English speakers are sensitive both to the distributional property of syllabic structure and to the distributional stress patterns of lexical classes. It has also been shown that stress patterns of known words play a role in stress assignment on new words for native English speakers (Wayland *et al.*, 2006).

Davis and Kelly (1997) tested both native and non-native English speakers' knowledge about the tendency of lexical stress placement in two-syllable English nouns that have initial stress and two-syllable verbs that have final stress. Subjects were a group of English learners from six L1 backgrounds (Cantonese, Finnish, German, Korean, Japanese and Spanish) with varying ages of acquisition (5–27 years). They found that words with final stress were more likely to be used in a sentence as verbs than were words with initial stress. For Davis and Kelly, these results indicated that the non-native speakers had learned the English noun–verb stress difference. However, age of arrival and length of residence did not correlate with the performance of the non-native English speakers.

Guion *et al.* (2004) studied the acquisition of the English word stress system by early and late Spanish–English bilinguals. In the production experiment, participants were required to concatenate non-words of four syllabic types that were presented as isolated stressed syllables in a single word and say it in a sentence frame. In the perception experiment, participants gave perceptual judgments on aurally presented paired sentences which differed only in the stress placement of non-words. Guion *et al.* found that in the production experiment, early Spanish–English bilinguals demonstrated near-native-like patterns of stress placement: that is, they used lexical class, vowel length and number of coda consonants to assign stress to non-words in a way almost identical to that of native English speakers. In the perception experiment, early bilinguals showed some deviations from the native speakers in using vowel length to place stress. This indicates that, given early and prolonged exposure to English, early bilinguals may be able to acquire knowledge of stress distributions by lexical class and syllabic structure in a way that is similar, but not identical, to that of native speakers. On the other hand, their study also found that the late Spanish–English bilinguals demonstrated a somewhat weaker knowledge of stress distribution by lexical class as well as syllabic structure compared to the early Spanish–English bilinguals in the production and the perception experiments.

Guion (2005) examined the English stress patterns of early and late Korean–English bilinguals and found that both the early and the late groups evidenced partial or native-like knowledge of syllabic stress placement in the production and perception experiments, although the early group was more native-like than the late group in the production experiment. The study also found that both the early and the late Korean–English bilinguals displayed non-native-like knowledge of stress patterns in the lexical classes of noun and verb; in comparison with native speakers, the performance of the late bilinguals was less successful than that of the early bilinguals. The results suggested that the late Korean–English bilinguals did not rely on their L2 knowledge of lexical class stress assignment in their production and perception of word stress in English. These findings differ from the study by Guion *et al.* (2004) with Spanish–English bilinguals, in which both the early and the late Spanish–English bilinguals evidenced knowledge of stress distributions by lexical class, and even the late Spanish–English bilinguals showed some native-like knowledge of the distributional patterns.

The two investigations (Guion, 2005; Guion *et al.*, 2004) thus indicate that acquisition of such patterns is affected by age of L2 exposure, as manifested in the fact that early learners demonstrated better performance than late learners in most cases. However, whether the acquisition of English stress patterns is affected by learners' L1 backgrounds seems to be more complicated than the age factor. Guion (2004: 223) offered a transfer account of the results involving syllabic structure for the late Spanish–English bilinguals' preference for and frequent production of initial stress in comparison with the early Spanish–English bilinguals as well as the native speakers. This is due to the fact that penultimate stress is the most common in the Spanish lexicon. However, Guion did not see any influence of Spanish on the results with reference to lexical class.

When Guion (2005) discussed one of the major differences between the studies (Guion *et al.* [2004] vs. Guion [2005]), she attributed the difference to participants' different linguistic backgrounds. The evidence of non-native-like knowledge of stress placement in the lexical classes of noun and verb among both the early and the late Korean–English bilinguals was assumed to have resulted from L1 transfer since prosodic prominence in Korean is defined at the phrase level rather than at the lexical level as in English (Guion, 2005, 2006). Guion (2005: 527) explained that early exposure to a phrase-level prosodic system may have reduced Korean–English bilinguals' sensitivity to English lexical patterns, and further that 'this effect might become more pronounced with increased delays of exposure to the L2'. Even so, Guion (2004: 223) did not interpret the Spanish–English bilinguals' use of distributional knowledge by lexical class as transfer from the L1 'as no such lexical differences exist' in Spanish. Instead, she offered an exposure account for the Spanish–English bilinguals' use of distributional knowledge by lexical class.

Guion's reluctance to see Spanish influence as a factor in the lexical class results creates a paradox. If Spanish–English bilinguals could demonstrate native-like knowledge of stress distributions by lexical class simply from exposure to English, similar results should be observed with the Korean–English bilinguals. Yet this was not the case since the Korean–English bilinguals showed much less sensitivity to English lexical class distinctions.

Despite the fact that Spanish has no contrastive stress patterns across nouns and verbs (Harris, 1994) as in English *cómbine* and *combíne*, stress differences across some other classes of words do exist. For example, the pronoun *éstas* 'these' (feminine plural) is in a minimal pair relation with the verb *estás* 'you are' (singular). Stress thus has a phonemic function in Spanish just as important as the phonemic function of stress in English. Accordingly, it may well be that both the early and the late Spanish–English bilinguals were sensitive to English stress contrasts in a way similar to native English speakers, which would therefore be positive transfer.

The difference between Spanish speakers and Thai speakers is also relevant in this regard. Wayland *et al.* (2006) studied adult Thai learners' knowledge of the L2 English prosodic system. They found that syllables with a long vowel attracted stress more often than syllables containing a short vowel, and nouns received initial stress more often than verbs for this group of L2 learners in their production of English non-words. The results might seem to suggest that the Thai learners possess native-like knowledge of the relationship between syllabic structure and stress pattern placement, which was interpreted as positive transfer from the Thai language. However, in the perception of English non-words, this group failed to demonstrate knowledge of English stress assignment. That is, neither lexical class nor syllabic structure influenced their perceptual judgments on English non-word stress placement. Regression analyses confirmed that neither syllabic structure nor lexical class was a significant factor in affecting Thai learners' stress assignments on non-words.

Recent work on Chinese has found some evidence of cross-linguistic differences affecting EFL learners' stress patterns. A corpus-based study (Gao & Deng, 2009) found that word stress misplacement was common among Chinese students. Stress errors often occurred in polysyllabic words in which the second syllable was often mistakenly stressed. Incomplete knowledge of English lexical stress rules was considered to be the cause of the learners' errors.

Nevertheless, investigations in some other settings have not always found L1 influence on the learning of L2 word stress patterns. Erdmann (1973) studied German learners' placement of stress in pronouncing English words and concluded that their performance did not accord with either English or German word stress rules. In a study with L2 learners whose native languages included Mandarin, Cantonese and Japanese, Archibald (1997) did not find evidence of transfer of L1 stress patterns into English as the errors in stress placement did not seem to be related to syllabic structure or the lexical class of the words in the learners' native language.

The studies reviewed thus show no consensus about L1 transfer. Moreover, results from Guion (2005) and Wayland *et al.* (2006) suggest that some aspects of a new prosodic system differing from that of the learner's native system can be learned well into adulthood. Even so, in their studies, the L1 prosodic system did exert a strong influence on the learning process, particularly for adult learners.

It should be noted, however, that most studies of L1 influences and age effects on the acquisition of L2 stress patterns have been conducted mostly in an L2 context. In China, English is learned as a foreign language, where learners' exposure to English is limited, by and large, to school, usually to a few hours of classroom instruction per week. In general, Chinese EFL learners have less exposure to English and fewer opportunities to use it for communicative purposes than do English as a second language (ESL) learners. Given the fact that Chinese prosody is different from the English system, the likelihood seems high that Chinese EFL learners may not develop general rules for English stress patterns and instead store stress patterns of each individual lexical item being learned. Such a possibility justifies an investigation into whether early exposure to English prosody is conducive to learning stress properties at the word level and whether Chinese prosody influences the learning of lexical stress patterns for both early and late Chinese EFL learners.

The Study

The present study was designed to investigate whether the age of L2 exposure affects foreign language learners in their acquisition of L2 native-like phonological knowledge in a school setting. It was also designed to determine to what extent the Chinese prosodic system might influence the learning of L2 English word stress patterns since the two languages differ so much in their suprasegmental systems. To this end, we examined early and late Chinese EFL learners' knowledge of English stress patterns. More specifically, we looked into the learners' knowledge of English stress patterns based on syllabic structure and distribution across the lexical classes of noun and verb. The following four research questions were addressed in our study:

(1) Do early or late Chinese EFL learners demonstrate native-like knowledge of English lexical stress patterns based on syllabic structure?
(2) Do early or late Chinese learners demonstrate native-like knowledge of English stress patterns based on lexical class?
(3) Does age of L2 exposure affect Chinese learners in acquiring English lexical stress patterns?

(4) How might Chinese suprasegmental patterns influence learners in acquiring English stress patterns?

Participants

Ninety adults took part in the experiment. Sixty participants were freshmen or sophomores in a university in southwest China, and 30 were native speakers of English from the USA. For all the participants in the Native Speaker group, English was their native language and they spoke no other language at home during childhood, although most of them had experience in foreign language learning in high school and/or college. Most of them were living in the USA at the time of the study and they took part in the experiment through the internet chat software SKYPE. All the participants in the Early and Late Learner groups spoke Chinese as their first language and studied EFL in a classroom setting. No participant in these two groups had been to any English-speaking country. The Early Learner group had started studying English between the ages of 5 and 9. As for the Late Learner group, the starting ages ranged from 12 to 13 (Table 9.2). Our decision about the cut-off age for the late group reflects our concurrence with Long (1990) that it would be impossible for learners older than 12 to acquire native-like phonological knowledge in an L2.

Instruments

Our study employed three measures: a dictation test, a stress placement test and an oral production test. The dictation test was designed to measure the participants' English proficiency. The test was based on the College English Test (CET) compound dictation test, one of the subtests in the CET, a nationwide standardized proficiency exam that is administered by the Higher Education Division of the State Education Commission. In this test, the participants were required to listen to a passage and fill in 10 words in 10 blanks. The mean score for the Early Learner group was 7.87 out of a possible 10, and the mean score for the Late Learner group was 7.63. A t-test indicated that there was no significant difference between the two mean scores.

Table 9.2 Information on the subjects

Groups	Sex (F/M)	AOL[a]	LOL[b]	Age[c]
Native speaker	14/16	0.0	26.8	26.8
Early learner	11/19	8.1	10.9	18.9
Late learner	11/19	12.2	7.5	19.7

[a] Mean age of English learning (in years).

[b] Mean length of English learning (in years).

[c] Mean age at time of testing (in years).

The stress placement test used real English words, and was in several respects similar to the one used by Guion *et al.* (2004). Eighteen words with regular English stress patterns and another 18 words which were not consistent with regular patterns were selected. Participants in the two groups were required to first write down the Chinese meaning for each word and then rate their confidence in their ability to pronounce the word on a five-point scale. Then, they were asked to underline the stressed syllable. The underlining procedure constitutes a methodological difference from the placement test used by Guion *et al.* (2004), who recorded the participants reading each of the words in the sentence frame 'I said ___ this time', with the elicited words being studied later for correct stress placement. We decided to employ the underlining procedure in order to avoid any possible slips of the tongue among participants during the reading.

The accuracy of stress placement on known English words was 85% or higher, and so the results from this measure indicated that both the Early and the Late Learner groups had the ability to correctly place stress on known English words, whether or not the words were consistent with the regular stress patterns.

In order to test early and late Chinese learners' knowledge of the English stress patterns in terms of syllabic structure and lexical class, an oral production experiment based on Guion *et al.* (2004) was administered to the two learner groups and the Native Speaker group. The participants were required to produce 40 non-words with four types of syllabic structures (Type 1: CVVCVCC, e.g. /beitist/; Type 2: CVCVCC, e.g. /dekips/; Type 3: CVCVC, e.g. /nilet/; Type 4: CVCVVC, e.g. /nili:t/). According to Guion *et al.*, the effect of long vowels predicts various response patterns, in that Type 1 should have more initial syllable stress than Type 2. Similarly, Type 3 should have more initial syllable stress than Type 4. The effect of final coda consonants predicts the following tendency: Type 3 should have more initial syllable stress than Type 2. The factor of lexical class involves whether nouns receive more initial syllable main stress than do verbs and verbs receive more final syllable main stress than do nouns.

In this production experiment, each of the non-words was presented twice, once with the noun frame and once with the verb frame. A total of 80 trials were randomized and divided into two counterbalanced blocks. Participants were trained with non-test items before the first block. The non-words were played with the software RealPlayer on a personal computer. For each trial, the non-words were first presented visually with a sentence frame; then, the two stressed, isolated syllables that constituted the non-word were presented with a three-second inter-stimulus interval. Participants could replay the trial if they chose to; after responding, they continued to play the next trial. The responses, which were recorded on tape, were coded as having main stress on either the first or the second syllable. For each non-word in each sentence frame (noun vs. verb) and in each syllabic type, the number of initial syllable stress responses was divided by the total number of responses for the 90 participants, resulting in a proportion of first syllable stress responses for each word in each sentence frame in each syllabic type.

Analysis and Results

Subject and item analyses of variance (ANOVA) were conducted in SPSS using a $3 \times 4 \times 2$ mixed design: 3 (Group: Native Speaker group, Early Learner group vs. Late Learner group) $\times 4$ (Syllabic Structure: Type 1, Type 2, Type 3 vs. Type 4) $\times 2$ (Lexical Class: noun frame vs. verb frame).

The main effects of Group ($F1 = 11.047$, $p < 0.001$; $F2 = 9.070$, $p < 0.001$), Syllabic Structure ($F1 = 23.092$, $p < 0.01$; $F2 = 8.167$, $p < 0.01$) and Lexical Class ($F1 = 132.346$, $p < 0.01$; $F2 = 220.420$, $p < 0.01$) were all significant, as well as the three-way interactions ($F1 = 4.491$, $p < 0.001$; $F2 = 8.784$, $p < 0.001$). The two-way interactions were also significant. To further investigate these effects, separate t-tests investigating the effect of Lexical Class for each of the three groups were performed. Then, separate one-way ANOVAs and pairwise comparisons examining the effect of Syllabic Structure for each of the three groups were performed. The results showed that there was a significant difference in the knowledge of English stress patterns based on syllabic structure and lexical class between the three groups (Figures 9.1 and 9.2).

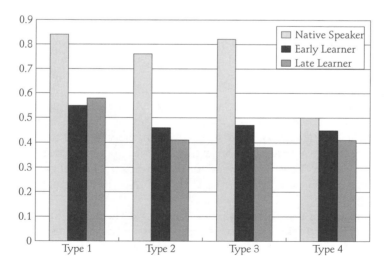

Figure 9.1 Mean proportion of initial stress productions for the noun frame for the three groups (n = 30). Four non-word types with different syllabic structures were produced in the noun frame

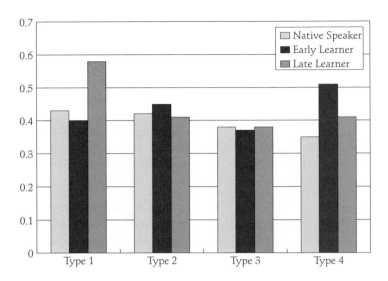

Figure 9.2 Mean proportion of initial stress productions for the verb frame for the three groups (*n* = 30). Four non-word types with different syllabic structures were produced in the verb frame

The effect of Lexical Class was significant for the Native Speaker group ($p < 0.01$), with 0.39 more first syllable stress productions in the noun frame than in the verb frame (0.73 vs. 0.34). However, separate *t*-tests did not reveal any significant difference of first syllable stress in the noun frame than in the verb frame for the other two groups: Early Learner ($p = 0.291$) and Late Learner ($p = 0.309$). The effect of Syllabic Structure was significant ($p < 0.05$) for the Native Speaker group, but it was not significant for the other two groups ($p > 0.05$). In the case of words produced in the noun frame, the Native Speaker group was found to have more initial syllable stress responses on Type 3 than Type 4 ($p < 0.01$). In the case of words produced in the verb frame, the Native Speaker group was found to have more initial syllable stress responses for Type 1 than the other three types ($p < 0.05$). The effect of Syllabic Structure in the verb frame for the Early and the Late Learner groups was not significant.

The results of the present study indicate that the Native Speaker group had more first syllable main stress responses in the noun frame than in the verb frame, while the effect of Lexical Class for the Early and the Late Learner groups was not significant. Accordingly, the native speakers seem to have used knowledge of distributional patterns based on lexical class (noun vs. verb) to assign main stress on disyllabic non-words, while both groups of Chinese EFL learners did not.

For the effect of Syllabic Structure on main stress placement, the native speakers produced stress patterns consistent with the distribution of stress across vowel types: that is, effects related to vowel length were found. For noun frame productions, more initial stress was found for Type 3 non-words than Type 4 non-words. For verb frame productions, more initial stress was found for Type 1 non-words than Type 2 non-words. Coda consonant effects were not found. In contrast, the Early and the Late Learner groups showed no effect of vowel length or coda consonants.

Discussion

Results from the study reveal that the early and the late Chinese EFL learners did not demonstrate native-like knowledge of English word stress patterns involving either syllabic structure or lexical class, and neither syllabic structure nor lexical class influences Chinese EFL learners' stress placement on English non-words. Our results were similar to those obtained in Wayland et al. (2006), in which neither syllabic structure nor lexical class proved to be an important factor in affecting Thai–English learners' decisions about stress on non-words. However, there was a difference between the two studies. For the Thai–English learners, a syllable with a long vowel attracted stress more often than a syllable with a short vowel or coda consonant(s) in their production of the English non-words, and this was seen as evidence of native-like knowledge of syllabic structure (Wayland et al., 2006: 298). This difference might be due partly to the linguistic backgrounds of the participants in the two studies. The differences between the decisions of Chinese and Thai speakers are, however, much smaller than the considerable differences between these two groups taken together and other groups that have been studied with similar methods, i.e. speakers of Spanish and Korean. Such great differences in performance argue strongly for language-specific influences on the response patterns of participants in the various studies.

The results of the current study also reveal that age of L2 exposure had no effect on Chinese EFL learners in the process of learning English word stress patterns by syllabic structure and lexical class, which differs from studies conducted by Guion et al. (2004) and Guion (2005). Those investigations found that early Spanish–English and Korean–English bilinguals demonstrated better performance than late Spanish–English and Korean–English bilinguals in the production and perception of English stress patterns related to syllabic structure and lexical class except in the case of stress patterns related to syllabic structure in the perception experiment where both the early and the late Korean–English bilinguals demonstrated native-like knowledge. However, in our study, both the early and the late Chinese EFL learners did not exhibit native-like knowledge of English lexical stress patterns involving syllabic structure or lexical class. Considering the high accuracy rate achieved by the early and the late Chinese EFL learners in the stress placement on known English words, it seems that both the early and the late learners rely more heavily on word-by-word learning of English stress patterns rather than abstract rules about stress placement by syllabic structure and lexical class. Therefore, the advantage of early exposure to the English prosodic system was not evident in our study, and this, to some extent, echoes the finding of a recent study by Hopp and Schmid (2013) suggesting that early acquisition cannot guarantee native-like pronunciation.

The high accuracy rate obtained by the two learner groups in the stress placement test on known words seems to suggest that, for the perception of English stress patterns of known words, Chinese EFL learners often rely on the analogy of the stress patterns of similar words which they have already learned. This is an easy L2–L2 inferencing process in which the influence of the native language may not be involved. However, as to the production process of English stress patterns based on English non-words, learners do not show much of an ability to abstract English stress placement patterns across a large set of lexical items, an ability which may be more difficult to develop.

What then is transferred from the L1 Chinese system? According to He (1987: 72), 'in the phonological system of all languages, people tend to be sensitive to the phonological features that can distinguish meaning but numb to other features that cannot'. As tone is a distinctive feature at the lexical level in Chinese, Chinese learners are likely to be sensitive to the tone features rather than the stress features. Such sensitivity may lead to an even distribution of strength on stressed and unstressed syllables or the misplacement of English stress patterns. As suggested by Moyer (2013), L2 learners' phonological/phonetic inaccuracies caused by L1 transfer may be natural and inevitable and are not necessarily indicative of age-related decline in phonological/phonetic competence.

We argue that what is transferred for the early and the late Chinese EFL learners may be their Chinese phonetic intuition. Once L1 phonetic intuition is developed, it becomes stable through time and use, and it is not easy to change. This may limit what late-starting Chinese EFL learners notice about English stress features as 'one language is already in place as a knowledge base, which can imply greater metalinguistic awareness' (Moyer, 2014: 418). With increasing exposure to the L2 prosodic system, ordinary Chinese EFL learners may learn L2 stress on a word-by-word basis (Guion, 2006). Chinese EFL learners may eventually develop stress rules closer to those of the target language, but learners who have the strongest phonetic sensitivity may successfully get rid of undesired influences of the L1 knowledge system (Odlin, 1989: 115). However, the limited exposure in the Chinese EFL context suggests that successful learning of English stress patterns may take a long time for many Chinese English classroom learners.

Conclusion

This chapter has shown that both early and late Chinese learners of EFL did not demonstrate native-like knowledge of English stress patterns based on lexical class and syllabic structure. One possible interpretation is that phrase-level prosodic prominence of Chinese may adversely affect Chinese speakers' ability to acquire a word-level prosodic system.

The findings in the study suggest some implications for foreign language learning in China. As detailed in the present study, Chinese EFL learners did not exhibit abstract knowledge of English stress patterns based on lexical class and syllabic structure. This might be attributed to two factors. First, Chinese EFL learners pay less attention to English word stress than to other aspects of English such as grammar. English teachers in China seem to spend little time teaching students English stress. Learners normally learn about English stress at the word level by reading lists of new words, by imitating their English teachers or by consulting phonetic information from a dictionary. Second, classroom learning does not provide adequate exposure for students to abstract knowledge of English stress patterns. To facilitate the process of developing native-like knowledge of English stress patterns, meaningful classroom learning activities need to be designed.

Acknowledgments

This research was supported by the Humanity and Social Science Fund of Ministry of Education, China (Project 08JA740048) and the National Social Science Fund, China (14XYY007). We thank Professor Yu Liming and Professor Terence Odlin for their helpful comments on earlier versions of this chapter.

Note

(1) Lexical class is not the only factor in the complicated English word stress patterns; words of different historical sources (Germanic, French and Latin) have different word stress patterns, while in Chinese, basic words do not have foreign sources. However, such historical factors do not impinge on the analysis offered in this study.

References

Archibald, J. (1997) The acquisition of English stress by speakers of nonaccentual languages: Lexical storage versus computation of stress. *Linguistics* 35, 167–181.

Chan, M.K.K. (2005) The processing and representation of lexical stress in the short-term memory of Cantonese-English successive bilinguals. Unpublished master dissertation, University of Hong Kong.

Chomsky, N. and Halle, M. (1968) *The Sound Pattern of English*. New York: Harper and Row.

Cutler, A. (1984) Stress and accent in language production and understanding. In D. Gibbon and H. Richter (eds) *Intonation, Accent, and Rhythm* (pp. 77–90). Berlin: de Gruyter.

Davis, S.M. and Kelly, M.H. (1997) Knowledge of the English noun-verb stress difference by native and nonnative speakers. *Journal of Memory and Language* 36, 445–460.

Depoux, E., Pallier, C., Sebastián Gallés, N. and Mehler, J. (1997) A distressing 'deafness' in French? *Journal of Memory and Language* 36, 406–421.

Depoux, E., Peperkamp, S. and Sebastián-Gallés, N. (2001) A robust method to study stress 'deafness'. *Journal of the Acoustical Society of America* 110, 1606–1618.

Erdmann, P.H. (1973) Patterns of stress-transfer in English and German. *International Review of Applied Linguistics* 11, 229–241.

Flege, J.E., Yeni-Komshian, G.H. and Liu, S. (1999) Age constraints on second-language acquisition. *Journal of Memory and Language* 41, 78–104.

Gao, L. and Deng, Y. (2009) The research of Chinese EFL learners' misplacement of English word stress: A corpus-based research. *Foreign Language World* 3, 10–16.

Guion, S.G. (2005) Knowledge of English word stress patterns in early and late Korean-English bilinguals. *Studies in Second Language Acquisition* 27, 503–533.

Guion, S.G. (2006) Knowledge of English stress in second language learner: First language and age of acquisition effects. *Korean Journal of English Language and Linguistics* 6, 465–492.

Guion, S.G., Harada, T. and Clark, J.J. (2004) Early and late Spanish-English bilinguals' acquisition of English word stress patterns. *Bilingualism Language and Cognition* 7, 207–226.

He, S. (1987) Several aspects of contrast between English and Chinese in English pronunciation teaching. *Journal of Foreign Languages* 6, 70–73.

Hopp, H. and Schmid, M.S. (2013) Perceived foreign accent in first language attrition and second language acquisition: The impact of age of acquisition and bilingualism. *Applied Psycholinguistics* 34, 361–394.

Houston, D., Jusczyk, P., Kuijpers, W.C., Coolen, R. and Cutler, A. (2000) Both Dutch- and English learning 9-month-olds segment Dutch words from fluent speech. *Psychological Bulletin and Review* 7, 504–509.

Long, M.H. (1990) Maturational constraints on language development. *Studies in Second Language Acquisition* 12, 251–285.

Long, M. (2013) Maturational constraints on child and adult SLA. In G. Granena and M. Long (eds) *Sensitive Period, Language Aptitude, and Ultimate L2 Attainment* (pp. 3–41). Amsterdam: John Benjamins.

Moyer, A. (2013) *Foreign Accent: The Phenomenon of Non-Native Speech*. Cambridge: Cambridge University Press.

Moyer, A. (2014) Exceptional outcomes in L2 phonology: The critical factors of learner engagement and self-regulation. *Applied Linguistics* 35, 418–440.

Odlin, T. (1989) *Language Transfer*. Cambridge: Cambridge University Press.

Trofimovich, P. and Baker, W. (2006) Learning second language suprasegmentals: Effect of L2 experience on prosody and fluency characteristics of L2 speech. *Studies in Second Language Acquisition* 28, 1–30.

Wayland, R., Guion, S.G., Landfair, D. and Bin, L. (2006) Native Thai speakers' acquisition of English word stress patterns. *Journal of Psycholinguist Research* 35, 285–304.

Wu, J. and Zhu, H. (2001) *Chinese Prosody*. Beijing: Language and Literature Press.

Zhang, L. and Li, H. (2011) Comparative study of elements that influence English and Chinese lexical stress patterns. *Journal of University of Electronic Science and Technology of China (Social Sciences Edition)* 5, 81–84.

10 SLA Perspectives on Language Contact: An Experimental Study on Retroflexion

David Mitchell

Introduction

Contact between speakers of Indo-Aryan (IA) and Proto-Dravidian (PDr) has been a highly debated issue for several years (e.g. Deshpande, 1979; Emeneau, [1956], 1980; Hock, 1996), particularly the issue of the development of retroflex consonants. In this chapter, the transfer of the retroflex feature onto IA dental stops by way of *imposition*[1] as the mechanism of transfer is tested and it is demonstrated that speakers of a language containing retroflex phonemes can impose that retroflex feature onto dental phonemes, even when the first language (L1) already has dental phonemes in its phonological inventory. The sounds under investigation are limited to apical alveolar stops and oral and nasal {ṭ, ḍ, ṇ, ṭh, ḍh}, and the phonological environments under question are word-initial, word-final and word-internal (in both C_C and V_V positions).

Before describing the experiment and results, it will help to consider three topics: (a) what is known about IA/PDr contact, (b) the issue of contact-induced change versus sound change proper and (c) phonological transfer. Consideration of these topics reveals the logic of considering imposition to be the mechanism most applicable to understanding the ancient language contact situation rather than other possibilities, such as transfer due to a massive influx of vocabulary borrowings or internal development (i.e. change not due to contact) alone.

Approximately 3500 years ago, in northwest India, there was contact between speakers of the Indo-European language Indo Aryan and speakers of the Proto Dravidian language family. The oldest text we have that shows the linguistic effects of this contact is the Rig Veda, which dates back to approximately 1500 BC. The consensus among scholars such as Thomason and Kaufman (1988: 39) is that the IA speakers were the dominant group.

However, the political and demographic circumstances are highly debated. At one extreme, scholars have argued that the IA speakers dominated the PDr speakers (the latter being considered by some scholars as primitive people) with military force, subsequently introducing their language, religion and other cultural traditions. However, scholars of a very different mind hold that it was the IAs who were less advanced and who found a more civilized lifestyle among the Dravidians (Deshpande, 1979; Emeneau, [1956], 1980; Hock, 1996). Due to a lack of solid evidence of any warfare between these two groups or of any invasion, of colonization or of racial hatred, a new view has taken shape, one that sees the two linguistic groups as highly integrated with relatively little ethnic conflict and with 'approximate social equality' (Hock, 1996). Southworth (1979), comparing two word lists, one showing borrowings from IA into PDr and the other showing borrowings from PDr into IA, saw the patterns as similar to modern colonial cases, with IA tending to borrow relatively few words, mainly flora and fauna, whereas words for technology and other cultural domains spread more from IA into PDr than the other way around. Thus, it appears that IA was probably the dominant language in the sense that it held a certain prestige rather than in the sense of it being the language of a military elite that had utterly subjugated speakers of PDr.

Both internal sound change (independent of language contact) and contact-induced change have been proposed as the cause of retroflexes now in the IA family of languages. Retroflexes are found in Sanskrit, the earliest attested daughter language of Proto-IA, but there is disagreement as to whether there were retroflex phonemes in Proto-IA before contact with PDr speakers (Deshpande, 1979; Southworth, 1979) or if they arose due to contact (Emeneau, 1956). The disagreement reflects a more general problem in historical linguistics over whether to identify a new sound pattern as due to *internally motivated sound change* (Joseph & Janda, 2003) or due to *external factors*, which often involve language contact. Retroflexion could have been internally motivated in IA languages and many sound change laws have been posited to connect earlier Indo-Iranian (the intermediate stage between Proto-Indo-European [PIE] and early IA) with the later IE languages of India (the IA languages), and some of the suggested laws involve retroflexion. Table 10.1 lists some of the more important historical patterns involving retroflexion (with the retroflex segment always marked with a dot underneath it). I provide a simplified look at each rule to give readers a basic idea of the sound changes that took place, as the precise details of each rule are numerous and go beyond the scope of this chapter. The rules in boldface (a–d) deal directly with {ṭ, ḍ, ṇ, ṭh, ḍh}, the target sounds that I am addressing (Collinge, 1985; Kobayashi, 2004). Rules (e–f) deal with dental sibilants becoming retroflex sibilants, but they are still important to mention because the resulting retroflex can go on to spread to a following {t, n}.

Table 10.1 Sound changes leading to retroflex phonemes (numbers in the rules refer to endnotes)

(a)	Fortunatov's law[2]	*lt³ > ṭ⁴	Compare **Skt. kuṭhāra-** ~ **Latin culter 'axe'**
(b)	NATI rule	*n > ṇ/{r, ṛ, ṣ...}_	*narena > nareṇa* 'with the man'
(c)	Rule I	*d(h) > ḍ(h) / *ž_	*liždha > līḍha* 'licked'
(d)	Rule II	*{tʰ⁽ʰ⁾} > {ṭ⁽ʰ⁾} / ṣ __	*sthā- > ti-ṣṭha-ti* 'he stands'
(e)	Rule III	*ḱ > š > ṣ / _*t	Compare Skt. *aṣṭa* ~ Latin *octo* 'eight'
(f)	RUKI rule	*s > ṣ / {r, u, k, i} __	*sthā- > ti-ṣṭha-ti* 'he stands'

Fortunatov's law (a) holds that when an *l precedes {t, d, n} in a cluster, the two consonants merge and become a retroflex (in the sketch of this rule in Table 10.1, only the case of the /**t**/ is specified, not the cases of the /d/ or the /n/). Thus *-lt- would become ṭ, *-ld- would become -ḍ- and *-ln- would become -ṇ-. The examples show the difference between a Sanskrit word which illustrates the outcome of the rule with a Latin word which did not undergo the retroflexion process. The NATI rule (b) requires that when a dental nasal is preceded in a word by {r, ṛ, ṣ} and is followed by a vowel or by {v, n, m, y}, it becomes a retroflex (for reasons of space, only the environment preceding the affected segment is given in the sketch of the rule in the table). The example shows the change acting on a hypothetical form (*narena*) to an actual Sanskrit word (*nareṇa*). Rule (c) states that *d and *dʰ become retroflexes when preceded by a voiced post-alveolar fricative. Using this along with certain other rules, we can thus posit the following changes: *žd⁽ʰ⁾ > *ẓd⁽ʰ⁾ > *ẓḍ⁽ʰ⁾ > ḍ⁽ʰ⁾. The example in (c) is like the one in (b), giving a hypothesized form that underwent change to an actual Sanskrit form. The example illustrating rule (d) shows that a voiceless aspirated dental stop /tʰ/ becomes /ṭʰ/ when preceded by a voiceless retroflex sibilant /ṣ/ in the word *ti-ṣṭha-ti*. The RUKI rule (f), however, is also involved in this example, since the root-initial s- changes to ṣ. This sibilant thus 'spreads' its retroflex feature to the following aspirated dental stop, changing tʰ to ṭʰ. in *ti-ṣṭha-ti*. In the example, the root *stha* ('to stand') requires repetition of a form (*ti*) in order to inflect for third singular present tense, that is, with the *ti-* at the beginning of the word as well as at the end; the vowel in the first *ti-* triggers the retroflexion of the /s/ and so contributes indirectly to the retroflexion of the ṭ in the root. (The RUKI rule, it should be noted, states that when the phonemes {r, u, k, i}[5] immediately precede the sibilant *s, retroflexion will occur.[6]) As for rule (e), it is argued that the voiceless palatalized velar stop became a voiceless post-alveolar fricative in Proto-Indo-Iranian (the proto stage dating before the split into Iranian and IA). Then, yet another change is posited, namely where a voiceless post-alveolar fricative became a voiceless retroflex fricative when it occurred before a voiceless dental stop. Thus, we can posit the following changes to account for the change from *okto to *aṣṭa* in the sequence *ḱt > *št > *ṣt > ṣṭ. (In contrast, the Latin *octo* did not undergo these changes.) The sound change laws in Table 10.1 (along with a few others) account for many of the retroflex phonemes found in attested Sanskrit (i.e. in written texts).

Even with these sound changes, however, we still have cases of retroflexion which cannot be accounted for in terms of their phonetic environment. Moreover, many Sanskrit words showing such unexplained cases are IE in origin, and thus cannot be directly attributed to the possibility of borrowing from PDr. Table 10.2 provides a sample of Sanskrit words with unexplained retroflexes along with their reconstructed PIE antecedents as well as cognates in certain other IE languages which do *not* show retroflexion.

These cases of retroflexion show that we cannot attribute the origin of retroflex phonemes in Sanskrit solely to the (possibly) internal sound changes listed in Table 10.1. On the other hand, PDr *is* reconstructed with retroflex phonemes (Krishnamurti, 2003: 120). With this in mind, PDr is a good candidate as a source for at least some of the retroflexion found in Sanskrit and later IA languages. Table 10.3 provides a short list of minimal pair examples from Tamil and Telugu, two daughter languages of PDr (Brown, 1994; Caldwell, 1875: 38), demonstrating how important retroflexion is in Dravidian languages. This does not prove that in PDr, dentals and retroflexes were phonemically contrastive or even that there were retroflex allophones (Hock, 1996), but the fact that they are contrastive in some of the daughter languages, coupled with the widespread existence of retroflexion in general throughout modern Dravidian languages, does make a good case for the existence of retroflex phonemes in PDr.

Table 10.2 suggests that not all retroflexion in Sanskrit or later IA languages can be explained through possibly internal sound change laws and Table 10.3 suggests that retroflexion is an essential part of Dravidian languages, dating back even to the PDr period. These findings among others have prompted many scholars to assert that retroflexion was incorporated into the IA language via contact with PDr speakers: Thomason and Kaufman (1988), for instance, claim that speakers of PDr shifted to a

Table 10.2 Examples of Proto-Indo-European words with retroflex phonemes imposed in Sanskrit

Sanskrit	Latin	Avestan	Lithuanian	Greek	English	PIE	Gloss
maṇi	monile	mainiš				*moni-	necklace
paṇḍú			spindeti			*(s)pend-	bright
daṇḍa				dendron		*dendr-	tree
vaṇij					win	*wVn-	merchant

Table 10.3 Proto-Dravidian daughter languages with dental/retroflex minimal pairs

Tamil		Telugu	
Dental	*Retroflex*	*Dental*	*Retroflex*
kudi	kuṭi	kuttu	kuṭṭu
en	eṇ	chittu	chiṭṭu
pudei	puṭei	dakku	ḍakku
manei	maṇei	tadi	taḍi

contact variety of IA. If this is the case, retroflexion could have entered the language by way of imposition on the part of the individual speakers (van Coetsem, 1988: 7–19). That is, people who spoke PDr as their L1 would have transferred the retroflex feature to the IA dental segments in question. There is, however, one formidable problem for a transfer analysis, namely, that PDr is reconstructed as having dental stops as well as retroflex stops. Why, therefore, would those speakers impose retroflexion when they were already capable of producing dental stops? The present experiment considers whether this phenomenon can take place either in the present or – by implication – in the past.

Retroflexion

Retroflexion need not have a single origin for both PDr and Sanskrit (or languages in the IA family that appeared after Sanskrit); they might have developed retroflexion separately. However, in this section, it is shown that Sanskrit and Dravidian have very similar phonotactic distributions with regard to phonemes containing the retroflex feature. Accordingly, it would be highly implausible to attribute such similarities to coincidence.

The two columns of Table 10.4 suggest somewhat different phonotactic constraints on retroflex consonants. For instance, PDr did not allow final retroflex stops yet Sanskrit did. However, according to Masica (1991: 157), those stops only occur in Sanskrit 'as a morphophonemic substitute for root-final {ch, ṣ, ś, j, h} finally, in compounds, and before certain inflections beginning with consonants'. These are all similar in that they come at a 'firm' morpheme boundary.[8] While PDr did not allow initial retroflex stops, some of the daughter languages do, but such instances result from metathesis of a word-initial vowel plus retroflex (#VR > #RV) and deletion of initial short vowels in all South Dravidian languages (Krishnamurti, 2003: 157). Sanskrit did allow initial retroflex stops, but again this is a highly restricted case, and Masica states that it happens 'practically never' (Krishnamurti, 2003: 157). Given the relatively small number of words with retroflex stops in this environment, it seems possible that these words came into the language as a result of influence from a Dravidian daughter language.[9] Therefore, initial retroflexes are also questionable as being an

Table 10.4 Distributions for retroflexes alveolars and dentals[7]

Distributions	Sanskrit	Dravidian
Word-initial retroflex stops	+	−
Word-medial retroflex stops	+	+
Word-final retroflex stops	+	−
Word-initial dental stops	+	+
Word-medial dental stops	+	+
Word-final dental stops	+	+
Word-initial alveolar stops	n/a	−
Word-medial alveolar stops	n/a	+
Word-final alveolar stops	n/a	−
Word-initial retroflex nasals	−	−
Word-medial retroflex nasals	+	+
Word-final retroflex nasals	−	+
Word-initial dental nasals	+	+
Word-medial dental nasals	+	+
Word-final dental nasals	+	+

early characteristic, and so the distribution of the retroflex consonants {ṭ ḍ ṇ} in Sanskrit and PDr was at least very similar, and perhaps at an early stage of IA, their retroflex distributions were the same.[10]

With the phonotactic distribution of retroflex stops aligning well in the two ancient languages, imposition by second language (L2) IA speakers becomes an even stronger possibility, though we are still left with the dilemma of appearances of retroflexes where we would expect dentals. Whether the sound change laws listed in Table 10.1 should be interpreted as contact phenomena is beyond the scope of this chapter, but the phonotactic similarities between IA and Dravidian languages (Table 10.4) do support a contact interpretation of those cases unexplained by the rules in Table 10.1 (i.e. those cases in Table 10.2). Considering that the social situation is so ancient, such a contact setting is no longer directly accessible for investigation. However, we can still appeal to the *theorem of uniformitarianism*, described in Joseph and Janda (2003: 26) as being a 'parsimony-derived principle that natural laws are constant across space and time'. This stems from Labov (1972: 275) and from even earlier non-linguistic fields of science. As Joseph and Janda put it,

> Yet probably another consideration would soon come to mind, one involving the slightly extended (and likewise previously mentioned) parsimony-derived assumption that such uniformity of law allows one to view the present as a key to the past: any process now observable thereby becomes available to be invoked as part of a plausible explanation

for past events – this principle is that of 'uniformity of process through time'. (Joseph & Janda, 2003: 26)

In the case of retroflexion in ancient India, one such process may have been imposition, more specifically, L1 → L2 phonetic transfer. Accordingly, an experiment resembling the hypothesized circumstances of the past was performed to see whether we would find similar results, i.e. that retroflexors (speakers using retroflex consonants) would transfer an important systemic property of their native language (retroflexion) to environments not well explained by traditional Indo-Europeanist analyses relying solely on internal change.

Methods

In order to recreate the circumstances of the past, it was necessary to employ two types of languages, one resembling pre-contact IA and the other resembling PDr. The former type served as a target language and the latter type as the source language (or languages) for the experiment. The target language selected was Spanish, and details about the speaker recruited appear in the next paragraph. As for the source language type, seven speakers of retroflexing languages functioned as proxies for speakers of the PDr source language: three Hindi speakers, one Bengali speaker, one Telugu speaker, one Tamil speaker and one Malayalam speaker. The former two languages descend from IA, the latter three descend from PDr. With regard to the Hindi and Bengali speakers, it should be kept in mind that retroflexion is common in the *modern* IA languages even while in the earliest contact (but not in the post-contact) situation, the IA target language which PDr speakers were acquiring had less retroflexion. In view of the extensive retroflex patterns found in Hindi and Bengali today, it is appropriate to include speakers of these modern IA languages to help assess the likelihood of transfer of retroflexion.

The Spanish words used in the experiment were spoken by a female speaker from Colombia in order to model dental consonants like those in the pre-contact IA target language. Table 10.5 details the aspects of the phonological inventories of Spanish, PDr, Proto-Indo-Iranian and Sanskrit that are relevant to this study. How closely the daughter languages of PDr and of Sanskrit resemble their precursors is a question that will be addressed in the discussion of the results.

The Spanish speaker was video-recorded while reading from a list of Spanish words which all contained at least one of the phonemes {t, d, n} either word-initially, word-medially or word-finally, in clusters and intervocalically. At word boundaries and intervocalically, the environment was usually kept free of phonetic motivation for inducing retroflexion. However, one exception involved clusters with /r/, from an expectation

Table 10.5 Phonological chart depicting Proto-Dravidian, Proto-Indo-Iranian, Indo-Aryan (after contact with Dravidian speakers) and Spanish

Dental	Alveolar	Retroflex
Proto-Dravidian		
*t	*t̠	*ṭ
*d	*d̠	*ḍ
*n	*n̠	*ṇ
Proto-Indo-Iranian		
*t/*th		
*d/*dh		
*n		
Sanskrit		
t/th		ṭ/ṭh
d/dh		ḍ/ḍh
n		ṇ
Spanish		
t		
d		
	n	

that this environment would induce retroflexion. The word list thus offered a wide variety of phonetic environments that might or might not elicit retroflexion (see the Appendix). The target phonemes were chosen for the following reasons:

(a) The phonemes (with the exception of Spanish /n/) are dental in Spanish and in pre-contact IA, and thus the two languages were a good choice for this study. It should be noted, though, that Spanish /n/ is alveolar (or, at best, an alveodental), and this place of articulation may make it more likely to be mistaken as a retroflex.
(b) PDr speakers seemed to have used retroflexes in place of dental phonemes in their attempts to pronounce IA words. So, again, appealing to the theorem of uniformitarianism, my hypothesis is that we should see a similar phenomenon in a modern context as in this experiment.

The retroflexors had to watch the video of the Spanish speaker saying the words and repeat them, to the best of their ability, with no option to rewind or hear the same word more than once. This was done to simulate the likely circumstances of the past as closely as possible because speakers in the ancient contact situation did not learn in a classroom environment but rather in an untutored setting by interacting with the speakers of the target language. Furthermore, while trying to learn a new word, L2 IA speakers may not have had the luxury of hearing the word repeated over and over in a social encounter; more likely, they heard words repeated gradually over days, weeks or months. L2 learners in this informal setting would thus have less than ideal opportunities for noticing phonetic norms of the target language.

The retroflexors watched the video of the Spanish speaker reading aloud on the 17-inch screen of an Acer laptop. The Sony headphones they used were of average quality, and participants were allowed to set the volume to a comfortable level; no one indicated an inability to hear the Spanish speaker clearly. They were recorded with a generic Radio Shack brand microphone, which was hooked up to the same Acer laptop and recorded at 44,100 Hz to WAV format using Pratt, a software package for analyzing speech. Each participant was recorded at different times and places, but the setting in all cases was a quiet room having minimal sonic disturbances.

The dependent variable was the place of articulation by the retroflexors (dental vs. retroflex) and the independent variables were language (Hindi, Bengali, Malayalam, Tamil, Telugu), language family (IE, Dravidian), phoneme (/t, d, n/), phonological environment (word-initial, medial intervocalic and medial clusters, word-final) and roundedness of the vowels surrounding the target sounds (rounded vowels vs. unrounded vowels).

The method for identifying retroflexion in the spectrograms used was to look for a precipitous drop or rise in the third and fourth formant (Bhaskararao & Ladefoged, 1983; Hamann, 2003). It is not the consonants themselves that reveal the retroflex feature, but the vowels which precede and/or follow the consonant. Figures 10.1 and 10.2 illustrate the crucial spectrographic region with arrows placed just above the third formant to show the sudden rising or dropping of the hertz value of the vowel. In cases where the vowel precedes the target sound, we expect to see a drop in the third formant as the vowel draws to a close. For instance, in Figure 10.2, when the Hindi speaker repeats the Spanish word *anillo* [aníjo], it is realized as [aṇíjo] and the third and fourth formant status of the initial [a] gives the needed evidence. The Spanish speaker's third formant when pronouncing

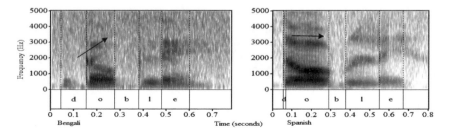

Figure 10.1 Sample of initial retroflex stop (*doble* 'double')

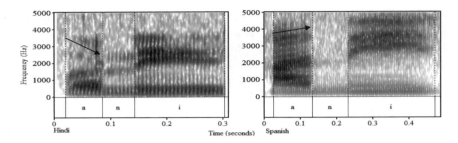

Figure 10.2 Sample of word-medial retroflex (*anillo* 'ring')

the initial vowel [a] is on a slow rise all the way to the point where it meets the onset of the [n], whereas the Hindi speaker's [a] shows a sharp drop to about the 2000 Hz level in the third formant just as it meets the onset of the [ɳ]. In cases where the vowel follows the target sound, we expect to see a sharp *rise* in the third formant at the onset of the vowel. Figure 10.1 shows where the Bengali speaker is imitating the Spanish word *doble* [dóble] but realizes the initial voiced dental stop as a voiced retroflex stop [ḍ]. At the onset of the vowel, the third formant is well below 2000 Hz, but quickly rises to around 2500 Hz. There are other non-retroflex occasions in which a sharp drop in the third formant is evident, such as with rounded vowels, and one might expect this to lead to some uncertainty. Even so, in cases of retroflexion there is a drop below the 2000 Hz level. If the level of the third formant is already lower than 2000 Hz, we can look to the fourth formant, which will also show a sharp drop down to the 2500 Hz level or lower. On the other hand, in all of the examples provided, the Spanish speaker's third formant remains between 3000 and 4000 Hz throughout the entire duration of the vowel. Gender could conceivably lead to some ambiguity in the results, considering that women generally have higher formants than men. Nevertheless, while the Spanish speaker's third formant is consistently higher than the retroflexors', it also travels along a more consistent path, not showing any signs of sudden rising or dropping, unlike patterns of the retroflexors.

Results

The stimuli were 33 words, 10 of which included two to three instances of the three target sounds {t, d, n}, providing 46 opportunities for each participant to impose retroflexion. There was one case, however, where a subject failed to repeat a word, and this case was counted as one where retroflexion was not imposed, which led to there being 45 instead of 46 opportunities. Accordingly, the total number of tokens to evaluate for retroflexion was 315 (45 opportunities × 7 talkers [see the Appendix]). Table 10.6 shows the results, broken down by environment.

Table 10.6 Percentage of retroflexion imposed in all environments

Environments	Retroflexion imposed	Not imposed	Total	% of imposed retroflexion
All word-initial (ex. total [totál])	13	43	56	23.00%
All word-medial intervocalic (ex. total [totál])	29	48	77	38.00%
All word-medial clusters (ex. cartel [kartél])	36	97	133	27.00%
All word-final (ex. cartón [kartón])	10	39	49	20.00%
Total	88	227	315	28.00%

In rounded environments, there can be a drop in the third formant much like those cues found for retroflexion, which could give the impression of retroflex phonemes where there were actually dentals. Thus, we have a more conservative account of imposed retroflexion in Table 10.7 and Figure 10.3 where rounded and unrounded environments are presented separately.

Word-initially, retroflexion was imposed a total of 23% of the time (26% in rounded environments; 19% in unrounded environments). Word-medially (intervocalically), the participants imposed retroflexion 38% of the time (75% in rounded environments; 29% in unrounded environments). In word-medial clusters, they imposed retroflexion 27% of the time (39% in rounded environments; 13% in unrounded environments). In the word-final position, they imposed retroflexion 20% of the time (21% in rounded environments; 29% in unrounded environments). In total, they imposed retroflexion 28% of the time (40% in rounded environments; 24% in unrounded environments). Significance levels were checked using logistic regression with a linear mixed effects model in the software package R (version 2.15.1). Fixed effects included the rounded vowel environment, other environments (namely, word-initial, word-final, word-medial inter-consonantal and word-medial intervocalic positions; Figure 10.3), the L1 of the participants and the phoneme type.

Random effects included participant and word. It was found that subjects were significantly more likely to impose retroflexion in rounded environments ($p < 0.00885$). Other factors did not have a significant effect

Table 10.7 Amount of retroflexion imposed on dental phonemes

Place of articulation	Unrounded	Rounded
Dental	113	105
Retroflex	27	70
Total	140	175
% of retroflexion imposed	24.00%	40.00%

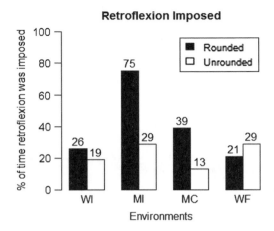

Figure 10.3 Comparison of retroflexion imposed in rounded and unrounded environments (WI, MI, MC and WF refer to word-initial, medial intervocalic, medial (consonant) cluster and word-final, respectively)

and were taken out of the model. When compared with the null model, rounding affected the place of articulation ($\chi^2(1) = 6.43$, $p = 0.01119$), raising the log odds of retroflexion being imposed by 0.884 units ± 0.338 (standard errors). In other words, the probability of retroflexion being imposed in rounded environments increased by about 0.88%.

It is true, of course, that there are many differences between modern Dravidian languages and their PDr precursor, and the same goes for differences between pre-contact IA and their daughter languages (including Sanskrit, an early post-contact IA language, as well as modern IA languages such as Hindi and Bengali). Yet, whatever the differences between the proto-languages and the daughter languages, they do not impinge on the results, nor do the differences between IA and Dravidian languages. As noted above, retroflexion is common in the modern IA languages so that retroflexing speakers of Hindi, for example, are not so different from the retroflexing speakers of PDr. Furthermore, the details of the individual performances in the Appendix show that participants sometimes used, as predicted, retroflexes in words such as Item 7 *borbotón* ('bubbling'), even where a straightforward interlingual identification between a Spanish dental /t/ and an L1 dental /t/ was possible (Hindi, Bengali, Tamil, Malayalam and Telugu all have both the dental and retroflex phonemes /t/ and /ṭ/). The logic of the hypothesis in this study was that if retroflexors even today would impose retroflexion on non-retroflex phonemes, despite the retroflexors having those non-retroflex phonemes at their disposal in their L1, then such imposition may well be what occurred in early contact, as suggested by the cases of unexplained retroflexion found in Sanskrit in contrast with other IE languages (Table 10.2). Participants in the experiment did indeed impose retroflexion patterns in a kind of transfer going beyond the typical interlingual identification of native language and target language segments.

Conclusions

The purpose of the experiment was to test whether speakers of retroflexing languages would impose retroflexion in a language contact situation as they seem to have done in the past, and the results show that the retroflexors often did use retroflexes instead of dentals, indeed at an average of 28% (Table 10.6). L2 learners thus seem able to transfer retroflex phonetic patterns even in places where a simplistic contrastive analysis would not predict it. In any case, an explanation involving language shift does plausibly account for the origins of retroflexion in post-contact IA languages. Some might still argue, however, for an explanation of the development of retroflexion in Sanskrit and later IA languages by appealing to internally motivated changes (arguably those in Table 10.1) and mass borrowing with subsequent phonemicization, so that after developing retroflexion in their own specific way, IA speakers in ancient India might have also begun overusing retroflexion. That is to say, native speakers of the IA precursor to Sanskrit could have picked up retroflexion on their own by means of borrowings of PDr words, and then they could have begun to use it in other places within the language (such as in place of dentals). However, there is no evidence of any mass borrowing at the early stages of PDr/IA contact to back up this claim. There is also the question of whether IA speakers would have gone so far as to begin using this newly found feature in unborrowed words, but that seems unlikely. We would have to assume that IA speakers borrowed massive amounts of words containing retroflexion, that those retroflex consonants then underwent phonemicization and that retroflexion became so prevalent that they then began using retroflexes sporadically in the place of dentals as well. With all of these assumptions, the burden of proof lies heavily on those who deny the likelihood of contact-induced change.

The variation among retroflexors in this study merits some attention. Even among the three Hindi speakers, there was never complete agreement as to whether the sound should be a dental or a retroflex (see the Appendix). There is not enough data in the present study to know if we should even expect consistency of this sort. One might speculate, though, that while it seems normal to expect similar responses, at least when the retroflexors speak the same language, there may be dialectal differences influencing the choices made. Given the large area in India inhabited by Hindi speakers, one methodological refinement for future study would be to elicit responses from retroflexors who not only speak the same language, but also the same dialect of that language. Language difference may have also been an important factor in the varying responses. While the participants were all speakers of retroflexing languages, the phonologies of their individual languages differed. Even so, the statistical analysis in the study found no significant effects involving the overall group outcome.

In light of the results indicating experimentally induced retroflexion, there is reason to explore possible causes for it. For one thing, preliminary evidence of a phonetic motivation has emerged. Retroflexors were significantly more likely to impose retroflexion in proximity to rounded vowels than unrounded ones. A similar phonetic motivation involving rounded segments may have also served as a trigger for the imposition of retroflexion for PDr speakers in ancient India.

Another causal factor in the ancient contact situation may have been social prestige. In some settings, retroflexion may have had a certain appeal and thus may have come to be overused in an attempt to sound fancy or intelligent, while in other settings perhaps little or no prestige was at stake. One useful contemporary example might be the case of Beijing Mandarin, where the retroflex sounds are thought to be smooth and pleasing to the ear of speakers of other dialects of Mandarin (Zhang, 2005). If researchers were to record native and non-native speakers of Beijing Mandarin speaking on different topics to elicit stylistic changes in speech patterns, it might turn out that non-native speakers overuse retroflex consonants somewhat as retroflexors in ancient India may have been doing with the IA target language. Interestingly, motivations for retroflexion have been investigated in the Indian context in a study of speakers of Telugu (Sastry, 1993).

We cannot turn back the clock to do a phonetic investigation of ancient India, but this study can shed some light on the Dravidian/Sanskrit controversy with regard to unexplained cases of retroflexion imposed on dental phonemes (Table 10.2). The evidence provided in this chapter shows that speakers of modern Indian languages can impose retroflexion on dental consonants when attempting to speak a new language. Therefore, the unexplained cases of retroflexion that surfaced in ancient times do not seem random or unmotivated.

Notes

(1) *Imposition* refers to what is also simply known as *transfer*, but it is used in order to show exactly what the mechanism of transfer is (van Coetsem, 1988). Here, specifically, *imposition* refers to a Dravidian speaker who has shifted to Sanskrit as his/her primary language, but is still 'imposing' some of his/her Dravidian speech patterns while speaking Sanskrit.

(2) Rules in bold represent target phonemes that are being dealt with directly in this chapter.

(3) An asterisk in diachronic studies signifies a hypothetical linguistic form for which we have no written evidence from the past.

(4) Consonants with a dot underneath are traditionally used to symbolize retroflex consonants in Sanskrit.

(5) The /r/ = [r], [ɾ] and [ɽ]. The /u/ = [u], [ū], [o] and [au]. The /i/ = [i], [ī], [e] and [ai].

(6) We see a similar sound change for the Slavic languages and even Avestan, a sister language of IA. However, for these two relatives of IA, the change is only *s > š / {r, u, k, i}_. (Note that here the denti-alveolar becomes some kind of post-alveolar, which is a retroflex in IA.) But it is claimed that, between Proto-Indo-Iranian and IA, the supposed post-alveolar fricative took yet another step and became a retroflex fricative, thus making the rule as stated in (f).

(7) Krishnamurti (2003: 120) describes the distribution of Dravidian stops, and Masica (1991: 157–159) and Kobayashi (2004) are the sources for the distribution of IA stops in Table 10.4.

(8) Masica gives the Vedic example of the root *prach-* 'ask' becoming *aprāṭ* (3sg. aorist). However, aside from these environments, there are no final retroflex stops in Sanskrit. Thus, final retroflexes could have been a later development and an earlier stage may be posited as not having final retroflex stops.

(9) Counting in Williams' (1899) *Sanskrit Dictionary*, I found 62 words with initial ṭ, 71 words with initial ṭ, 2 words with initial ō, 9 words with initial ṭh and 18 cases of initial ṭh. This comes to a total of 162 words with initial retroflex consonants.

(10) The list of word-initial retroflexes in Sanskrit is riddled with cases of onomatopoeia (*ṭaṅka* 'stone cutter's chisel', *ṭha* 'loud noise', *ṭambara* 'great noise', *ṭhakkana* 'shutting of a door'). There are also words such as proper names, flora and fauna, places and names of instruments that replicate sounds (*ṭaṭṭanī* 'small house lizard', *ṭunaka* 'Curculigo orchioides', *ṭuṇṭula* 'small owl', *ṭheṅka* 'name of a bird', *ṭhāla* 'shield'). Very few of these are old (of Vedic age).

References

Bhaskararao, P. and Ladefoged, P. (1983) Non-quantal aspects of consonant production: A study of retroflex consonants. *Journal of Phonetics* 11, 291–302.

Brown, C. (1994) A *Telugu-English Dictionary* (2nd edn). New Delhi: Asian Educational Service.

Caldwell, R. (1875) *A Comparative Grammar of the Dravidian or South-Indian Family of Languages*. Madras: University of Madras.

Collinge, N. (1985) *The Laws of Indo-European*. Amsterdam: Benjamins.

Deshpande, M. (1979) Genesis of Rigvedic retroflexion: A historical and sociolinguistic investigation. In N. Deshpande and P. Hook (eds) *Aryan and Non-Aryan in India* (pp. 235–315). Ann Arbor, MI: Center for South and Southeast Asian Studies, University of Michigan.

Emeneau, M. ([1956] 1980) India as a linguistic area. In A. Dil (ed.) *Language and Linguistic Area: Essays by Murray B. Emeneau* (pp. 90–127). Stanford, CA: Stanford University Press.

Hamann, S. (2003) *The Phonetics and Phonology of Retroflexes*. Utrecht: LOT Press.

Hock, H. (1996) Subversion or convergence? The issue of pre-Vedic retroflexion reconsidered. *Studies in the Linguistic Sciences* 23, 73–115.

Joseph, B. and Janda, R. (2003) On language, change, and language change – Or, of history, linguistics, and historical linguistics. In B. Joseph and R. Janda (eds) *Handbook of Historical Linguistics* (pp. 3–180). Oxford: Blackwell.

Kobayashi, M. (2004) *Historical Phonology of Old Indo-Aryan Consonants*. (Study of Languages and Cultures of Asia and Africa Monograph Series 42.) Tokyo: Institute for the Study of Languages and Cultures of Asia and Africa.

Krishnamurti, B. (2003) *The Dravidian Languages*. Cambridge: Cambridge University Press.

Labov, W. (1972) *Sociolinguistic Patterns*. Philadelphia, PA: University of Pennsylvania Press.

Masica, P.C. (1991) *The Indo-Aryan Languages*. Cambridge: Cambridge University Press.

Sastry, J. (1993) Retroflexion as an act of identity in Telugu speech. *Osmania Papers in Linguistics* 19, 71–83.

Southworth, F. (1979) Lexical evidence for early contacts between Indo-Aryan and Dravidian. In N. Deshpande and P. Hook (eds) *Aryan and Non-Aryan in India* (pp. 191–234). Ann Arbor, MI: Center for South and Southeast Asian Studies, University of Michigan.

Thomason, S. and Kaufman, T. (1988) *Language Contact, Creolization, and Genetic Linguistics*. Berkeley, CA: University of California Press.

Williams, M. (1899) *A Sanskrit–English Dictionary*. Oxford: Clarendon Press.

Van Coetsem, F. (1988) *Loan Phonology and the Two Transfer Types in Language Contact*. Dordrecht: Foris.

Zhang, Q. (2005) A Chinese yuppie in Beijing: Phonological variation and the construction of a new professional identity. *Language in Society* 34, 431–466.

Appendix

Words	Environments	Rounded vowel	Hindi (1)	Hindi (2)	Hindi (3)	Tamil	Telugu	Malayalam	Bengali	Retroflex imposed
1. car**t**a	MC	a	n	n	n	n	n	n	n	0
2. cuer**n**o	MC	o	n	n	y	y	y	n	y	4
3. **cartel**	MC	a	n	n	n	n	n	n	n	0
4. car**t**ón	MC, WF	o, o	y/n	y/n	n/n	n/n	n/n	n/n	y/n	3 and 0
5. **carnaval**	MC	a	n	n	y	n	y	n	n	2
6. **carne**	MC	a	y	n	n	y	y	y	n	4
7. borbo**t**ón	MI, WF	o, o	n/n	n/n	y/y	y/y	y/y	n/n	n/n	3 and 3
8. **birlan**	WF	a	y	n	y	n	n	y	n	2
9. cor**d**ón	WF	o	n	n	n	n	n	y	n	2
10. **cornada**	MC	o	n	n	n	n	y	y	n	2
11. coro**n**acion	MI, WF	o, o	y/n	n/n	y/y	n/n	y/n	y/n	n/n	4 and 1
12. **corne**ta	MC, MI	o, a	n/y	y/y	y/n	n/n	y/n	y/n	n/n	4 and 2
13. **impor**t**ante**	MC, MC	o, a	n/n	y/n	n/n	n/n	y/n	n/n	n/n	2 and 0
14. **verte**	MC	a	n	n	n	n	n	n	n	0
15. birma**n**o	MI	o	n	n	y	y	y	n	n	3
16. compu**t**ador	MI	o	n	skipped	y	n	y	n	n	2
17. **incarnacion**	MC, MC, WF	a, a, o	n/n/n	n/n/n	n/n/n	n/n/n	y/n/n	n/n/n	n/n/n	1, 0, 0
18. **ordinario**	MI	a	n	n	n	n	n	n	n	0
19. **mantengo**	MC	a	n	n	n	n	y	n	n	1
20. **boni**ta	MI, MI	o, a	n/n	n/n	y/y	y/n	y/n	y/y	n/y	4 and 3
21. **bonda**d	WF	a	y	n	n	n	y	n	n	2
22. to**t**al	WI, MI	o, o	n/n	y/n	n/n	n/y	y/n	n/y	n/y	2 and 3

(Continued)

Words	Environments	Rounded vowel	Hindi (1)	Hindi (2)	Hindi (3)	Tamil	Telugu	Malayalam	Bengali	Retroflex imposed
23. duermo	WI	o	n	n	n	n	n	n	n	0
24. doble	WI	o	n	n	n	N	n	n	y	1
25. dormir	WI	o	n	n	n	N	n	n	y	1
26. dame	WI	a	n	n	n	N	n	y	y	2
27. nocturno	WI, MC, MC	o, o, o	n n n	y/n/y	y/y/y	y/n/y	n/y/y	y/y/y	y/y/y	5, 4 and 6
28. dime	WI	a	n	y	n	N	n	n	n	1
29. quererte	MC	a	n	y	n	N	n	n	n	1
30. tirar	WI	a	n	y	n	N	n	n	n	1
31. obtener	MC, MI	o, a	n/n	y/y	n/n	n/n	n/y	n/n	n/n	1 and 2
32. anillo	MI	a	n	n	y	Y	n	y	n	3
33. portable	MC	o	n	y	n	N	n	n	n	1
Total	WI = 56 MC = 133 MI = 77 WF = 49	a = 20 o = 25	7/46	45	46	46	46	46	46	315
Unrounded = a Rounded = o			a = 4/20 o = 2/25	a = 5/20 o = 8/25	a = 4/20 o = 12/25	a = 2/20 o = 18/25	a = 6/20 o = 13/25	a = 4/20 o = 9/25	a = 2/20 o = 8/25	a = 27/140 o = 70/175 a = 19% o = 40%

Part 4

Cognitive Perspectives

Virtually all of the chapters in this volume arguably have insights relevant to cognition, but the chapters in Part 4 focus on issues best treated in a separate section. In Chapter 11, Terence Odlin considers how transfer affects the relation between comprehension and production. Comparing the written English as a foreign language (EFL) performance of first language (L1) Finnish and L1 Swedish speakers (210 individuals altogether), he identifies very different reproductions of the same input, and the differences indicate cross-linguistic influence. The input, two titles in English in a silent movie, varied in length, with one of the titles being rather short and the other considerably longer. Although the length factor is clear in the case of the longer title, which no one reproduced verbatim in his/her written synopses of the film scene, very few individuals reproduced verbatim even the much shorter title ('It was the girl, not the man'): only 4 of the 210 participants did so. Accordingly, the reproductions of the short (and the long) title should not be viewed as attempts at mimicry but rather as reconstructions – and as reconstructions influenced by distinct grammatical patterns in the native languages of the participants. For example, almost none of the reconstructions of the L1 Swedish speakers showed omissions of English articles, but those of the L1 Finnish speakers often did, results consistent with the fact that Swedish has articles while Finnish does not. While the evidence comes from production data, it suggests language-specific factors also at work in comprehension and memory. Odlin observes that the approach labeled thinking for speaking by Slobin envisions an important role for comprehension as well as production (despite the emphasis in the label on speaking), and the evidence of distinct transfer patterns among the L1 Finnish and L1 Swedish groups thus supports other thinking for speaking studies.

Chuming Wang's chapter, 'Context and Language Transfer', draws on usage-based theories to stress the importance of both linguistic and non-linguistic contexts in the acquisition of a new language. He considers in detail cases of transfer in EFL contexts where learners typically have relatively little exposure to target language input outside the classroom. Accordingly, when communicative pressures require learners to call on their interlanguage resources, the contexts of use of the native language can affect comprehension and production, and such contexts are thus the focus of what the author calls the compensation hypothesis. Although using L1 contexts as the frame of reference can sometimes facilitate acquisition, such dependence on already-familiar resources can often lead to negative transfer. Regarding this dilemma, Wang advocates early pedagogical intervention to create appropriate contexts: in effect, students should learn together and use together, according to what the author calls the learn-together-use-together (LTUT) principle.

11 Language Transfer and the Link between Comprehension and Production

Terence Odlin

Introduction

Understanding a language and using it are the typical practical goals of second language acquisition (SLA). Sometimes, of course, learners may settle for a minimal knowledge of a second language (L2) that will enable them, for example, to read it (and perhaps even then only certain kinds of texts). Conversely, users of a foreign language phrasebook may learn just enough to be able to speak a little of the L2, which could help these users, sometimes even when they do not understand a spoken reply but do understand gestures or other paralinguistic cues. Yet, apart from such cases, the practical goals of listening and speaking and of reading and writing are complementary: that is, comprehension should normally help production, and production can foster encounters with users of the target language that lead to better comprehension. Not surprisingly, the interaction between comprehension and production has prompted interest in part because of the significance of such interaction for seeing how L2 learners increase their L2 proficiency (e.g. Izumi, 2003).

While the practical goals are complementary, the complex processes involved in comprehension and in production remain only imperfectly understood, and in the study of the exact ways in which comprehension interacts with production there remains much unexplored territory. One important dimension of the interaction is the role that cross-linguistic influence may play, and a recent study of transfer by Ringbom (2007) offers an interesting assessment of the relation:

> Similarity of grammar appears to be especially important in facilitating *learning*…, both learning for comprehension and learning for production. Lexical similarity, which facilitates the learner's linking words to other formally similar words, is also basic for learning, but may not work in exactly the same way for comprehension, as comprehension can be

merely approximate, and comprehension does not leave a permanent mark in the mental lexicon. (Ringbom, 2007: 17, emphasis in the original)

The similarity that Ringbom alludes to is the set of resemblances seen between two languages, and for Ringbom a high degree of cross-linguistic similarity makes an especially important contribution to the kinds of transfer seen in SLA. In this chapter, the exact claims seen in the above quotation will not be tested, but the evidence will indeed support Ringbom's position that cross-linguistic similarity in grammar and vocabulary can enhance both comprehension and production, and thus promote learning.

Comprehension and Manifestations of it in Production

Before the empirical study of certain consequences of lexical and grammatical similarity, some aspects of comprehension and production warrant attention. As Ringbom notes, comprehension can be less than full, and apart from an imperfect knowledge of an L2, there can be a wide range of reasons for only 'approximate' comprehension, even when the context involves only native speakers. Foss and Hakes (1978: 100–101) make a useful distinction between three levels of comprehension: *structural* (what has the speaker [S] said?), *intentional* (what does S actually want?) and *motivational* (why does S want it?). One can understand the structural product yet have no clue as to a speaker's (or writer's) intentions or motivations; an obvious example is where two people (be they spies, lovers or bankers) communicate using sentences which say one thing yet actually 'mean' another. The three levels imply that listeners must have the capacity to analyze meanings communicated in relation to all three questions. Such capacity involves both individual mental processes and cultural norms of interpretation (e.g. French *Bon appétit!*, which is often used in France before starting a meal). Also relevant to the three-level notion is the complex interaction of the levels (e.g. understanding the intentional correlates of a syntactic pattern). Some work in pragmatics has looked closely at such interaction (e.g. Kortmann, 1991; Wilson & Sperber, 1993), and there are certainly implications for transfer research (e.g. Odlin, 2008a).

Another key aspect of theories of comprehension is their relation to memory. Although memory and comprehension are distinct capacities in many respects, they also interact a great deal. Especially important for this chapter will be the reconstructive nature of some memory processes. A classic psycholinguistic experiment by Loftus and Palmer (1974) well illustrates some aspects of the role of reconstruction in remembering. Participants were shown a film of an accident and were later asked, 'About how fast were the cars going when they smashed into each other?' or 'About how fast were the cars going when they hit each other?' or other questions in which only the verb denoting the collision was different. In the case of *smash* and *hit*, the former verb elicited significantly higher estimates of the speed of the cars, even though everyone had seen the same film. The different verbs clearly encouraged somewhat different reconstructions of the non-verbal event witnessed.

The notion of cognitive construction also applies when what is to be recalled is linguistic input, whether it is speech or writing. As with the recall of non-linguistic input, productions in response to linguistic input can be seen as reconstructions, and here they may involve both linguistic comprehension and linguistic production. In fact, work on child language and L2 acquisition has employed techniques such as repetition testing and (in the case of literate individuals) dictation. Assessing empirical work on repetition in child language research, Slobin and Welsh (1973: 496) conclude that 'sentence recognition and imitation are filtered through the individual's productive linguistic system'. In a discussion of both first language (L1) and L2 research, Natalicio (1979: 169) likewise stresses that repetition and dictation require 'the full comprehension and production processes—the internalized grammar of expectancy'. By such analyses, the techniques often elicit more than just mimicking the spoken or written input: changes in the repetitions from what language learners have heard show that the input is not so much copied as reconstructed, and the same result is evident in the difference between the spoken input and the written output of dictation. For Natalicio and for Slobin and Welsh, the products evident in dictation and repetition often reflect comprehension processes, and the errors seen in the products can offer insights into how the developing language system interacts with what learners understand. To extend the 'filter' metaphor of Slobin and Welsh to L2 contexts, the interlanguage (IL) is the filter (Natalicio's 'grammar of expectancy'). Apart from the testing research, there has also been some attention in SLA to the constructive nature of the comprehension process, where listeners or readers recreate, to some extent, what seems to them to be the form and meaning of what they have heard or read (e.g. Grabe, 2002).

If an IL filter affects how the input to comprehension is used, it quite plausibly has language-specific dimensions whereby the particular target language and native language (and perhaps other previously encountered languages) affect the path from input to comprehension to recreation and production. In fact, there is already some evidence of the IL having language-specific processing characteristics in various stages of comprehension from the apprehension of word forms to the recreation of syntactic structure (e.g. Fender, 2003). The research to be discussed in this chapter accordingly considers the question of whether or not cross-linguistic influence affects the path from input to output. The evidence will show that such influence is strong.

Background on the Two Main Languages of Finland

To demonstrate cross-linguistic influence, a variety of methods can be employed, but work on the language contact situation involving Finnish, Swedish and English in Finland has led to an especially promising methodology (Jarvis, 2000; Odlin, 2012). Finland has a bilingual language policy for many purposes, though the relation between Finnish and Swedish is certainly one of a majority language (around 93% native speakers of Finnish) and minority language (around 6% native speakers of Swedish). In schools, both are taught as the L1 and L2, and English is normally a required foreign language, even though the details of who may study what language and for how long have varied in the past 20 or 30 years (Ringbom, 1987, 2007).

The main evidence used in this chapter will be data collected in Finland by Jarvis (1998). The methodology that Jarvis used has a number of strengths. His study compared speakers of two quite different languages: Swedish, a Germanic language similar to English in many ways (despite some divergences), and Finnish, a non-Indo-European language showing numerous points of contrast with English. Moreover, the speakers in the Jarvis study had similar social backgrounds, all of the participants being students attending schools in Finland. (For brevity, the native Finnish speakers will be called 'Finns' and the native Swedish speakers 'Swedes', though it should be kept in mind that the participants were Finnish citizens.) A third strong point of the Jarvis study is that the data elicited come from performances of a task given to all the participants, with details of that task provided in the next section. Finally, the fact that Jarvis collected data from Finns and Swedes varying in the number of years of English studied allows for some inferences about IL development. Table 11.1 summarizes the relevant characteristics of the different groups.

As noted above, there have been changes in when and how long particular languages are studied as L2 or third (L3) languages, and groups such as F9B (Table 11.1), who had an early start with Swedish relative to English, are not as common as they were in earlier decades, as indicated by details given by Ringbom (1987, 2007). Ringbom, a member of the Swedish-speaking minority, considers the socio-economic and cultural differences between Finns and Swedes to be minimal, and so the results of comparisons that he, Jarvis and others have made of the two groups' performance in English seem largely due to the linguistic differences and not to sociocultural factors. The role of these linguistic differences can be assessed in detail because Jarvis collected data not only from the groups described in Table 11.1, but also from native speakers of Finnish, Swedish and English writing in their native languages, and some examples of constructions used by native speakers will be considered in the discussion of the results.

Table 11.1 Experimental participant groups

Group	n	L1	Ages	Grade	English instruction	Swedish instruction
F5	35	Finnish	11–12	5	3rd year	None
F7	35	Finnish	13–14	7	5th year	1st year
F9A	35	Finnish	15–16	9	7th year	3rd year
F9B	35	Finnish	15–16	9	3rd year	7th year
						Finnish instruction
S7	35	Swedish	13–14	7	3rd year	5th year
S9	35	Swedish	15–16	9	5th year	7th year

Source: Jarvis (1998).

Task and Procedures

The main language task was the same for both the non-native speakers of English and the three native speaker groups. All wrote accounts of certain episodes in the Charlie Chaplin film *Modern Times*, starring Chaplin and Paulette Goddard. The groups described in Table 11.1 wrote their narratives in English and, as noted, the other native speaker groups wrote narratives in Finnish, Swedish and English (in the latter group, students from the state of Indiana participated). Two scenes of the film were presented in separate segments, first a 5-minute sequence and later a 3-minute sequence. After each sequence, participants were given intervals of about 30 minutes (for the first sequence) and 14 minutes (for the second) to write their narratives. Additional details about the elicitation procedure and materials are provided by Jarvis (1998: 85–93).

The entire film is a silent movie even though it was produced in the 1930s, when sound was available; in fact, some music is heard but no spoken language. In the two segments viewed, there were nine titles with the words of the characters printed on the screen. The two scenes will be referred to as the Rich Lady Scene (RLS) and the Dream Scene (DS). The following are synopses of the main details.

Rich Lady Scene

Goddard looks in a bakery window and then turns to see the bakery truck, which the baker is just leaving. As Goddard takes a loaf from the truck and runs away, a rich lady comes round the corner and sees what has happened, and she seems to tell the baker (although there is no title yet). In her dash away, Goddard collides with Chaplin. When the baker goes after Goddard, he tells a policeman (in a title) that she took the bread. Chaplin then says (in a title) that he himself did. After the policeman starts to take Chaplin away, with Goddard being left free, the rich lady says to the baker, 'It was the girl, not the man'.

The baker and the lady approach the policeman and both seem to tell him this (although no title is used at this point). The policeman then releases Chaplin and takes Goddard.

Dream Scene

After Chaplin as well as Goddard got arrested, they managed to escape. As they sit on a grassy space, they dream of a happy life together, complete with a house and orange trees. At the end of this reverie, Chaplin says in a title, 'I'll do it! We'll get a home even if I have to work for it'.

Results

In both of the scenes just described, the words of the titles made an impression on many Finns and Swedes, who attempted to quote them or to use at least some of the words in reported speech (often preceded by words such as *said that*). The actual words of the titles in question are

RLS: 'It was the girl, not the man'.
DS: 'I'll do it! We'll get a home even if I have to work for it'.

As will be seen, the attempts at using words or paraphrases were often not successful in verbatim accuracy, but virtually every attempt offers insights. If comprehension and production of the information in the titles were completely independent of the native language of the writers, there should be no difference in the grammatical patterns used by Finns and Swedes in supplying the information. However, the results of the analysis indicate that there are in fact considerable differences, differences that correspond to particular patterns in Finnish and Swedish. By the same token, the results indicate that reproducing the information of the titles was not mere parroting of the words. In the case of the RLS, only two Finns and two Swedes reproduced the words of the title verbatim, and in the case of the DS no one at all did. Later, a more detailed discussion of the implications of this result will be provided, but in general the finding of so few verbatim reproductions will serve as preliminary evidence that the reproductions of the vast majority of Finns and Swedes were reconstructing – not copying – what they had read.

In analyzing the learner-supplied information in the titles, the first step was to determine who used the RLS title or DS title information at all. In general, identifying the use of such information proved easy, but an illustration of some of the decisions that had to be made will prove helpful. The following comes from the first part of the narrative of a ninth-grade Finn (F9A 04), with misspellings and other errors retained:

Young girl walk a town.

She gomes to the breadshop.

She is hungry.

She see how man take bread at the breadbil [the bakery truck] and go in.

She steal a bred.

Old woman see everything and tell a shopkeeper.

Shopkeeper tell a polis ho [who] goes stoping a rober.

Girl run stright on Chaplin.

They fall, and polise rest a rober.

Girl say police att [that] she isn't a rober.

Chaplin say, 'She didn't do it, I did.'

Polie rest Chaplin men old woman tell shopkeeper, 'That's not a man, it's woman'.

The first italicized line does not contain information derived from the title 'It was the girl, not the man' but rather from an earlier line ('She stole a loaf of bread'). However, the second italicized line does constitute a reproduction (albeit with lexical and grammatical errors) of the information in 'It was the girl, not the man'. Only cases where the information given by the student indicated use of that particular title were counted. In the example, the errors involving *a man* and *woman* with no article are, incidentally, characteristic of many reproductions of the Finns and will be discussed further on.[1]

Analysis of the use of the information in the RLS title

In the case of the RLS, the information used thus involved reports about who really stole the bread: Goddard, not Chaplin. Table 11.2 details the use of the information according to group. With the exception of the F5 learners, who had only two years of English, the various groups showed a high use of the information: about 80% or more of the individuals in two of the other Finnish groups and in both of the Swedish groups used the information. As for those who did not use the information in these groups or even for those in the F5, it would be unsound to conclude that they did not understand the information in the title, although, of course, there is also no evidence that they did understand. In any event, the title in the RLS proved accessible for most of the learners in most of the groups, and so

Table 11.2 Information from title in the RLS used or not by numbers of Finns and Swedes

	F5	F7	F9A	F9B	S7	S9
Used	23	27	28	28	28	30
Not used	12	8	7	7	7	5

it proves relatively easy to compare what these groups did with the same information.

One indication that the Finns and Swedes made different use of the information is the different rates of occurrence of cleft sentences such as *It was the girl, who stole the bread* (S7 04). Swedish learners frequently produced them in using the title information to indicate contrast in the RLS, and the results in Table 11.3 are consistent with analyses of transfer and focus constructions. The high proportions of cleft sentences among Swedes is especially striking in view of the difference in years of study: the S7 group had only two years of English, yet the students in this group who produced clefts outnumbered by over five to one the F9A group, who had had six years of English.

As noted earlier, native speakers wrote accounts of the same episodes in their native languages, and in the case of the Swedes, cleft sentences were quite common: e.g. *...det var kvinnan som stal brödet...* (it was the woman who stole the bread, SX 12) and *...det var flickan som tog det och inte mannen* (it was the girl who took it and not the man, SY 11; SX and SY designate different native speaker groups and the numbers refer to different individuals in these groups). The formal patterning and also the pragmatic functions of clefts in Swedish are similar to what is found in English clefts, and so the cross-linguistic similarity is consistent with a transfer explanation for the Swedes' frequent use of the structure, as are also errors in their use of the target language pattern (Odlin, 2008a). A cleft pattern was sometimes evident in the Finnish narratives of native speakers: e.g. *... kyllä se oli se nainen joka sen leivän varasti...* (indeed it was the woman who the bread stole, FY 20). However, such uses were quite rare in the Finnish texts, which is not surprising in view of the fact that Finnish relies heavily on other devices, especially word order, to achieve focus. Accordingly, while three of the four Finnish groups writing in English used the information in the RLS title about as much as the Swedes did, they used the cleft pattern far less. A chi-square test indicates that the distribution of results in Table 11.3 is statistically significant ($\chi^2=22.1$, df 5, $p < 0.001$), and the lopsided pattern seems attributable to the frequent influence from L1 Swedish on individuals in the S7 and S9 groups.

Besides clefts, another way to indicate the contrast between Chaplin and Goddard in the RLS is through pairs of noun phrases (NPs) juxtaposed in the same clause or contiguous clauses (and indeed the actual wording of the RLS title is one example: 'It was the girl, not the man'). The Finns and Swedes used a variety of NP types (including erroneous ones), as seen

Table 11.3 Cleft sentences used by numbers of Finns and Swedes

F5	F7	F9A	F9B	S7	S9
1	3	2	3	11	12

Table 11.4 Rich lady scene: NP types used in pairs contrasting Chaplin and Goddard

Proper noun	...the girl stole a bread, not *Chaplin*
Pronoun	...'*she* stole the bread'
Demonstrative and noun	It wasn't *that man*, it was the girl.
Definite article and noun	It wasn't that man, it was *the girl*.
Indefinite article and noun	'It wasn't *a man*. It is *a lady*'.
Zero and noun	It wasn't *man*. It was the girl!

in Table 11.4: a proper noun (usually *Chaplin* or *Charlie*), a pronoun, a noun with a demonstrative determiner, a noun with either a definite or (erroneously) an indefinite article or a noun with the article erroneously omitted (the omission being termed a *zero article*).

Finns and Swedes differed greatly in their use of zero and indefinite articles. In Table 11.5, the number of pairs of NP references to Chaplin and Goddard used by each group of Finns appears in the first row while in the last row a figure twice the value appears. For example, in the F5 group, 19 individuals produced referential pairs (e.g. *It wasn't that man, it was the girl*), and so there were 38 references (19 to Chaplin and 19 to Goddard). There were two proper noun references in this group, thus about 5% of the total 38, while there were 10 references with a definite article (which therefore correctly reproduced the determiner in the title), and thus about 26% of the total. Errors with an indefinite article constituted 21% of the total, while zero articles constituted 26%. The F7 and F9A groups used fewer zero articles, and the percentages of tokens showing the correct definite article were larger: 50% and 44%. Remarkably, the percentage was even higher in the F9B group (who had only two years of English but six years of Swedish), with a figure of 58%. This group also had a much lower error rate in using an indefinite article (8%) than did the other three groups.

As Table 11.6 indicates, the Swedes far more often produced the correct definite article in the same references and their sentences almost never

Table 11.5 NP types used by Finns in pairs contrasting Chaplin and Goddard

	F5	F7	F9A	F9B	Total
NP pairs	19	14	9	17	59
Proper	2 (5%)	2 (7%)	1 (5%)	4 (11%)	9 (7%)
Pronoun	2 (5%)	1 (3%)	0 (0)	2 (5%)	5 (4%)
Demonst	6 (15%)	2 (7%)	3 (16%)	1 (2%)	12 (10%)
Def Art	10 (26%)	14 (50%)	8 (44%)	20 (58%)	52 (44%)
Indef	8 (21%)	6 (21%)	4 (22%)	3 (8%)	21 (17%)
Zero	10 (16%)	3 (10%)	2 (11%)	4 (11%)	19 (16%)
NP total	38	28	18	34	118

Table 11.6 NP types used by Swedes in pairs contrasting Chaplin and Goddard

	S7	S9	Total
NP pairs	16	6	22
Proper	1 (3%)	1 (8%)	2 (4%)
Pronoun	3 (9%)	0 (0)	3 (6%)
Demonst	1 (3%)	0 (0)	1 (2%)
Def Art	26 (81%)	10 (83%)	36 (81%)
Indef	1 (3%)	0 (0)	1 (2%)
Zero	0 (0)	1 (8%)	1 (2%)
NP total	32	12	44

showed errors involving either indefinite articles or zero articles.[2] Like English, Swedish has definite and indefinite articles whereas Finnish has neither, and so positive transfer from Swedish seems clear. The Swedes' success also suggests a role for positive transfer in the greater success of the F9B group (who had six years of L2 Swedish) in comparison with the other Finns in producing definite articles and avoiding indefinite articles. As for zero articles, the incidence among the F9B group was not different from the F7 or F9A groups, although the F9B group showed greater success compared with the F5 group, who likewise had only two years of English.

The frequent use by Finns of indefinite articles in the title information of the RLS suggests that these learners have not yet understood the meaning difference between *a* and *the*. However, such incomprehension does not arise from any absence of definiteness as a meaning category in Finnish (Chesterman, 1991), and so it is doubtful if any kind of conceptual transfer is involved (cf. Han, 2010; Jarvis, 2002; Jarvis & Pavlenko, 2008; Odlin, 2008b). The use of zero likewise does not indicate any absence of definiteness in the Finns' L1 but rather insufficient awareness of the usually obligatory mapping of definiteness meanings onto articles in English. In contrast, the Swedes nearly always prove sensitive to the mapping requirements, which are similar in their native language.

Analysis of the use of the information in the DS title

While the above analysis of responses to the RLS title indicates clear-cut transfer effects related to the link between comprehension and production, the performance of Finns and Swedes with other titles in *Modern Times* also provides evidence of transfer but with complications. The somewhat different results are evident in the apparently greater difficulty of the DS title 'I'll do it! We'll get a home even if I have to work for it!'. Table 11.7 shows that far fewer individuals in each group used the information of this title. The main source of difficulty is probably the large number of

Table 11.7 Information from title in the DS used or not by numbers of Finns and Swedes

	F5	F7	F9A	F9B	S7	S9
Used	5	14	19	17	9	21
Not used	30	21	16	18	26	14

words in the title, a factor which would likely affect the Swedes as well as the Finns. Indirect support for this interpretation comes from work on repetition and dictation which indicates that length is a factor (Natalicio, 1979: 174–175). More direct support comes from the fact that no one reproduced the exact words of the title even though a small but equal number of Finns (two) and Swedes (two) managed to reproduce the words of the RLS title, which is much shorter. For the DS, the result is the same even when the count of reproductions was limited to how many students correctly reproduced just the second sentence in the title (i.e. 'We'll get a home even if I have to work for it!'). That is, no one provided a verbatim reproduction of this sentence.

Despite the difficulty of the DS title, Swedish influence seems to have helped, as has years of studying English. Swedes with four years of English (S9) used the title information the most, whereas Finns with only two years of English and no Swedish (F5) used it the least. It also seems that years of study and Swedish influence are largely independent factors, since Finns with six years of English study (F9A) used the title more than any other group of Finns, yet the second highest group was F9B, which had only two years of English study but six years of Swedish. The importance of Swedish influence is also suggested by the S7 group, which had only two years of English yet used the information almost twice as often as the F5 group. As in the case of the RLS, the simple non-use of information in the title of the DS cannot be equated with non-comprehension. Even so, the difference in the use of the two titles is striking and it suggests that the DS title was much harder to process.

When Swedish influence aided the comprehension of the DS title, as the results for S7, S9 and F9B suggest, the facilitating effects were probably more global than local, that is, no single structural similarity between Swedish and English likely explain the entire facilitating effect. Nevertheless, there are some specific differences in the performance of the Finns and Swedes in reproducing the title information that are due to differences in Finnish and Swedish. Among those learners who did use information from the title, there is a remarkable difference in the presence of the subordinating conjunction *if* by Finns and Swedes, with the former tending to use it less, as seen in Table 11.8, a pattern which proves to be statistically significant (χ^2=19.1, df 5, p < 0.005).

Table 11.8 Use of the subordinating conjunction *if* by Finns and Swedes

F5	F7	F9A	F9B	S7	S9
1	1	8	4	7	13

While Table 11.8 indicates that Swedish confers an advantage in processing *if*, the analysis is necessarily complicated for a number of reasons. One is that in a few cases a different subordinating conjunction besides *if* appears, as in *They dream little while about own house. Chaplin promise that he will get* [a house] *for them altought* [*sic*] *he must go to work* (F9A 23). These cases are rare, however, and are straightforward to interpret (and they are counted as instances of using the information in the title). More challenging are the several instances involving the word *even*, which accompanies *if* in the title and which counts as an adverb in the target language. However, in several cases, only *even* is present: e.g. *After that dreaming Charlie deside* [*sic*] *that he get home* [for] *them, even he have work for it* (F9B 33). Another possibility, but one consistent with the target language, is for *if* to appear but without the *even*, as in *Chaplin says – We can have a home – if I have work for it* (F5 14). As shown in Table 11.9, the three possible outcomes involving *even* and *if* pattern differently in the writing of the Finns and Swedes. The chi-square test of the distribution in the table indicates a non-random response pattern despite the nearly equal number of Finns and Swedes supplying one of the three choices ($\chi^2 = 10.0$, df 2, $p < 0.01$).

No Swede used *even* without *if*, in contrast to nine Finns. The omission of *if* by several Finns suggests that they did not understand its meaning or its syntactic status as a subordinating conjunction. Perhaps some other test would indicate that these learners have at least a passive understanding of what *if* means, but it cannot be said that the conjunction is part of their productive IL vocabulary. Neither partial nor complete incomprehension is necessarily attributable to Finnish influence – not knowing vocabulary is simply not knowing. However, the comparative success of the Swedes that is evident in avoiding the omission of *if* suggests positive transfer from Swedish, but it is transfer where cross-linguistic lexical similarity seems to play an important role. The adverb has a clear cognate in Swedish *även*, e.g. *även om han måste arbeta för det* (even if he must work for it, SX 12). The transparent similarity of the adverbs no doubt makes identifying English *if* with Swedish *om* easier and also makes it unlikely that *even* will be considered as anything other than an adverb.

One plausible analysis of the cases of *even* without *if* in Table 11.9 is that the Finns using it thus have erroneously classified *even* as a subordinating conjunction. Reclassifications of words are not unusual in IL, and indeed speakers of fairly similar languages such as English and Spanish may misjudge the grammatical class of a target language word

Table 11.9 Use of *even if, even* (and no *if*) and *if* (and no *even*) in the DS title

	Finns	Swedes
even if	11	17
even	9	0
if	3	3

(Odlin & Natalicio, 1982). How much of a role Finnish influence may play in this hypothesized reclassification remains an open question, but there is a candidate word in Finnish, *vaikka*, which seems a likely source. *Vaikka* has different translations in different contexts, but one common correspondence is with English *even if*, as in

Teen	sen	vaikka	minun	pitäisi	mennä	yliopistoon
I-do	it	even-if	I	must	go	to-university[3]

I will do it even if I have to go to the university.

Thus, *vaikka* can function as a special kind of conjunction, one which functions in clauses that König (1988) terms *concessive conditionals*. König's analysis details important semantic similarities between ordinary conditionals (typically marked with *if*) and concessives (typically marked with *although*), and his analysis can help in explaining why a learner might use a concessive in recounting the DS as was the case with *altought he must go to work*. In any event, *vaikka* codes a concessive notion (which in English is coded by *even*) and a conditional one (coded in English by *if*). Indeed, many native speakers of Finnish writing in Finnish translated *even if* as *vaikka* as in this example:

Silloin	Chaplin	lupaa,	että	hän	hankkii		heille	kodin,
Then	Chaplin	promises	that	he*	gets		them	home
vaikka	hänen	pitäisi	tehdä	töitä	sen eteen. (FY 36)			
even-if	he	must	do	work	it			

Then Chaplin promises that he (will) get them a home, even if he has to work for it.

The titles of *Modern Times* were not translated into Finnish, and so the use of *vaikka* in such cases offers an insight into what many Finns (the native speakers in the groups in Jarvis' research) regard as a valid interlingual identification – and translation – between English and Finnish.

Since *vaikka* codes both a concessive and a conditional notion, any Finn not so familiar with the English vocabulary item *if* might conclude that the other form, *even*, would serve as an adequate translation of both the conditional and the concessive element. Such an interpretation is erroneous in terms of the target language norms, of course, but such transfer-induced reinterpretations are evident in the case of other grammatical morphemes such as those used in the English perfect (Odlin & Alonso-Váquez, 2006). By this analysis, then, the *even* in *even he have work for it* is an IL conjunction despite its status as an adverb in the target language.

Summary of Findings on Transfer

The main empirical findings of this study involve the different patterns of reproduction of the same target language input, with the different patterns reflecting differences between Finnish and Swedish. These patterns include:

- Greater use by Swedes than by Finns of cleft sentences in English to reproduce information from the RLS (and cleft sentences are frequent in the Swedish accounts of this scene).
- Few cases of errors involving articles in the RLS among the Swedes in contrast to frequent errors among the Finns, especially in the inappropriate use of indefinite articles and zero articles. (This finding is consistent with the obligatory use of articles in Swedish and the absence of articles in Finnish.)
- Greater use of the subordinating conjunction *if* from the DS title by Swedes (whose native language has a transparent parallel between English *even if* and Swedish *även om*).
- Frequent use of *even* as what seems to be a conjunction among the Finns (a pattern probably implicated with the Finnish conjunction *vaikka*).
- A superior performance by Finns with six years of Swedish and only two years of English (the F9B group) in comparison with a group with two years of English but no study of Swedish (the F5 group), in terms of using the title information in the RLS and DS and also in article use, with such results suggesting L2 → L3 transfer effects.

In general, the similarities between Swedish and English proved helpful in processing the target language input and avoiding errors in production. For Finns, the dearth of cross-linguistic similarities seems to have impeded processing and to have occasioned more errors. The evidence thus indicates that the degree of cross-linguistic similarity affects the link between comprehension and production. Put more concisely, the reconstructing of input does not seem immune to transfer.

Implications of Transfer in Comprehension and Production

The empirical findings presented thus offer evidence of cross-linguistic influence on how L2 learners use target language input to produce sentences. As with earlier research on dictation and repetition testing, the results in this investigation do not support any claim that reproducing the titles of the Chaplin film involved just mimicry. Indeed, it could be argued that the use of information by Finns and Swedes owes even less to mimicry than might affect performances on repetition or dictation tests. As noted above, there were very few exact reproductions of the wording of the RLS title and none at all of the DS title.

The scarcity of verbatim reproductions points not only to the constructive nature of comprehension processes, but it also raises very complex issues of memory, especially issues related to comprehension and acquisition. Although the importance of constructive processes in memory is not in doubt, the exact nature of the processes is unclear, including how they contribute to further acquisition of an L2 or to stabilization or what some consider fossilization (cf. Han, 2010; Han & Odlin, 2006; Long, 2003). It is beyond the scope of this chapter to address all the issues in detail, much less offer a detailed model. Nevertheless, the following discussion may help to identify factors that will warrant close study in any future attempts to build or test a model of the role of transfer in the constructive processes of memory, comprehension, production and acquisition.

Central to any specific model should be the broader concerns raised by Slobin in what he and others have called thinking for speaking (e.g. Cadierno, 2008; Slobin, 1996, 2000). As Slobin (2000) puts it, the focus of such concerns is on

...the fact that one cannot verbalize experience without taking a *perspective*, and further, that the language being used favors particular perspectives. The world does not present itself as 'events' to be encoded in language. Rather, in the process of speaking or writing, experiences are filtered through language into verbalized events. (Slobin, 2000: 107, emphasis in the original)

Slobin argues, furthermore, that the filtering of experience is a language-specific process. Although the label 'thinking for speaking' suggests that production, not comprehension, is the sole focus of this approach, Slobin asserts that

...we can go at least one step beyond on-line production to examine the *memory* that remains after receiving and processing a verbalized event...Thus while the speaker thinks for speaking, the listener listens for understanding and, ultimately, for remembering. (Slobin, 2000: 126, emphasis in the original)

Following this logic, Slobin proceeds to discuss listening for remembering and reading for remembering. Unlike in some earlier work (e.g. Slobin, 1996), he does not directly address transfer or other issues of SLA, although he does consider translation. In any case, the picture of memory that Slobin sketches requires attention to concerns specific to transfer in comprehension and memory.

A natural point of departure for considering memory and transfer is the oft-made distinction between long-term memory (LTM) and short-term memory (STM). Different tasks obviously make different demands on LTM and STM, and so while reconstruction is a common thread in dictation, repetition and reporting titles in the Chaplin film, the differences of the tasks likely mean different relations between different memory capacities (cf. Robinson, 2001). In dictation and repetition, much of the performance depends on STM capacities, but in the narrative task, the demands for recall exceed normal STM capacities. As noted above, the two film segments viewed were about 5- and 3-minutes long, and recall of the words of the RLS and DS titles would be affected not only by the extended intervals of the film segments (and possibly distracting events in them) but also by the intervals given to students to write their narratives (30 and 14 minutes for the writing tasks). In view of just the time factor in the writing tasks, the relation between STM and LTM would probably have to be quite different from the relations in tasks such as dictation and repetition.

While the STM/LTM dichotomy is a helpful point of departure, alternatives to the classic distinction are at least worth keeping in mind. Not all psychologists accept the distinction, and perhaps a more flexible concept of 'working memory' can compensate for the limitations of STM capacity (e.g. Harrington & Sawyer, 1992; Jarvis et al., 2013). By such an analysis, perhaps a learner's retention of the title information remains in the working memory for a longer period than what a conventional model of STM might predict. Furthermore, it may prove best to see the narrative recall tasks as involving a continuum of capacities whereby LTM is not a monolith. Chafe (1973, 1994) views LTM as divisible into 'shallow' (less permanent) and 'deep' (more permanent) capacities. This distinction seems attractive since any acceptable model will have to distinguish the relatively permanent storage of the native language as well as the more stable parts of the IL from the more *permeable* (to use a term favored by Selinker [1992]) parts of the IL. Yet, it also seems likely that many of the skills needed to reproduce the information in the film titles interact with shallow capacities which produce several possible IL variants. For instance, the highly diverse patterns of NP references among Finns, seen in Table 11.5, contrast with the more uniform (and accurate) patterns of the Swedes in Table 11.6. In the latter group, the similarity of the L1 and English seems to limit any experimenting with the NP structure in the IL. However, the Finns, who find little reliable help from their L1 on how English articles work, employ a wider range of patterns including NPs marked for indefinite articles and zero NPs, patterns that in other contexts would be appropriate recall though not in the case of the RLS title.

Still another alternative to the classic STM/LTM distinction holds that they are not altogether separate even while the former uses activated knowledge and focused attention (e.g. Cowan, 1995: 133–134). Such activation could survive long enough to report recent information such as that in the titles of film scenes. This approach is also compatible with Robinson's (2003: 655–656) emphasis on the role of *rehearsal* in SLA. That is, by reproducing input, learners can create new structures that become memory traces in their IL. It is important to note, accordingly, that the whole issue of memory in IL is complicated by the fact that in any task, such as the retelling of parts of the Chaplin film, the IL of any learner may undergo certain changes because of the task itself. Perhaps, for example, the Finns who seem to believe that *even* is a conjunction had never hypothesized the possibility before. In this case, the hypothesis turns out to be false, of course, but it might become a more or less permanent (and perhaps fossilized) part of the IL. Alternatively, after trying out their initial hypothesis, some learners might decide to consult a bilingual dictionary and thereby arrive at a pedagogically more desirable outcome, i.e. the discovery that *even if*, not *even*, is a better translation of *vaikka*.

New IL structures can and do draw on native language lexical and grammatical structures as well as on structures in an L2 in cases of L3 acquisition (and the performance of the F9B group indeed suggests L2 Swedish influence on L3 English). In either L2 or L3 acquisition, the result may be positive transfer as in the cleft sentences and definite articles of Swedes or negative transfer as in the use of zero articles or *even* by Finns. The diverging patterns in this study are compatible with the notion of a language-specific dimension in the reconstruction of L2 input. Although the approach known as thinking for speaking might seem to focus exclusively on production, it is as Slobin (2000) has argued, an approach that also has major implications for comprehension and so for the link between comprehension and production.

Notes

(1)   In the second italicized example, the word *men* is probably not a misspelled attempt to use English *man* but rather an inappropriate use of the Swedish conjunction *men* (=but). Ringbom (1987) offers many examples of Swedish words that L1 Finnish learners use, apparently believing that they are also English words.

(2) Unlike the results for Table 11.3, those for Tables 11.5 and 11.6 involve a wider range of choices, and any inferential statistics would thus be less straightforward. Even so, the figures in the tables are consistent with the results of inferential tests done on zero articles in the same corpus (Odlin, 2012).

(3) Some Finnish grammatical details in this and the following examples have been deliberately ignored in the English glosses for the sake of simplicity, as in the translation of *yliopistoon*, which is not a prepositional phrase but rather an inflected noun.

References

Cadierno, T. (2008) Learning to talk about emotion in a foreign language. In P. Robinson and N. Ellis (eds) *Handbook of Cognitive Linguistics and Second Language Acquisition* (pp. 239–275). New York: Routledge.

Chafe, W. (1973) Language and memory. *Language* 49, 261–281.

Chafe, W. (1994) *Discourse, Consciousness, and Time*. Chicago, IL: University of Chicago Press.

Chesterman, A. (1991) *On Definiteness: A Study with Special Reference to English and Finnish*. Cambridge: Cambridge University Press.

Cowan, N. (1995) *Attention and Memory: An Integrated Framework*. Oxford: Oxford University Press.

Fender, M. (2003) English word recognition and word integration skills of native Arabic- and Japanese-speaking learners of English as a second language. *Applied Psycholinguistics* 24, 289–315.

Foss, D. and Hakes, D. (1978) *Psycholinguistics: An Introduction*. Englewood Cliffs, NJ: Prentice Hall.

Grabe, W. (2002) Reading in a second language. In R. Kaplan (ed.) *Oxford Handbook of Applied Linguistics* (pp. 49–59). New York: Oxford University Press.

Han, Z. (2010) Grammatical inadequacy as a function of linguistic relativity: A longitudinal case study. In Z. Han and T. Cadierno (eds) *Linguistic Relativity in Second Language Acquisition: Evidence of First Language Thinking for Speaking* (pp. 154–182). Bristol: Multilingual Matters.

Han, Z. and Odlin, T. (2006) Introduction. In Z. Han and T. Odlin (eds) *Studies of Fossilization in Second Language Acquisition* (pp. 1–20). Clevedon: Multilingual Matters.

Harrington, M. and Sawyer, M. (1992) L2 working memory capacity and L2 reading skill. *Studies in Second Language Acquisition* 14, 25–38.

Izumi, S. (2003) Comprehension and production processes in second language learning: In search of the psycholinguistic rationale of the Output Hypothesis. *Applied Linguistics* 24, 168–196.

Jarvis, S. (1998) *Conceptual Transfer in the Interlanguage Lexicon*. Bloomington, IN: Indiana University Linguistics Club.

Jarvis, S. (2000) Methodological rigor in the study of transfer: Identifying L1 influence in the interlanguage lexicon. *Language Learning* 50, 245–309.

Jarvis, S. (2002) Topic continuity in L2 English article use. *Studies in Second Language Acquisition* 24, 387–418.

Jarvis, S. and Pavlenko, A. (2008) *Cross-Linguistic Influence in Language and Cognition*. New York: Routledge.

Jarvis, S., O'Malley, M., Jing, L., Zhang, J., Hill, J., Chan, C. and Sevostyanova, N. (2013) Cognitive foundations of crosslinguistic influence. In J. Schwieter (ed.) *Innovative Research and Practices in Second Language Acquisition and Bilingualism* (pp. 287–308). Amsterdam: Benjamins.

König, E. (1988) Concessive connectives and concessive sentences: Cross-linguistic regularities and pragmatic principles. In J. Hawkins (ed.) *Explaining Language Universals* (pp. 145–166). Oxford: Blackwell.

Kortmann, B. (1991) *Free Adjuncts and Absolutes in English*. London: Routledge.

Loftus, E. and Palmer, J. (1974) Reconstruction of automobile: An example of the interaction between language and memory. *Journal of Verbal Learning and Verbal Behavior* 13, 585–589.

Long, M. (2003) Stabilization and fossilization in interlanguage development. In C. Doughty and M. Long (eds) *Handbook on Second Language Acquisition* (pp. 487–535). Oxford: Blackwell.

Natalicio, D. (1979) Repetition and dictation in language testing. *Modern Language Journal* 63, 163–176.

Odlin, T. (2008a) Focus constructions and language transfer. In D. Gabryś-Barker (ed.) *Morphosyntactic Issues in Second Language Acquisition Studies* (pp. 3–28). Clevedon: Multilingual Matters.

Odlin, T. (2008b) Conceptual transfer and meaning extensions. In P. Robinson and N. Ellis (eds) *Handbook of Cognitive Linguistics and Second Language Acquisition* (pp. 306–340). New York: Routledge.

Odlin, T. (2012) Nothing will come of nothing. In B. Kortmann and B. Szmrecsanyi (eds) *Linguistic Complexity in Interlanguage Varieties, L2 Varieties, and Contact Languages* (pp. 62–89). Berlin: de Gruyter.

Odlin, T. and Natalicio, D. (1982) Some characteristics of word classification in a second language. *Modern Language Journal* 66, 34–38.

Odlin, T. and Alonso-Vázquez, C. (2006) Meanings in search of the perfect form: A look at interlanguage verb phrases. *Rivista di Psicolinguistica Applicata* 6, 53–63.

Ringbom, H. (1987) *The Role of the First Language in Foreign Language Learning*. Clevedon: Multilingual Matters.

Ringbom, H. (2007) *Cross-Linguistic Similarity in Foreign Language Learning*. Clevedon: Multilingual Matters.

Robinson, P. (2001) Task complexity, task difficulty, and task production: Exploring interactions in a componential framework. *Applied Linguistics* 22, 27–57.

Robinson, P. (2003) Attention and memory during SLA. In C. Doughty and M. Long (eds) *Handbook of Second Language Acquisition* (pp. 631–678). Oxford: Blackwell.

Selinker, L. (1992) *Rediscovering Interlanguage*. London: Longman.

Slobin, D. (1996) From 'thought and language' to 'thinking for speaking'. In J. Gumperz and S. Levinson (eds) *Rethinking Linguistic Relativity* (pp. 97–114). Cambridge: Cambridge University Press.

Slobin, D. (2000) Verbalized events: A dynamic approach to linguistic relativity and determinism. In S. Niemier and R. Dirven (eds) *Evidence for Linguistic Relativity* (pp. 107–138). Amsterdam: John Benjamins.

Slobin, D. and Welsh, C. (1973) Elicited imitation as a research tool in developmental psycholinguistics. In C.A. Ferguson and D.I. Slobin (eds) *Studies of Child Language Development* (pp. 485–497). New York: Holt, Rinehart and Winston.

Wilson, D. and Sperber, D. (1993) Linguistic form and relevance. *Lingua* 90, 1–25.

12 Context and Language Transfer

Chuming Wang

Usage-based linguistics views language knowledge as experience, and it inevitably emphasizes the significance of context in language acquisition and use. The present chapter addresses the issue of language transfer from a contextual perspective. The central role of contextual interaction in language learning and use is considered in relation to transfer, with special attention to what I call the compensation hypothesis (CH).

The Usage-Based Perspective

As a point of departure, a translation puzzle might help illuminate the role of context. In a political speech by the former Chinese president Hu Jintao, a Chinese expression *buzheteng* was used to encourage Chinese people to concentrate on the construction of their country. *Buzheteng* consists of two words: *bu* ('not') and *zheteng*, a colloquialism which can translate as *turn from side to side* (as a sleepless person might do in bed), as *do something over and over again* or as *cause physical or mental suffering*. How best to translate *buzheteng* prompted considerable debate on the internet, with several alternatives being offered, including *Don't make trouble* and *Don't do much ado about nothing* [*sic*], but none seems satisfactory. Each alternative captures only part of the meaning, especially since the idiom has developed special political connotations in the tumultuous years since the Cultural Revolution (1966–1976) in China. As one participant in the debate asserted,

> The mention of *buzheteng* evokes myriads of feelings and thoughts particularly for those who are in their fifties and sixties. It is impossible to make us understood in a few words to foreigners living outside China. The literal translation *buzheteng* in the form of its Chinese spelling strikes me as most apt, better than any other possible renderings.

For this individual, the best translation is in effect no translation. The challenges of translation well illustrate a basic tenet of usage-based linguistics (e.g. Tomasello, 2003), namely, that linguistic knowledge is viewed as experience acquired through use; use is, moreover, always context bound. By the same logic, acquisition entails the learning of forms in specific contexts, thus making language acquisition and use essentially inseparable (Firth & Wagner, 1998; Larsen-Freeman, 2006). How language knowledge is acquired and mentally represented is crucial to its retrieval and use in real-life situations. It is this point, as will be shown shortly, that is particularly pertinent to language transfer in second language (L2) learning.

Usage-oriented research has emphasized the interaction among variables related to language learning (e.g. Verspoor *et al.*, 2011). In this framework, the L2 learning process entails a multitude of variables, linguistic and non-linguistic, interacting with each other in diverse domains including the language system, the social environment and the psychological make-up of an individual. For Ellis (1998) and many others, language and language learning emerge from interactions involving phenomena as different as the brain and society. This interactive view concurs with the dynamic systems theory (DST), a field that studies changes and views our world as constantly changing systems of varying magnitudes, systems made up of related variables. Application of the theory to the study of L2 development is fairly recent, building partly on Ellis's conception of the L2 learner as a dynamic system, in effect a network of many variables, both cognitive and social (cf. de Bot *et al.*, 2007; de Bot & Larsen-Freeman, 2011).

The interactive view in DST suggests that the accurate and appropriate use of a linguistic form depends on the proper integration of contextual variables in the learning process, that is, what co-occurs with a linguistic form being learned will affect its storage, retrieval and use. This is what I have called the learn-together-use-together (LTUT) principle (Wang, 2009), which maintains that the right kind of contextual variables concomitant with a linguistic form being learned enhances the likelihood of its correct use, whereas inappropriate contextual variables that co-occur with the form increase its deviant uses.

Evidence for the LTUT is not hard to come by. In a study looking into a group of Russian–English bilinguals' recall of specific life experiences, Marian and Neisser (2000) found that participants accessed more Russian memories when interviewed in Russian than when interviewed in English. Furthermore, participants accessed English memories more quickly when the interview language was English than when it was Russian. The findings confirm the researchers' hypothesis that memories become more accessible when the language most involved in retrieval matches the language most involved in encoding, which thus suggests that language and context of use are mentally stored in an interconnected manner. Similarly, in a longitudinal study observing how a Spanish-speaking learner of English used English in class, Eskildsen (2009) found that situational context primed the use of L2 constructions. Some English expressions learned through interactions in the classroom context could be recalled for use in the same context after a lapse of seven months, suggesting that contextualization of a language form facilitates recall and use of the form learned.

Not only situational context but also linguistic context influences storage and retrieval of memories. In a study on the effect of linguistic context on the processing and recall of English words, Schooler (1993) showed that a particular word is more likely to be recalled when other words that co-occurred with it previously are present. It is more difficult to complete words shown alone out of context (as in SEA____? or FAC___?) than it is for the second word of a strong context collocation (as in HERMETICALLY SEA____? or LANGUAGE FAC___?), which can evoke the phrases *hermetically sealed* and *language faculty*. Such studies indicate that the processes of learning, storing and using linguistic forms are tied up with context, and that such findings, as will be seen, have implications for language transfer.

An Interactive and Dynamic Perspective of Context

Whether a linguistic form is properly learned and whether it can be put to correct use depend largely on concomitant variables. Accordingly, all the variables within the system can be conceived of as the background against which the form is learned and can be broadly defined as the context of learning. Among the myriad variables that may be relevant in any given context are the relationship between interlocutors, their psychological states, their proficiency in the target language and their sociocultural background and values, along with factors such as the time and location of a conversation, bodily activities, discourse type, non-verbal reactions and, of course, the linguistic forms and meanings. Any change in the combination of the component variables of a context may indeed affect the context, including changes in the meaning.

Contexts can be subcategorized according to the characteristics of the contextual variables involved in the use and learning of a linguistic form. For example, variables characteristic of a social situation constitute the social context. Likewise, we have the cognitive context, the psychological context, the linguistic context and so on, each of which can be still further specified. Within the linguistic context, for example, there is a phonetic context, a phrasal context, a sentential context, etc. In the dynamic process of a speech event, an incoming utterance is also capable of shaping a new context for subsequent linguistic action. Contexts and utterances thus interact in multiple dimensions (cf. Duranti & Goodwin, 1992: 29–31).

Some researchers distinguish between external and internal context (e.g. Batstone, 2002; Kramsch, 1993), which, as will be shown later, can help to understand language transfer. The external context refers to the context of a speech event with its components visible and/or audible to the participants. Conversely, the internal context involves the background schematic knowledge that resides in the learner's mind, embracing such factors as 'the intentions, assumptions and presuppositions of speakers and hearers' (Kramsch, 1993: 36) in their use of a language. Speakers and hearers have assumptions about what forms are pragmatically appropriate in native language contexts, and these assumptions partly constitute 'our culturally determined predisposition to perceive and assimilate' (Gumperz, 1982: 12) and affect what we perceive and retain in our mind. Thus, internal contexts are dynamic, adjustable and responsive to the external context and can be enriched through communicative interaction.

Given that L2 learning is an interactive process involving at least two languages along with a multitude of non-linguistic factors, the interlanguage (IL) has features different from either the first language (L1) or the target language due to the differences in contextual variables. If more L1-based variables are engaged in the L2 learning process, the IL will resemble the L1. If more L2-based variables go into interactions, the IL will be more native-like. In contrast to the normally successful ultimate attainment of the L1, L2 learning results in diverse outcomes, largely due to the existence of the L1 in the learner's mind. The longer the L1 is used, the more deeply entrenched it becomes. The existing L1 system along with its associated contextual variables will inevitably interact and exert a pervasive influence.

Interaction and interconnectedness among variables within a dynamic system suggest that activating one variable will inevitably trigger other interrelated variables. Thus, language transfer can be conceptualized as a process of activating one language in the use of another and as an outward manifestation of the internal workings of the dynamic system. Such an interactive view proves highly compatible with many findings about transfer, such as the fact that transfer is bidirectional rather than a one-way path from L1 to L2 (e.g. Brown & Gullberg, 2008; Pavlenko & Jarvis, 2002). Prominent in bidirectional research about L2 → L1 and L1 → L2 influences are contextual factors such as L2 proficiency, the nature of the structures used and whether the participants were using their L1 or L2. Such an interactive view of transfer has yet further ramifications as will be seen.

The Compensation Hypothesis

As considered above, contextual interaction is essential for L2 development and use, and language transfer is a concomitant phenomenon. The significance of interaction for L2 learning and use is twofold. First, a linguistic form being learned is made meaningful through contextualization and meaning drives learning of the form. Second, the linguistic form becomes contextually marked, and this marking serves to facilitate the recall and retrieval of the form for communicative use. At this point, one might ask what will happen if the appropriate external context is not available for interaction during the process of L2 learning, as is often the case in foreign language learning (FLL). Accordingly, it will help to consider transfer and context in relation to certain ideas in cognitive linguistics.

In the absence of an appropriate external context for meaningful interaction, FL learners have no alternative but to draw on their L1 contextual knowledge (including pragmatic and other cultural knowledge) to make L2 input comprehensible. Through repeated mappings in the course of learning, the integration of the L1 contextual knowledge with L2 forms becomes entrenched, often resulting in IL mixtures (in other words, negative transfer) that are not welcome. The consequences of providing or not providing an appropriate context in the learning of L2 forms not properly contextualized are analyzed in detail in the CH (Wang, 2003, 2007): To compensate for a lack of knowledge about appropriate L2 contexts, L1 contextual knowledge is activated. The compensatory process may involve more than literal translation, however, and will depend on the specific L1 contextual knowledge put into play. The CH assumes that acquisition is basically meaning driven (VanPatten, 1996) and that meaning involves negotiable social interaction (Firth & Wagner, 1997). The CH also assumes that the mental representation of linguistic forms is inseparable from contextual knowledge. The CH is thus consistent with the cognitivism of Goldberg (2006), who maintains that a construction is a form–meaning pairing that constitutes the basic unit of language use. In the absence of a proper external context, when L2 learners are assigning meaning to an L2 form, the internal context is simultaneously activated and mapped onto the form. In the CH, the mapping of forms and meanings arises from the context-bound nature of language use and occurs automatically.

The CH can be taken as a special case of the LTUT principle. Negative L1 transfer can be traced back to improper L2 learning in an L1-based context, thus resulting in a mismatch between context and form. The mismatch in mental representation blocks the retrieval of appropriate L2 forms for communicative use (cf. Ellis, 2008). Overcoming the mismatch proves challenging because the influence of the L1-based internal context on L2 learning is pervasive and deep-rooted. A case in point is Shen's (1989) experience as a Chinese-born scholar in learning to write L2 English compositions when he went to the United States to study. At first, he had a hard time overcoming the differences between Chinese and American culture and developing an 'English self' in the course of learning to write English. When it came to writing Chinese compositions, he resumed his old ways of thinking. In his English writing, however, transfer of the Chinese way of thinking was so apparent that he had to 'reprogram' his identity. When he wanted to write appropriate English compositions, he had to deliberately detach himself from the Chinese context.

The impact of the internal context on language learning and transfer as exemplified in Shen's experience is also consistent with Slobin's (1996) thinking-for-speaking hypothesis. According to this hypothesis, the conceptualization of a given situation is often influenced by the language one speaks because languages differ in their ways of coding reality or experience of the world. For example, Talmy (1985) found that a motion event is lexicalized in different ways in different languages. The manner component of a motion event can be conflated in English verbs whereas Spanish requires manner to be expressed separately. A semantic component such as manner in Spanish is therefore foregrounded and becomes more salient than in its English counterpart where it 'attracts little direct attention' (Talmy, 2000: 128). Evidence for the transfer effects related to thinking for speaking in spatial constructions comes from a series of L2 learning studies focusing on the expression of motion events in different languages reviewed by Cadierno (2008) as well as from other studies (e.g. Han & Cadierno, 2010). It is noteworthy that even for those advanced L2 learners who can speak a fluent and target-like variety of the L2 and whose L1 differs typologically from the L2 in the expression of motion events, their gestures still suggest L1 cognitive patterns while speaking the L2 (Brown & Gullberg, 2008).

The CH and Conceptual Transfer

Crucial to the analysis of Jarvis and Pavlenko (2008: 115) of conceptual transfer is 'the influence of the language-mediated conceptual categories of one language on verbal performance in another language', where 'language-mediated concepts' are distinguished from 'language-independent' ones. The emphasis on context in the CH is demonstrably relevant to conceptual transfer because in the CH (and the LTUT principle), L1 contextual compensation occurs online in the dynamic process of comprehending, learning and using the L2. Consistent with the analysis of Pavlenko (1999), the CH argues for the necessity of a non-linguistic level of representation by positing a distinction between semantic and conceptual representations in bilingual memory. Pavlenko considers this distinction crucial for the study of bilingualism since different contexts are involved in the learning of two languages and lead to different conceptual representations. She contends that L2 word meanings which are learned in 'decontextualized' classroom environments foster considerable L1 conceptual transfer. Furthermore, context makes a significant difference in how or if L2 learners change in non-linguistic behavior associated with the L2 because meaningful social interaction is required for conceptual representations to develop fully.

To support this analysis, Pavlenko compared the performances of monolingual speakers of Russian, monolingual speakers of English, L1 Russian learners of English as an L2 and Russian learners of English as a foreign language (EFL; the latter group living in the United States). She found that while both the EFL and the English as a second language (ESL) groups were able to define words like *privacy* and *personal space* (indicating that they all understood the basic semantics of the words), the performance of the EFL learners resembled that of Russian monolinguals. The ESL learners, in contrast, used these English words in a target-like manner when their classroom learning was supplemented by interactions in a naturalistic environment. As with the CH, Pavlenko's interpretation of the results emphasizes the importance of context:

> The FL learners don't have enough context to form an experiential multi-modal representation which goes beyond the word definition and forms a concept. Due to the scarcity of associations and the weakness of their links, such a word may be better available for recognition than for recall (what was long ago in SLA deemed to be 'passive knowledge'). On the other hand, natural environment learners acquired new concepts contextually, interactively and experientially, and, as a result, incorporate them into their restructured conceptual systems, whereby they can be available for both recognition and recall ('active knowledge and use'). (Pavlenko, 1999: 222)

Different contexts of L2 learning thus lead to qualitative differences in concept development, which in turn affects L2 use. Active knowledge and use of the L2 are premised on the availability of L2-based contexts for meaningful interaction during the L2 learning process; otherwise, L1-based conceptual transfer is likely to occur. As FLL is characterized by a dearth of target-like contexts, contextual compensation involving concepts is unavoidable.

More Evidence for the Context-Based Account of Language Transfer

The CH puts a premium on the role of context in the transfer process. Further support for such an emphasis is evident in an investigation of how Japanese-speaking learners of English realized L2 English requests (Takahashi 1996), with the results indicating that well-established conventions in the native language affected performance more than L2 proficiency did. Due to learners' unfamiliarity with the functional equivalence of L1 and L2 conventions, instead of choosing the pragmatically more appropriate but syntactically more complex English forms, the learners equated the honorific auxiliary verbs *itadaku* and *morau* with the English modals *would* and *could*. This occurred because the polite expressions in Japanese are encoded relatively simple forms such as *itadaku* and *morau*. Such interlingual identifications occurred even when other target language forms were pragmatically more appropriate, forms coded through more complex syntactic structures, as with the mitigators in *I wonder if I could borrow your notes just for today*. Takahashi's findings support the CH in two respects. First, the learners' knowledge of L1 use plays a crucial role in transfer; second, unfamiliarity with the L2 context occasions transfer. (See also Chapter 9 by Li *et al.*)

The role of context can also be seen in the learning of L2 pronouns. Kinginger (2000) examined L2 use of the French pronouns *tu* and *vous*, both forms translatable into English as *you*. Unlike English, French makes a number distinction: second person singular (*tu*) and second person plural (*vous*), which normally also signal levels of formality (*tu* being less formal and *vous* being more formal). Kinginger's participants were students of a French class in the United States who were linked by computers to an English class in France, with the groups socializing through email exchanges and videoconferencing. Results showed socialization processes at work in the email messages, as the learners' pragmatic use of the French pronouns improved. This finding suggests that fluent and accurate use of such pronouns requires not only familiarity with the L2 forms but also an integration of these forms into contexts in which the forms can be used appropriately. Beyond the elementary semantic distinction between *tu* and *vous* lies the challenge of acquiring the contextual knowledge needed for pragmatic success.

Pronouns also pose learning challenges for Chinese-speaking learners of English, as often seen in the unwitting use of *he* in place of *she*. A plausible explanation of the difficulty is that the Mandarin equivalent of both *he* and *she* is the third person singular pronoun *ta*, which is not specified for gender. Students' attempts at using pronouns often show an exclusive and indiscriminate use of *he* and thus suggest transfer. Inadequate contextual support during instruction may also contribute to the challenges. What seems desirable is providing a clear context in which the two English pronouns are linked with meaningful and salient distinctions in gender. In the absence of such contextual support, fossilization may result, and in such cases, the multiple effects principle of Selinker and Lakshmanan (1992: 198) seems relevant: 'When two or more SLA factors work in tandem, there is a greater chance of stabilization of interlanguage forms leading to possible fossilization', and if so, transfer may be either a privileged co-factor or, indeed, a necessary one.

Implications and Conclusions

The LTUT principle in general and the CH in particular emphasize the role of context in language transfer. In L2 settings, negative transfer results from interactions in the L1 context during the learning and use of the L2, whereas focusing on properly contextualized L2 forms promotes their correct use. This conceptualization has important implications for understanding some transfer-specific concerns and for overcoming interference to achieve success in L2 learning.

One issue of concern is the predictability of transfer. Since activation of L1 contextual knowledge occasions transfer, a pertinent question to ask is whether we can in any way predict what structures will or will not get transferred. In light of the CH, predictability of L1 transfer ought to be based primarily on learners' knowledge of the L1 context. For example, the L1 context is clearly relevant in Takahashi's finding that two structures (*would you please* and *would you*) formally congruent with common request strategies in Japanese constitute highly conventionalized and frequently used patterns in L2 English IL.

The contextual account of language transfer takes into account the distinction between positive and negative transfer. As Ringbom (2007) has emphasized, the positive/negative distinction should not lead anyone to assume that there exists some fundamental difference in terms of the underlying cognitive process involved. Positive transfer typically involves an L1 form being matched in comprehension or production with something similar in the target language form. Where the L1 carryover deviates from a correct L2 usage in context, negative transfer can occur. In accord with the LTUT principle, we can envision positive transfer as L2-based contextual variables interacting in successful matches instead of in the mismatches so common in negative transfer (even while such interference is hard to suppress, especially in L1-related contexts).

Because language transfer stems from interactions of more than just linguistic forms, difficulties often arise from learners' lack of experience with non-linguistic contexts that support the use of L2 forms. Acquisition involves not only learning a new complex set of properly contextualized forms in conformity with target language norms, but also developing a new internal context compatible with target language norms of usage. Studies in pragmatics have shown that this adjustment does not easily take care of itself (e.g. Rose & Kasper, 2001). In L2 pragmatics (and elsewhere), learning can be seen as a mental process of matching between context and L2 forms, in effect, form–meaning mapping through which constructions emerge. During this process, it is highly desirable to provide proper contextual support for incoming L2 forms not only because of the role of context in providing new intake (Batstone, 2002), but also because adequate form–context interaction ensures a long-term effect on learning and inhibits negative transfer. A form that is not so contextually supported, regardless of its grammaticality, is not suited for communicative use.

Technology can certainly contribute to practicing an L2 form with an appropriate external context (e.g. while watching a video), and exposure to authentic external contexts compatible with target forms will help suppress the L1-based internal context. Such forms should be learned in a supportive context from the very start in order to maximize the learning effect and minimize L1 interference.

To conclude, language transfer is a context-mediated cognitive process and it involves internal context or contextual knowledge interacting with external contexts. To understand how a language form gets transferred, it is necessary to examine how contextual variables interact with the form as part of a dynamic system. The CH and the LTUT principle have been formulated to account for why and how language transfer occurs in FL settings.

Note

(1)   Preparation of this chapter was supported by a grant from the National Social Science Fund of China (12 and ZD224). The author thanks Terence Odlin for his very helpful comments and suggestions for improving this chapter.

References

Batstone, R. (2002) Contexts of engagement: A discourse perspective on 'intake' and 'pushed output'. *System* 30, 1–14.

Brown, A. and Gullberg, M. (2008) Bidirectional crosslinguistic influence in L1–L2 encoding of manner in speech and gesture. *Studies in Second Language Acquisition* 30, 225–251.

Cadierno, T. (2008) Learning to talk about motion in a foreign language. In P. Robinson and N. Ellis (eds) *Handbook of Cognitive Linguistics and Second Language Acquisition* (pp. 239–275). New York: Routledge.

de Bot, K. (2007) A dynamic systems theory approach to second language acquisition. *Bilingualism: Language and Cognition* 10, 7–21.

de Bot, K. and Larsen-Freeman, D. (2011) Researching second language development from a dynamic system theory perspective. In M.H. Verspoor, K. de Bot and W. Lowie (eds) *A Dynamic Approach to Second Language Development* (pp. 5–23). Amsterdam: Benjamins.

Duranti, A. and Goodwin, C. (1992) Rethinking context: An introduction. In A. Duranti and C. Goodwin (eds) *Rethinking Context: Language as an Interactive Phenomenon* (pp. 1–42). Cambridge: Cambridge University Press.

Ellis, N. (1998) Emergentism, connectionism and language learning. *Language Learning* 48, 631–664.

Ellis, N. (2008) Usage-based and form-focused language acquisition: The associative learning of constructions, learned attention, and the limited L2 endstate. In P. Robinson and N. Ellis (eds) *Handbook of Cognitive Linguistics and Second Language Acquisition* (pp. 372–405). New York: Routledge.

Eskildsen, S.W. (2009) Constructing another language: Usage-based linguistics in second language acquisition. *Applied Linguistics* 30, 335–357.

Firth, A. and Wagner, J. (1997) On discourse, communication, and (some) fundamental concepts in SLA research. *The Modern Language Journal* 81, 285–300.

Goldberg, A. (2006) *Constructions at Work: The Nature of Argument Structure Generalizations.* Oxford: Oxford University Press.

Gumperz, J. (1982) *Discourse Strategies.* Cambridge: Cambridge University Press.

Han, Z. and Cadierno, T. (2010) *Linguistic Relativity in SLA: Thinking for Speaking.* Bristol: Multilingual Matters.

Jarvis, S. and Pavlenko, A. (2008) *Crosslinguistic Influence in Language and Cognition.* New York: Routledge.

Kramsch, C. (1993) *Context and Culture in Language Teaching*. Oxford: Oxford University Press.

Larsen-Freeman, D. (2006) The emergence of complexity, fluency, and accuracy in the oral and written production of five Chinese learners of English. *Applied Linguistics* 27, 590–619.

Marian, V. and Neisser, U. (2000) Language-dependent recall of autobiographical memories. *Journal of Experimental Psychology: General* 129, 361–368.

Pavlenko, A. (1999) New approaches to concepts in bilingual memory. *Bilingualism, Language and Cognition* 2, 209–230.

Pavlenko, A. and Jarvis, S. (2002) Bidirectional transfer. *Applied Linguistics* 23, 190–214.

Ringbom, H. (2007) *Cross-Linguistic Similarity in Foreign Language Learning*. Clevedon: Multilingual Matters.

Rose, K.R. and Kasper, G. (eds) (2001) *Pragmatics in Language Teaching*. Cambridge: Cambridge University Press.

Schooler, L.J. (1993) Memory and the statistical structure of the environment. PhD dissertation, Carnegie Mellon University.

Selinker, L. and Lakshmanan, U. (1992) Language transfer and fossilization: The 'multiple effects principle'. In S. Gass and L. Selinker (eds) *Language Transfer in Language Learning* (pp. 197–216). Amsterdam: Benjamins.

Slobin, D. (1996) From 'thought and language' to 'thinking for speaking'. In J. Gumperz and S. Levinson (eds) *Rethinking Linguistic Relativity* (pp. 70–96). Cambridge: Cambridge University Press.

Takahashi, S. (1996) Pragmatic transferability. *Studies in Second Language Acquisition* 18, 189–223.

Talmy, L. (1985) Lexicalization patterns: Semantic structure in lexical forms. In T. Shopen (ed.) *Language Typology and Syntactic Description, Vol. 3: Grammatical Categories and the Lexicon* (pp. 36–149). Cambridge: Cambridge University Press.

Talmy, L. (2000) *Toward a Cognitive Semantics: Concept Structuring Systems*. Cambridge, MA: MIT Press.

Tomasello, M. (2003) *Constructing a Language: A Usage-Based theory of Language Acquisition*. Cambridge, MA: Harvard University Press.

VanPatten, B. (1996) *Input Processing and Grammar Instruction*. New York: Ablex.

Verspoor, M.H., de Bot, K. and Lowie, W. (eds) (2011) *A Dynamic Approach to Teaching and Second Language Acquisition*. Amsterdam: Benjamins.

Wang, C. (2003) The compensation hypothesis in L2 learning. *Foreign Language Research* 1, 1–5.

Wang, C. (2007) A good beginning is more than half the battle. In W. Hu and Q. Wen (eds) *Selected Papers from the 4th International Conference on ELT in China* (pp. 74–85). Beijing: Foreign Language Teaching and Research Press.

Wang, C. (2009) A study of the interrelationship between L2 learning variables and L2 use. *Foreign Languages in China* 5, 53–59.

13 Conclusion: A Few More Questions

Terence Odlin

The first chapter in this volume broached the topic of transfer through a series of questions. Many more might also have been asked, given the complexity of the topic, yet a few seem especially appropriate to conclude a volume having, as this one does, a wide range of perspectives on cross-linguistic influence. Two questions will focus on theoretical and methodological concerns running through various chapters. A third question addresses an even broader concern: the reasons that anyone might have to be interested at all in transfer.

How Much Cognitive Processing is Language Specific?

One of the most common beliefs about learning a new language is that one has to start 'thinking' in that language. This conviction, which can be found among highly proficient bilinguals as well as among novices, might seem so obvious as to be irrefutable. Even so, it is a belief at odds with a universalist philosophy that has proven very influential in the linguistics and psychology of the past 50 years. One introduction to linguistics (Pinker, 1994: 81) clearly states some of the universalist assumptions on this point: 'People do not think in English, Chinese, or Apache; they think in a language of thought. This language of thought probably looks a bit like all of those languages'. The phrase *language of thought* likely comes from the title of a book by Jerry Fodor (1975) that proposes certain principles of language and cognition deemed to be applicable to humans in general. Pinker takes an especially skeptical stance on linguistic relativity, but his commitment to a universal cognitive code argues for a model in which any kind of processing such as the perception of sounds or the production of sentences is language-neutral apart, of course, from language-specific rules needed for the comprehension or production of anything in a particular language. Such rules, however, would presumably function only as specific settings for the operation of a language-neutral processor.

It would be difficult if not impossible to argue that universalist assumptions such as those of Pinker are utterly wrong; even so, some work in psycholinguistics suggests that certain processing routines are in fact language specific, and the routines can vary even in the case of highly similar languages. Work by Caramazza *et al.* (2001), for example, indicates that native speakers of French, Italian and Spanish show remarkable intergroup differences in how they employ determiners in picture-naming tasks, with comparable findings also evident in intergroup differences between speakers of Dutch and German. Caramazza *et al.* hold that a major source of the differences is cross-linguistic variation in how categories such as number and gender interact in the process of determiner selection.

Work *outside of* second language acquisition (SLA) thus offers important reasons to take seriously the question of language-specific processing, and *within* SLA, transfer research constitutes a domain where the question can be pursued. Several of the results in this volume suggest effects compatible with a language-specific view of processing. For example, the analysis of Paribakht and Wesche (Chapter 5) finds the difference in first language (L1) writing systems to be one factor among others that can explain the results of tests of lexical inferencing of second language (L2) English words. Their results showed an intergroup difference between L1 French and L1 Persian speakers, with the latter group showing a greater reliance on the overall discourse context. Paribakht and Wesche explain this intergroup difference mainly in terms of a difference in the alphabets of French, a language where written vowels normally make the identification of morphemes easier than does Persian, a language often showing no vowels in the written word forms. By this analysis, readers of Persian are more likely to find the written words in their L1 less easy to ascertain unless they consider a larger discourse context, and this processing routine transfers to L2 reading. The authors' explanation posits interaction between lexical inferencing and writing systems, thus between the domains of pragmatics and graphemics. The interpretation of Paribakht and Wesche resembles to some extent other work that suggests language-specific processing effects related to cross-linguistic contrasts in writing systems (e.g. Mori, 1998; Wang *et al.*, 2003). However, the intriguing idea of a relation between graphemics and pragmatics offers new prospects for research and warrants further testing. One possible test would be to compare the performance of the Persian speakers with speakers of Tajik, the official language of Tajikistan, which is historically quite closely related to Persian but which – crucially – uses a Cyrillic alphabet in which, like French, vowel phonemes are normally represented with written letters. If Tajik speakers perform more like the French speakers than like the Persian speakers in the Paribakht and Wesche study, this result would corroborate their explanation about the language-specific effects of the Persian alphabet.

Chapter 9 by Li, Zhang and Zhou involves a more localized processing domain where L1 prosodic patterns affect the way that L2 prosodic patterns are perceived and produced. The authors concur with He (1987) about the perceptual consequences of being a native speaker of a tone language. Lexical tones in spoken Chinese often vary from one syllable to the next and with roughly equal prominence given to each toned syllable. The perceptual demands on listeners to notice (at some level of awareness) each distinct syllable engender a language-specific predisposition that becomes manifest when L2 learners face the challenges of a language such as English where the syllables in a sequence normally vary quite a lot in their phonetic prominence. As Li, Zhang and Zhou put it, 'Chinese learners [of English] are likely to be sensitive to the tone features rather than stress features'. In their analysis, the sensitivity to lexical tones is coupled with a diminished ability to perceive differences between stressed and unstressed syllables involving phonetic features such as syllable length. As for using stress in speech production, the likely consequences of L1 Chinese influence are, in the analysis of Li, Zhang and Zhou, 'an even distribution of strength on stressed and unstressed syllables or the misplacement of English stress patterns'. Indeed, the results of their perception and production tests indicate divergences from the patterns characteristic of native speakers of English and also divergences from other bilingual groups studied by Susan Guion and others. The differences in findings offer support as well to the emphasis of Wang (Chapter 12) on the importance of the context of acquisition. The Chinese academic setting in the study of Li, Zhang and Zhou differed considerably from some other settings where stress placement has been studied, and such differences seem probable factors in why age-related effects were not prominent in the results in Chapter 9.

The study by Li, Zhang and Zhou suggests that the predispositions of L1 phonological processing influence how L2 prosodic patterns will be perceived, with the transfer affecting perception and production. However, the link between perception and production sometimes involves complications not fully explained in terms of simple interlingual identifications. One such complication is seen in Mitchell's analysis of the retroflexion patterns of speakers of Hindi, Tamil and other languages who were asked to repeat Spanish words. While participants did *impose* retroflexion (to use Mitchell's term) on Spanish consonants, they often did so even when a simple interlingual identification between an L1 and L2 consonant would have led to positive transfer, as in the word *borbotón* ('bubbling'), where the target language /t/ is phonetically similar to a non-retroflex /t/ in L1 Hindi. Mitchell's findings about this asymmetry in perception and production recall some earlier work, as in a detailed study by Nemser (1971). One result in Nemser's investigation showed that Hungarian learners normally perceived the English voiceless interdental fricative /Θ/ as a voiceless labio-dental (/f/), but the same individuals produced a voiceless apical stop (/t/).

The findings in Chapters 9 and 10 indicate language-specific links between perception and production in phonetics and phonology, but the notion of language-specific processing also seems relevant with regard to syntactic patterns considered in Odlin's study of the link between comprehension and production (Chapter 11). L1 Finnish and L1 Swedish speakers wrote accounts in English of what they had seen in a film, and their narrations often included attempts at quoting the words they had read in the titles in the silent film. Out of 210 individuals, only 4 reproduced the words of one of the titles verbatim ('It was the girl, not the man'), and no one at all reproduced another, longer title verbatim. Despite the rarity of verbatim recalls, many learners did attempt quotations, and their attempts indicate group differences suggesting L1 influence, as where significantly more L1 Swedish speakers used *it*-cleft sentences (e.g. *It was the girl, who stole the bread*) than did L1 Finnish speakers. Both Swedish and Finnish have syntactic structures very similar to English *it*-clefts, yet while film narrations in L1 Swedish showed a similar preference for cleft sentences, the L1 Finnish narratives did not. The predilection of Swedes to use clefts both in their L1 and in their English as a foreign language (EFL) narrations suggests a memory pattern in which recall of the wording of the English title is influenced by a construction especially characteristic of Swedish usage.

Language-specific effects are also evident in prepositional choices, as seen in the analysis of Li and Cai (Chapter 4). In contrast to a demonstrated preference of native speakers of English to construe, for example, the location of someone near a waterfall as *above* it or *below* it, speakers of Chinese tend to construe the same relation just as one of distance. The likelihood of L1 Chinese influence is bolstered by the facts of native speaker usage that the authors discuss and also by results from other research (e.g. Ijaz, 1986) showing different L1 groups making different L2 prepositional choices. Li and Cai clearly detail the differences in construals between native speakers of English and Chinese in their choices of English prepositions, but the wider implications of such differences remain an important research challenge, a challenge with many unanswered questions. For instance, could the upstream and downstream perspectives seen in English usage involve any effects on non-verbal memory? If the answer to the question is yes, some testing procedure using pictures with no verbal task might provide the necessary evidence, with such results resembling those of Lucy (1992). It is conceivable, however, that results might not be consistent with the kind of linguistic relativity posited by Lucy, but instead with processing effects that are language specific but not 'Whorfian', to use the adjective often employed to characterize strongly relativistic analyses. Language-specific yet non-Whorfian processing would be consistent with analyses such as thinking for speaking (Slobin, 1996, 2000, 2004), where the cognitive consequences of cross-linguistic variation are more limited.

Many recent analyses have addressed similar concerns about thinking for speaking and about what is called conceptual transfer (e.g. Han & Cadierno, 2010; Jarvis, 2007, 2011; Jarvis & Pavlenko, 2008; Odlin, 2005, 2008a). Further progress in understanding the issues and making new empirical discoveries will depend on both theoretical advances and methodological innovations such as those that Jarvis describes in Chapter 2. While a variety of long-established methods including picture tests, films and translation procedures have helped make an empirical case for transfer (as in some chapters of this volume), new tools have also intrigued SLA researchers, such as eye-tracking technology as well as methods to study brain activity. As Jarvis considers in this chapter and elsewhere (e.g. Jarvis *et al.*, 2013), the new tools seem especially promising for getting at problems such as the non-linguistic dimensions of conceptualization that interact with linguistic processes in conceptual transfer.

Research into language-specific processing should consider not only widely recognized areas of interest such as cross-linguistic differences in the representation of space and time, but also more elusive topics such as emotion. As noted above, bilinguals and multilinguals often have the impression of there being different modes of thinking in different languages, and this impression often stretches the notion of *thinking* in a language to include *feeling* in a language. Indeed, there exist interesting contrasts in how languages express various emotions, and there remains the challenge of deciding whether all languages share a common core of emotions for whatever cross-linguistic differences do exist (Pavlenko, 2005). The challenges of investigating transfer and affective states seem possible to meet at least in part through methods already established such as the comparison of different L1 groups with regard to particular structures. For example, considerable work has been done on the transfer of focus constructions such as cleft sentences in various language-contact settings, and while not all cases of such constructions will count as instances of transfer of affect, some indeed appear to be (Odlin, 2008b).

How Much Do Translation Tasks and Grammaticality Judgment Tasks Concur or Diverge in What They can Say About Language Transfer?

Two of the chapters in the section on syntactic transfer used translation as their main empirical procedure. In Chapter 6, Li and Yang required L1 Chinese learners of English to translate two Chinese passages into the target language. The translation task in Chapter 8 by Chang and Zheng involved something similar except that the L1 was English and the L2 Chinese (and with another difference being that the structures to be translated were sentences in isolation instead of sentences in a cohesive text). In contrast to those two chapters in Part 2, Chapter 7 by Gao employed a grammaticality judgment task (GJT) and also a related forced-choice procedure (in the interest of brevity, only the GJT will be discussed).

The procedures in all three chapters help make a serious case for transfer. The back-translation task used by Li and Yang indicates frequent omissions consistent with what several analysts see as a characteristically Chinese pattern of topic chaining. Chang and Zheng likewise conclude that their translation data offer evidence of L1 influence (though in this case English is the native language), with the data indicating an overreliance on the Chinese causative verb *shi*, often translatable as English *make*; *shi* is an appropriate form in some syntactic contexts but not in others where a wide variety of causative verbs are required. In Gao's chapter, on the other hand, the evidence for transfer comes largely from differences in intuitions between L1 Chinese and L1 Korean learners of English in how tolerant they are of ungrammatical sentences such as *The Eiffel Tower sees easily from this window,* which seemed aberrant to many Koreans but acceptable to many Chinese and the group differences in judgments are consistent with typological differences between Chinese and Korean.

With regard to Gao's GJT results, it would be interesting to see if a translation task would produce results pointing to cross-linguistic influence; by the same token, it would be possible to develop a GJT involving omissions such as those typically found in the topic chains analyzed by Li and Yang to see if Chinese and Korean learners, for example, were equally tolerant of such omissions. Other GJT studies (e.g. White, 1985) have indeed indicated that different L1 groups show differing degrees of tolerance of omissions. There would also be good reasons to try to elicit oral production with methods such as retelling stories or describing pictures. Even so, the similarities or dissimilarities between GJTs and translation tasks constitute a particularly intriguing challenge because they raise the issue of what kinds of knowledge sources may be involved in transfer, including sources not always evident when learners use their target language in conversation or in writing.

Concerns in SLA about knowledge and use go back several decades, as seen in an early study of GJTs (Schachter *et al.*, 1976). The authors took exception to an assertion by Selinker (1972) that studies of phenomena such as learners' intuitions had little to offer researchers seeking to understand interlanguage systems. To make an empirical case, Schachter *et al.* presented several ill-formed sentences to English as a second language (ESL) learners with different L1s, including Arabic, Chinese, Japanese and Persian. Some results proved straightforward where, for instance, L1 Persian speakers were especially likely to accept as grammatical a sentence with an aberrant relative clause structure having what is sometimes called a resumptive pronoun, e.g. *The problems that a tourist guide must have them are numerous*, where the *them* refers to the problems (cf. Odlin, 1989: 100). The argument that Schachter *et al.* advanced for the soundness of GJTs included evidence of transfer. One result in their study nevertheless complicated the picture since some of the Arabic speakers did not judge relative clause anomalies so positively as Persian speakers did, even though Arabic also employs resumptive pronouns. Schachter *et al.* attributed the difference in judgments to the fact that some Arabic participants were Algerians who also spoke L2 French, a language that, like English (the third language [L3]), does not allow the relativization pattern used in the GJT. By the researchers' interpretation, then, L2 French influence overrode L1 influence, which is a conclusion consistent with a transfer explanation but clearly more complex than the case of the L1 Persian speakers.

Since the Schachter *et al.* article, countless SLA studies have likewise used GJTs to make inferences and, as Gass and Polio (2014) argue, such tests are now usually considered to be one more tool in a toolbox with many methods. Even so, the concerns about knowledge and use seen in the disagreement between Selinker and Schachter *et al.* remain significant, as do distinctions between *knowledge* and *knowledge about* a language. Knowledge about a language, which is also termed *metalinguistic awareness*, clearly comes into play in any GJT, but some of the difficulty of interpreting such tests resides in the question of how much any metalinguistic performance may say about any deeper knowledge underlying such awareness (whether such knowledge reflects aspects of universal grammar posited by Noam Chomsky and others or, perhaps, reflects a different kind of knowledge system).

The study of metalinguistic awareness has a long history in research on L1 acquisition by monolingual children (e.g. Hakes, 1980) and has continued, with recent work on not only grammaticality judgments (e.g. Cairns *et al.*, 2006) but also on topics as diverse as children's understanding of word meanings (Marazita & Merriman, 2004), pragmatic intuitions (Olson & Astington, 2013) and the awareness of lexical tones (e.g. Lin *et al.*, 2013). Metalinguistic awareness has likewise interested many researchers focusing on bilingual and multilingual contexts (e.g. Birdsong, 1989; Foursha-Stevenson & Nicoladis, 2011; Jessner, 2006, 2014). Among the metalinguistic abilities present even in young bilinguals is translation (Malakoff, 1992; Malakoff & Hakuta, 1991). Malakoff (1992) sees the translation abilities of young bilinguals as often sound, allowing them to avoid pitfalls such as false cognates, e.g. English *blessed* and French *blessé* (which means 'wounded'). For Malakoff, translation is a 'natural' metalinguistic ability.

The investigations by Malakoff consider, as do many other studies, what James (1996) calls 'cross-linguistic awareness'. As such awareness develops, it can often filter out misleading parallels between languages.

The study by Schachter *et al.*, for instance, suggests that such awareness aided Algerian learners in judging an L2 French pattern to be a more reliable translation equivalent than an L1 Arabic one to the normal L3 English relative clause pattern. Such a filtering process is also evident in the analysis of Singleton (Chapter 3) of how Japanese and Korean learners of English use loanword vocabulary. In his analysis, learners engage in 'exploring' (his word) how close the parallels may be between many Japanese or Korean words originally borrowed from English and transformed in the East Asian context but also available as a way to expand vocabulary available for use in L2 English. In Singleton's analysis, such exploration also takes place when English-speaking learners of French seek to profit from many parallels despite pitfalls such as *blessed/blessé*.

For all the potential that cross-linguistic awareness has, however, some multilingual research suggests that stresses on such awareness often occur and can sometimes lead to behaviors that seem counterintuitive. A study of L3 Spanish by Bono (2011), for example, found L2 English to be a greater influence than L1 French in some lexical choices. Thus, one learner produced the following interlanguage Spanish sentence: **Actualmente se suicidó.* Bono details the discourse context, involving an exchange between two learners and their tutor, with the context clearly requiring that the Spanish target form be *en realidad* ('in reality') instead of *actualmente*, with an accurate sentence thus being *En realidad se suicidó* ('In fact he committed suicide'). French *actuellment* and Spanish *actualmente* are both temporal adverbs often translatable as *currently* while English *actually* is an epistemic adverb, one that signals the speaker's commitment to the truth of the statement to follow. Despite a virtually identical meaning of the adverbs in French and Spanish, the learner's attempt to make *actualmente* an epistemic form shows that L1 French did not prevail over L2 English even though in this case the L2 influence was utterly unhelpful.

Multilingual research shows other paradoxical cases, but similar findings are not unusual in L2 studies either. As described in Chapter 1, widely recognized work by Kellerman (1977) focused on the suspicions of some L1 Dutch speakers that idioms such as *dyed-in-the-wool* are translatable virtually word for word between Dutch and English. Moreover, comparable studies in Syria and Finland have drawn conclusions similar to those of Kellerman (Abdullah & Jackson, 1998; Sjöholm, 1983). Also relevant is the phenomenon of hypercorrection (likewise discussed in Chapter 1), as when Finns use the spelling *gomes* instead of *comes* or *komes* (where the latter misspelling at least reflects the real correspondence between English /k/ and Finnish /k/). Such cases may arise from a conviction that English and Finnish do not have much in common either in their spoken consonants or in the letters representing consonants. In any case, hypercorrections are not restricted to L2 or L3 learners. Janda *et al.* (1994) discuss a range of pronunciations among native speakers of English that they call *hyperforeignisms*, which often involve proper and common nouns native to one language but used in another with some counterintuitive changes. One example that Janda *et al.* give is of the name of an Israeli prime minister, Yitzhak Rabin, whose surname is pronounced in Hebrew with a stress on the first syllable, a pattern quite like the way many English proper nouns are pronounced (e.g. Robin, Robert and Roger); even so, as the authors observe, some speakers of English choose to hyperforeignize Rabin's name by placing the stress on the second syllable, making it in effect more exotic sounding than the actual native Hebrew form.

The many examples given by Janda *et al.* should not be considered cases of L1 → L2 or L2 → L1 transfer since the hyperforeign pronunciations probably do not result very often from attempts by English speakers to learn Hebrew or any other language from which the nouns come. What hyperforeignisms do have in common with the L2 and L3 examples previously considered are the apparent doubts about some cross-linguistic correspondences despite the authenticity of the correspondences. Furthermore, the behaviors involving *actualmente, gomes, dyed-in-the-wool* and *Rabín* all come from *individual decisions* about how similar or different structures in two languages are. Bono's *actualmente* example came from just one learner (although it seems likely that some other individuals might have made a similar choice); similarly in Kellerman's study, students varied in their suspicion or trust of parallels between Dutch and English idioms (the variation made clear in charts showing a wide range of individual choices). Moreover, social contexts outside of the formal ones in instructed SLA have sometimes shown bilinguals spontaneously using L1 idioms in their L2 (e.g. Odlin, 1991). Such facts indicate that cross-linguistic awareness is subject to social as well as individual variation.

Variation concerns thus urge caution in making inferences about metalinguistic awareness in relation to transfer. It would be premature to assert that whenever learners of an L2 (or L3) participate in a grammaticality judgment test, they will engage consciously or unconsciously in translations or related cross-linguistic comparisons. Moreover, such an assertion, while intriguing, entails complexities that will likely take many years (or even decades) before a consensus emerges as to how true the assertion is. The awareness of a new language or of any language already acquired varies considerably from one individual to the next, and therefore many of the contextual factors considered by Wang in Chapter 12 could possibly contribute to variations either in grammaticality judgments or in translations. Along with individual or social variation, the dynamic nature of acquisition itself complicates the research challenge (Jessner, 2006). As learners' knowledge develops, changes in cross-linguistic awareness also seem likely. Such changes make it plausible to expect that, for example, French learners of Spanish who are explicitly warned about the false friend that English *actually* is would be more cautious in judging *any* sentence where an L2 English structure might or might not be consistent with the L3 pattern.

Whatever the challenges that metalinguistic awareness poses, it is a cognitive capacity that thoughtful teaching practices can put to good use. For example, Otwinowska-Kasztelnic (2010, 2011) has considered the problem of cognate recognition in L2 and L3 acquisition among university students in Poland. While it might seem obvious to some professionals that Polish *optymistyczny*, German *optimistisch* and English *optimistic* are cognate forms, Otwinowska-Kasztelnic found that university students who had not had explicit training on recognizing cognates did not perform as well on a reading test as students who did have such training. Like several other studies, Otwinowska-Kasztelnic's research also indicates that becoming multilingual can often encourage a more general ability to note details in form–meaning relations.

Why Should Anyone Care About Transfer Research?

The consciousness raising about cognates illustrates the potential to develop metalinguistic awareness, which is consistent with earlier work (e.g. Kupferberg & Olshtain, 1996; Spada & Lightbown, 1999). Moreover, many recent studies of multilingualism tend to show that acquiring an L3, L4 or still another language can do much to raise awareness (De Angelis, 2007; Gibson & Hufeisen, 2011; Jessner, 2006, 2014). Taken together, these findings on SLA and on multilingualism suggest a synergy in which increasing success in acquisition can lead to greater awareness, and greater awareness can itself promote further acquisition.

However promising the synergy seems to be, caveats are necessary. Factors such as the motivations of learners and teachers and the overall conditions of instruction obviously can do much to enhance or diminish any actual learning. Researchers, moreover, remain uncertain about what the full potential may be of any consciousness raising. This uncertainty arises partly from challenges related to language-specific processing, which was the focus of the first question in this chapter. There has long been an awareness of the potential significance of such processing. As early as 1836, Wilhelm von Humboldt considered SLA to be inherently incomplete because, he believed, something of the L1 always 'carries over' (i.e. transfers). Nevertheless, another well-known relativist, Benjamin Lee Whorf, considered it possible to overcome the 'binding power' of the L1 through consciousness raising (Odlin, 2005, 2008a). Echoes of Humboldt's pessimism and of Whorf's optimism are easy to find in research circles nowadays, but most of those who take a position either way would probably agree that much more needs to be understood about language-specific processing before science confirms just how deep-rooted the influences underlying language transfer are.

Somewhat independently of the aims of researchers and teachers, the goals of individual learners themselves may change somewhat when benefitting from the synergy referred to above. The benefits may come not only in some fairly immediate ways (as in the apparently greater ability to identify cognate vocabulary) but also in the long-term advantages that bilingualism or multilingualism can confer. Despite past controversies about the effects of bilingualism on mental development, much recent work makes the case for special cognitive advantages linked directly to bilingual abilities (Bialystok, 2005) and even neurological advantages also linked to those abilities (Luk *et al.*, 2011).

Such benefits may, in turn, foster other kinds of growth as well as in the ability to make new friends, to appreciate more fully the cultures of other countries or regions and to reflect more insightfully on one's own culture. Modern literature abounds in examples of such reflection, and interestingly, some authors have chosen to create their own kind of bilingual style to give a sense of life in a language different from that of the text of the literary work. The Indian author Raja Rao (1977), for instance, wrote a novel in English having a narrator who did not speak any English, yet through some creative uses of word order and other devices, Rao was able to give a sense of a person speaking Kannada, a Dravidian language of South India. Similar efforts can be seen in work of the Irish playwright John Millington Synge (1937) and of the American novelist Ernest Hemingway (1940), and such examples suggest a detailed, if only implicit, contrastive analysis employed by the authors. Even while writing in English, Synge showed a clear awareness of the vocabulary and syntax of Irish (aka Gaelic), as did Hemingway of Spanish. In these cases as well as in several others, the authors needed considerable proficiency in a new language, with their efforts no doubt guided by a sense of wonder about the people they sought to portray. Even among everyday language learners who do not aspire to write novels or plays, reflecting on similarities and differences in languages and cultures can also encourage a strong sense of wonder.

References

Abdullah, K. and Jackson, H. (1998) Idioms and the language learner: Contrasting English and Syrian Arabic. *Languages in Contrast* 1, 83–107.

Bialystok, E. (2005) Consequences of bilingualism for cognitive development. In J.F. Kroll and A. De Groot (eds) *Handbook of Bilingualism: Psycholinguistic Approaches* (pp. 417–432). Oxford: Oxford University Press.

Birdsong, D. (1989) *Metalinguistic Performance and Interlinguistic Competence.* Berlin: Springer.

Bono, M. (2011) Cross-linguistic interaction and metalinguistic awareness in third language acquisition. In G. De Angelis and J.-M. Dewaele (eds) *New Trends in Cross-Linguistic Influence and Multilingualism Research* (pp. 25–52). Bristol: Multilingual Matters.

Cairns, H., Schlisselberg, G., Waltzman, D. and McDaniel, D. (2006) Development of a metalinguistic skill. Judging the grammaticality of sentences. *Communication Disorders Quarterly* 27, 213–220.

Caramazza, A., Miozzo, M., Costa, A., Schiller, N. and Alario, F. (2001) A crosslinguistic investigation of determiner production. In E. Dupoux (ed.) *Language, Brain, and Cognitive Development* (pp. 209–226). Cambridge, MA: MIT Press.

De Angelis, G. (2007) *Third or Additional Language Acquisition.* Clevedon: Multilingual Matters.

Fodor, J. (1975) *The Language of Thought.* Cambridge, MA: MIT Press.

Foursha-Stevenson, C. and Nicoladis, E. (2011) Early emergence of syntactic awareness and cross-linguistic influence in bilingual children's judgments. *International Journal of Bilingualism* 15, 521–534.

Gass, S. and Polio, C. (2014) Methodological influences of 'interlanguage'. In Z. Han and E. Tarone (eds) *Interlanguage 40 Years Later* (pp. 147–171). Amsterdam: John Benjamins.

Gibson, M. and Hufeisen, B. (2011) Perception of preposition errors in semantically correct and erroneous contexts by advanced multilingual English as a foreign language learners: Measuring metalinguistic awareness. In G. De Angelis and J.-M. Dewaele (eds) *New Trends in Cross-Linguistic Influence and Multilingualism Research* (pp. 74–85). Bristol: Multilingual Matters.

Hakes, D. (1980) *The Development of Metalinguistic Abilities in Children.* Berlin: Springer.

Han, Z. and Cadierno, T. (2010) *Linguistic Relativity in SLA: Thinking for Speaking.* Bristol: Multilingual Matters.

He, S. (1987) Several aspects of contrast between English and Chinese in English pronunciation teaching. *Journal of Foreign Languages* 6, 70–73.

Hemingway, E. (1940) *For Whom the Bell Tolls.* New York: Scribners.

Ijaz, I.H. (1986) Linguistic and cognitive determinants of lexical acquisition in a second language. *Language Learning* 36, 401–451.

James, C. (1996) A cross-linguistic approach to language awareness. *Language Awareness* 5, 138–148.

Janda, R., Joseph, B. and Jacobs, N. (1994) Systematic hyperforeignisms as maximally external evidence for linguistic rules. In S. Lima, R. Corrigan and G. Iverson (eds) *The Reality of Linguistic Rules* (pp. 67–92). Amsterdam: Benjamins.

Jarvis, S. (2007) Theoretical and methodological issues in the investigation of conceptual transfer. *Vigo International Journal of Applied Linguistics (VIAL)* 4, 43–71.

Jarvis, S. (2011) Conceptual transfer: Crosslinguistic effects in categorization and construal. *Bilingualism: Language and Cognition* 14, 1–8.

Jarvis, S. and Pavlenko, A. (2008) *Cross-Linguistic Influence in Language and Cognition.* New York: Routledge.

Jarvis, S., O'Malley, M., Jing, L., Zhang, J., Hill, J., Chan, C. and Sevostyanova, N. (2013) Cognitive foundations of crosslinguistic influence. In J. Schwieter (ed.) *Innovative Research and Practices in Second Language Acquisition and Bilingualism* (pp. 287–308). Amsterdam: Benjamins.

Jessner, U. (2006) *Linguistic Awareness in Multilinguals: English as a Third Language.* Edinburgh: Edinburgh University Press.

Jessner, U. (2014) On multilingual awareness or why the multilingual learner is a specific language learner. In M. Pawlak and L. Aronin (eds) *Essential Topics in Applied Linguistics and Multilingualism, Second Language Learning and Teaching* (pp. 175–184). Wien/New York: Springer.

Kellerman, E. (1977) Toward a characterization of the strategy of transfer in second language learning. *Interlanguage Studies Bulletin* 2, 58–145.

Kupferberg, I. and Olshtain, E. (1996) Explicit L2 instruction facilitates the acquisition of difficult L2 forms. *Language Awareness* 5, 149–165.

Lin, C. Wang, M. and Shu, H. (2013) The processing of lexical tones by young Chinese children. *Journal of Child Language* 40, 885–899.

Lucy, J. (1992) *Grammatical Categories and Cognition*. Cambridge: Cambridge University Press.

Luk, G., Bialystok, E., Craik, F. and Grady, C. (2011) Lifelong bilingualism maintains white matter integrity in older adults. *Journal of Neuroscience* 31 (46), 16808–16813.

Malakoff, M. (1992) Translation ability: A natural bilingual and metalinguistic skill. In R. Harris (ed.) *Cognitive Processing in Bilinguals* (pp. 515–529). Amsterdam: North Holland.

Malakoff, M. and Hakuta, K. (1991) Translation skill and metalinguistic awareness in bilinguals. In E. Bialystok (ed.) *Language Processing in Bilingual Children* (pp. 141–166). Cambridge: Cambridge University Press.

Marazita, J. and Merriman, W. (2004) Young children's judgment of whether they know names for objects: The metalinguistic ability it reflects and the processes it involves. *Journal of Memory and Language* 51, 458–472.

Mori, Y. (1998) Effects of first language and phonological accessibility on kanji recognition. *Modern Language Journal* 82, 69–82.

Nemser, W. (1971) *An Experimental Study of Phonological Interference in the English of Hungarians*. Bloomington, IN: Indiana University Linguistics Club.

Odlin, T. (1989) *Language Transfer: Cross-Linguistic Influence in Language Learning*. Cambridge: Cambridge University Press.

Odlin, T. (1991) Irish English idioms and language transfer. *English World-Wide* 12, 175–193.

Odlin, T. (2005) Cross-linguistic influence and conceptual transfer: What are the concepts? *Annual Review of Applied Linguistics* 25, 3–25.

Odlin, T. (2008a) Conceptual transfer and meaning extensions. In P. Robinson and N. Ellis (eds) *Handbook of Cognitive Linguistics and Second Language Acquisition* (pp. 306–340). New York: Routledge.

Odlin, T. (2008b) Focus constructions and language transfer. In D. Gabryś-Barker (ed.) *Morphosyntactic Issues in Second Language Acquisition Studies* (pp. 3–28). Clevedon: Multilingual Matters.

Olson, D. and Astington, J. (2013) Preschool children conflate pragmatic agreement and semantic truth. *First Language* 33, 617–627.

Otwinowska-Kasztelnic, A. (2010) Language awareness in using cognate vocabulary: The case of Polish advanced students of English in light of the theory of affordances. In J. Arabski and A. Wojtaszek (eds) *Neurolinguistic and Psycholinguistic Perspectives on SLA* (pp. 175–190). Bristol: Multilingual Matters.

Otwinowska-Kasztelnic, A. (2011) Awareness and affordances: Multilinguals versus bilinguals and their perception of cognates. In G. De Angelis and J.-M. Dewaele (eds) *New Trends in Cross-Linguistic Influence and Multilingualism Research* (pp. 1–18). Bristol: Multilingual Matters.

Pavlenko, A. (2005) *Emotions and Multilingualism*. Cambridge: Cambridge University Press.

Pinker, S. (1994) *The Language Instinct: How the Mind Creates Language*. New York: Morrow.

Rao, R. (1977) *Kanthapura*. Westport, CT: Greenwood Press.

Schachter, J., Tyson, A. and Diffley, F. (1976) Learner intuitions of grammaticality. *Language Learning* 26, 67–76.

Selinker, L. (1972) Interlanguage. *International Review of Applied Linguistics* 10, 209–231.

Sjöholm, K. (1983) Problems in 'measuring' L2 learning strategies. In H. Ringbom (ed.) *Psycholinguistics and Foreign Language Learning* (pp. 174–194). Turku: Obo Akademi Foundation.

Slobin, D. (1996) From 'thought and language' to 'thinking for speaking'. In J. Gumperz and S. Levinson (eds) *Rethinking Linguistic Relativity* (pp. 97–114). Cambridge: Cambridge University Press.

Slobin, D. (2000) Verbalized events: A dynamic approach to linguistic relativity and determinism. In S. Niemeir and R. Dirven (eds) *Evidence for Linguistic Relativity* (pp. 107–138). Amsterdam: John Benjamins.

Slobin, D. (2004) The many ways to search for a frog: Linguistic typology and the expression of motion events. In S. Strömquist and L. Verhoeven (eds) *Relating Events in Narrative; Volume 2: Typological and Contextual Perspectives* (pp. 219–257). Mahwah, NJ: Lawrence Erlbaum.

Spada, N. and Lightbown, P. (1999) Instruction, first language influence, and developmental readiness in second language acquisition. *Modern Language Journal* 83, 1–22.

Synge, J. (1937) *Complete Plays*. New York: Random House.

Wang, M., Koda, K. and Perfetti, C. (2003) Alphabetic and nonalphabetic L1 effects in English word identification: A comparison of Korean and Chinese English L2 learners. *Cognition* 87, 129–149.

White, L. (1985) The 'pro-drop' parameter in adult second language acquisition. *Language Learning* 35, 47–62.

Index of Persons Cited